4/

Business Logic for Sustainability

Business Logic for Sustainability

A Food and Beverage Industry Perspective

Aileen Ionescu-Somers and Ulrich Steger

First published 2008 by
PALGRAVE MACMILLAN
Houndmills, Basingstoke, Hampshire RG21 6XS and
175 Fifth Avenue, New York, N.Y. 10010
Companies and representatives throughout the world

PALGRAVE MACMILLAN is the global academic imprint of the Palgrave
Macmillan division of St. Martin's Press, LLC and of Palgrave Macmillan Ltd.
Macmillan® is a registered trademark in the United States, United Kingdom
and other countries. Palgrave is a registered trademark in the European
Union and other countries.

ISBN 13: 978–0–230–55131–2   hardback
ISBN 10: 0–230–55131–9   hardback

This book is printed on paper suitable for recycling and made from fully
managed and sustained forest sources. Logging, pulping and manufacturing
processes are expected to conform to the environmental regulations of the
country of origin.

A catalogue record for this book is available from the British Library.

A catalogue record for this book is available from the Library of Congress.

10   9   8   7   6   5   4   3   2   1
17   16 15 14 13 12 11 10 09 08

Printed and bound in Great Britain by
CPI Antony Rowe, Chippenham and Eastbourne

Contents

List of Tables

List of Figures

Acknowledgements

This may be the first attempt to write a book specifically on the business logic for sustainability in the food & beverage sector. For their support with this ground-breaking initiative, we would first like to thank the member companies of the Forum for Corporate Sustainability Management (Forum for CSM) at the International Institute for Management Development (IMD) that pushed for an all out effort to 'crack' the business case for sustainability (BCS) in nine industry sectors (see www.imd.ch/research/ centers/csm). For their contributions to the content of this book we would like to acknowledge the food & beverage contingent amongst the CSM member companies; Hans Jöhr (Nestlé), Claus Conzelmann (Nestlé), Niels Christiansen (Nestlé), Tim Wolfe (Nestlé), Hans-Joachim Richter, (Nestlé Nespresso), Dean Sanders (Nestlé Nespresso), Richard Heathcote (Scottish & Newcastle), Jan-Kees Vis (Unilever), Anne Weir (Unilever), Dierk Peters (Unilever), Jens Rupp (Coca Cola HBC) as well as the many others to whom we had access within these companies. Both Unilever and Nestlé acted as 'reference companies', giving us exceptional access either to company information or to their senior management staff. This enabled us to carry out valuable in-depth interviews in these companies over a prolonged period of time (2002 to 2007) to explore many of the dimensions of the business logic for sustainability in the food & beverage industry.

We would also like to thank other managers that facilitated extensive interviewing at non-Forum for CSM member companies that also participated in our research: Lars Krause-Kjær (Aarhus United), Georges Jaksch (Chiquita), Salvatore Gabola (Coca Cola), Will Peskett (Diageo), Bruno Kistner (DSM), Paul Hebblethwaite (Cadbury Schweppes), Soren Hjuler Vogelsang (Danisco), Bernard Giraud (Danone), Kerr Dow (Heinz) Albrecht Schmidt (Kraft), Reid Hole (Nutreco), and Peter White (Procter & Gamble). All of these managers, and those to whom they facilitated access, ensured that we were able to 'join the dots' and present as holistic a picture of the status of business logic for sustainability in the F&B industry as possible. The strong survey response was also mainly due to their support.

We thank our partner and friends from the World Wide Fund for Nature (WWF International) for the invaluable support they gave to this book: Jim Leape (Director General), Paul Steele (Chief Operating Officer), and Jean-Paul Jeanrenaud and Maria Boulos of WWF's Business and Industry Unit. The food & beverage sector research presented in this book benefited greatly from WWF's keen interest in bringing many of the difficult challenges of sustainable development to executive's 'front of mind'. Jean-Paul was also a member of the BCS advisory council and we also kindly acknowledge the other members: Margaret Flaherty of WBCSD, Thomas Streiff of Swiss Re, Jeroen Bordewijk and Jan-Kees Vis of Unilever as well as Reinier de Mann and Heike Leitschuh-Fecht. The European Academy for Business in Society (EABIS), and in particular Dr. Gilbert Lenssen provided invaluable opportunities to present the findings of the food & beverage research in several forums.

We would like to especially thank IMD president Peter Lorange, IMD faculty Professor Benoit Leleux, IMD staff Philip Koehli, John Evans and Petri Lehtivaara for their continued interest in corporate sustainability and enthusiastic support for the objectives and continued existence of IMD's Forum for CSM.

We are also most grateful to the other members of the CSM team, Oliver Salzmann and Kay Richiger. Kay provided all manner of support during this project and without Oliver's painstakingly careful and thoughtful contributions to data analysis and as a 'sounding board' for many of the conclusions reached in this book, things would have been a lot more difficult. Thanks also to Elaine Holt for much needed administrative support, and to Michelle Perrinjaquet (IMD editorial team) and Keith Povey for their professional help with preparation of the manuscript.

Finally, warm thanks to Professor Robert (Bob) Briscoe of the National University of Ireland (University College Cork) and who gave invaluable support to the doctoral work of Aileen Ionescu-Somers that contributed valuable content to this book.

The authors take full responsibility for any flaws, errors and/or omissions in the book.

List of Abbreviations

BCS	Business case for sustainability
BOP	Bottom of pyramid
BSE	Bovine Spongiform Encephalopathy
CAP	Common Agricultural Policy
CARU	Children's Advertising Unit
CGIAR	Consultative Group on International Agricultural Research
CIES	Comité International d'Entreprìses à Succursales – International Committee of Food Retail Chains
vCJD	variant Creutzfeldt-Jacob disease
CNIE	Canadian Network for Innovation in Education
CS	Corporate sustainability
CSA	Community Supported Agriculture
CSL	Corporate Social Leadership
CSM	Corporate sustainability management
CSR	Corporate Social responsibility
EABIS	European Academy for Business in Society
EAS	Early Awareness System
ECR	Efficient Consumer Response
EFFAT	European Federation of Food, Agriculture and Tourism Trade Unions
EHS	Environmental, health & safety
EMS	Environmental Management System
ESP	Environmental and social performance
EU	European Union
EurepGAP	Euro Retailer Produce Working Group
F&B	Food and beverage
FAO	Food and Agriculture Organization
FDA	Food and Drug Administration
FMCG	Fast-moving consumer goods
Forum for CSM	Forum for Corporate Sustainability Management
FSA	Food Standards Agency
GATT	General Agreement on Tariffs and Trade
GM	Genetically Modified
GMO	Genetically modified organisms
GRI	Global reporting initiative

H&S	Health and Safety
HCR	Harvest Control Room
IACFO	International Association of Consumer Food Organizations
IGO	International Governmental Organizations
IIASA	International Institute for Applied Systems Analysis
IIED	International Institute for Environment and Development
ILO	International Labour Organisation
IMD	International Institute for Management Development
KPI	Key Performance Indicators
LTO	Licence to operate
MAP	Management Appraisal Process
MSC	Marine Stewardship Council
MSCI	Morgan Stanley Capital International
NGO	Non-governmental organization
NPV	Net present value
OECD	Organization for Economic Cooperation and Development
P&G	Procter and Gamble
R&D	Research and Development
SAI	Sustainable Agriculture Initiative
SAIN	Sustainable Agriculture Initiative Nestlé
SD	Sustainable Development
SFL	Sustainable Food Laboratory
SHGs	Self-help groups
SME	Small and/or medium-sized enterprise
SRI	Socially responsible investing
TNC	Transnational corporation
UNEP	United Nations Environmental Program
UNICEF	United Nations International Children's Emergency Fund
VCJD	Variant Creutzfeldt-Jakob Disease
WBCSD	World Business Council for Sustainable Development
WHO	World Health Organization
WWF	World Wide Fund for Nature

Foreword

by James P. Leape, Director General, WWF International

From the time we wake up in the morning to a cup of coffee until we toast another day at sundown, the food and beverage industry plays a vital role in the lives of billions of people every day. Over the years, social and economic trends have had an impact on the industry, but ultimately it is the environment – which has been largely undervalued to date – that will decide the industry's future.

Freshwater is a good example. Only 3 per cent of all water on earth is freshwater, and only 1 per cent of this amount is useable. So it is amazing to think that while it takes three litres of water to produce one litre of carbonated soda, it takes up to 250 litres of water to produce the sugar used to flavour it. Even more astounding is the fact that it takes five thousand litres to produce one fast-food hamburger meal. With increasing threats to freshwater ecosystems – from climate change to pollution – the business case for sustainability (BCS) in the food and beverage industry should no longer be an open debate, but unfortunately it is.

This timely and in-depth study follows on the heels of an earlier publication that WWF supported from 2002 to 2004, which explored the BCS across a broad range of industry sectors from aviation to pharmaceuticals. Surprisingly, according to this latest work, most companies in the food and beverage industry are not yet taking sustainability seriously enough in order to assure sustainable development for future generations.

WWF has recently partnered with Coca-Cola, which publicly committed to reduce, recycle and replenish the water that it uses. WWF hopes such partnerships will serve as both a catalyst and a standard for others to follow. More broadly, we hope this study will challenge the sector to identify its critical path to sustainability before it is too late for business and the planet.

Preface

This book presents the food and beverage (F&B) sector results of the IMD Forum for Corporate Sustainability Management's research on the business case for corporate sustainability (the BCS project) across nine industry sectors from 2002 to 2004. It also reflects additional qualitative work carried out up to mid-2007 to further benchmark the results already available and update developments within the industry on emerging business logic for sustainability.

Very often, perception defines reality when it comes to sustainability, and it is also difficult to break through the current 'hype' around these concepts. The topic of sustainability, or sustainable development, is often perceived as 'fuzzy' by hard-nosed managers impatient for more measurable and tangible criteria by which to make their judgements. The topic is fascinating for researchers and a real 'head-scratcher' for sustainability professionals keen to make breakthroughs.

We reveal the economic logic behind the sustainability strategies of globally active companies in the industry. We assumed that such companies, being economic entities, will only take serious action upon sustainability issues beyond compliance if there is inherent business logic for so doing, and as long as that business logic can be communicated internally within companies. Our findings from a cross-industry comparison were that the BCS is definitely industry-specific, and can even be company or unit-specific; hence the value of this book for F&B managers, and also for any manager who is working on integrating sustainability concepts in business strategy.

The F&B industry is a 'front-line' industry; given that people around the world have to eat every day, it is 'front of mind' for consumers and for industry stakeholders. That is reflected in many of the detailed conclusions presented in this book. Within, you will find industry-specific data that is extensively analysed, processed and compared also to the overall BCS project results. A related diagnostic toolset can be downloaded free of charge at: http://www.imd.ch/research/centers/csm.

The book is organized as follows. First we present an executive summary with our general findings, assessing the business case and discussing what can reasonably be expected of companies in response to articulated expectations of NGOs, governments and other stakeholders. The rest of the book has two parts, one devoted to our findings

about how managers build the business case for sustainability in the
F&B industry. Here we focus mainly on the competitive framework of
the industry, the economically relevant issues with which companies
are confronted, the nature of stakeholder pressure and the perceived
contribution of sustainability to corporate value drivers. The second
part of the book looks in detail at how F&B managers roll out the business case within companies and covers the full waterfront of activities
involved in aligning F&B organizations behind strategies.

While it is clear that the business case in the F&B industry is probably
stronger than any other sector considered in IMD's BCS research, the
case is nevertheless not fully exploited by the industry and there still is
a long way to go before sustainable development is fully integrated into
business strategy. We hope that this book will provide some of the tools
required by managers to bolster their business cases, so that it appears
less and less elusive to the grand majority.

Executive Summary

Assessment of the Business Logic for Sustainability in the Food and Beverage Industry

1 Introduction

In this volume, we address the complexities and challenges of building and implementing a business case for the integration of environmental and social (sustainability) aspects into business strategy in the food and beverage (F&B) industry. Our preliminary literature review revealed that research contributing to the conception, building and roll out of industry-specific cases was lacking. Using comprehensive industry surveys, desk research and interviews with managers at global F&B companies as well as industry stakeholders carried out over a period of five years, we propose 'building blocks' for the business case for sustainability (BCS) in the F&B industry. In our study, we also cover the full waterfront of management aspects related to the potential for a BCS for globally active companies in the F&B industry, from strategy conception to implementation.

Since our research is primarily based on the perception of managers – what one could call an 'inside out' perspective – hard-lined, pragmatic managers may be tempted to write it off as too 'soft' an approach. But our view and experience are that the successful promotion of a BCS depends on how managers react to the related concepts as and when they are confronted with them. The 'Smart Zone' – the business area in which companies create additional economic value by improving environmental and social performance beyond that required by legislation – is thus dependent on whether managers see a business reason for action and whether they are able to build, communicate and implement that business case. Manager's perception of business logic for sustainability is fundamental to the development of a BCS and also to its successful roll out within companies.

It will always be a challenge for managers to work out the extent to which they should go beyond a focused corporate profit objective and regulation to take responsibility for the host of unregulated yet negative social and environmental consequences of their economic decisions.

The Smart Zone will therefore be unfixed and dynamic, and will depend on how much effort companies put into defining their business rationale, the level of pressure companies receive from stakeholders, the changing political climate, the corporate culture and type of people within organizations and so on.

In the following sections, we summarize our findings.

2 Building the business case

Is there a BCS in the F&B industry, a business case for internalizing social and environmental issues? Is the case robust, or elusive? One of our advisory council members put it in a nutshell:

The business case is not just 'found', it has to be built.

The BCS is not only industry specific, but business unit and project specific. Its foundations must take account of both the tangible and the quantifiable actions that are based on incremental continuous improvement mechanisms, as well as the more intangible value constructs; reputation/brand value, licence to operate, attracting and retaining talent, which allow corporate sustainability management (CSM) to contribute to important company value drivers.

However, the BCS is challenging for F&B companies to build, even though we identified many sustainability issues that had a direct relationship with the industry's core business. While the financial consequences of F&B companies not internalizing key social and environmental issues are rarely permanent, sustainability issues have nevertheless shown themselves to impact the bottom line, at least on a short-term basis, increasingly regularly. Given the increasingly short-term earnings orientation of major shareholders, and the reliance of share price on a host of criteria including corporate image and reputation, this should be is a cause for concern for senior managers, who very often are on a short-term mandate themselves, and are thus concerned about not 'rocking the boat'.

However, the risks and opportunities presented by sustainability issues are often not immediately apparent to business managers. The multiplicity of both the issues and relevant stakeholders serve to create a complex and fragmented business context over which companies will only ever have very partial control. Many F&B companies still lack even basic capacity to gather and process economically relevant data, and those that do manage to do this cannot hope to solve many of the sustainability issues they identify as relevant without working within the scope of stakeholder alliances and partnerships.

2.1 The F&B industry competitive framework

The personal and cultural nature of F&B implies that societal trends are of key importance for the sustainability agenda of companies in this sector. Since the sector's potential customer base is, ultimately, made up of the entire population of the planet – assuming that one day even the poorest may be prospective customers – focusing on consumer and societal trends (health, traceability, consumer behaviour) are of paramount importance for the industry. Here, the F&B sector has recourse to a considerable store of economic arguments that lend themselves to a robust BCS. These arguments have causal relationships based on industry dynamics that would not hold the same weight in other industries.

Consumer power is weak in key countries where population growth is at its highest. Consumption is stagnating in key markets such as the United States and Europe where populations are falling. Companies will have to be increasingly creative to capitalize on the potential of developing markets. However, we noted that the F&B industry has been relatively slow to innovate in order to anchor a foothold in these markets – yet innovate it must. We observed that exploiting reputation and brand value constructs through radical strategic innovation around sustainability concepts is currently not part of the inbuilt DNA of the industry. To a large extent, this is because this industry is inherently conservative and, like many mature industries, risk-averse. Also, there is still substantial scope to exploit already existing products and processes and make substantial profits, without the risk and investment involved in more radical innovation.

However, sustainability can present an opportunity for learning about new markets and this may have been underestimated by F&B companies. And we are all the more convinced of this since, even in developed markets, the industry was late to 'get on the boat' with the obesity issue and was forced into a race to product redevelopment and review of product strategies as a result. And even in spite of the formidable pressure still building around this specific issue, much of the industry still remains anchored to old business models. Throughout the study, we have argued that with an integrated and strategic approach to sustainability issues, companies will be more in tune with their current societal realities. This is in their business interest. A statistical 'buying' trends approach will not be enough in the future given rapidly changing consumption scenarios.

In addition, the differentiation opportunities that sustainability presents are not being exploited to the full by companies. Yet, in an increasingly consolidated market, with easily imitable products, F&B companies probably need to be looking at and analysing each and every opportunity available. Accessing immediate and short-term profits using familiar, time-tested formulas and incremental improvements on existing processes and systems is still dominating the agenda. It is simply still too profitable in the short-term to do this than for the industry to invest in research and development in radical innovation and to take the associated risks. Some leading companies are already demonstrating that this may well be a blinkered strategy.

2.2   The business relevance of the key social and environmental issues

The diversity and number of social and environmental issues faced by the F&B industry is exceptional, given the way food permeates the daily lives of each and every living being on the planet. This compromises the identification of a focused company-specific corporate sustainability agenda. Within the factory gates, managers in the industry demonstrate a quiet confidence in their companies' ability to manage environmental issues directly related to production, while managing social issues are somewhat taken for granted in Europe. But the industry's major issues of economic relevance are outside those gates, much further up – sustainable agriculture, human rights, child labour – or down – public health, alcohol abuse, animal welfare – the supply chain. The sandwiched positioning of the industry between its suppliers and retailers, which in turn are often interfacing with increasingly worried, health-conscious consumers, exposes the industry to sustainability related business risks right through the value chain. However, because of the complexity, we discovered that even the primary players in the industry have a long way to go, and much to learn on the way, before they can state that they are 'on top of' these issues. In any case, it is important for economically squeezed F&B companies to identify which of many sustainability issues 'out there' are of economic importance to them, and to clarify for their shareholders the materiality of social and environmental risks and potential links to the bottom line.

Some sustainability issues touch the 'soft underbelly' of the F&B industry and the simple equation 'no resource = no business' presents a strong economic argument for adopting and promoting a more sustainable approach. Experiencing a decrease in the raw material base upon which the industry relies is a considerable threat and a true business risk to the industry's economic viability. However, this generates considerable complexity in the work place, given the way the industry's current socio-economic framework is currently set up. Disappearing fish resources allowed some companies in the industry to use a tangible example to build an industry business case for the key issue of agricultural sustainability. It makes a lot of sense to use such a model to analyse similar risk with bigger bottom-line effects, and to learn from the experience of a solid business case based on significant business risk within a tight time perspective of five years – and thus, within a time horizon to which most managers relate.

During the period of research, we were able to observe and learn from the lack of readiness of the industry to handle major issues that hit the bottom line of companies and that have both socially and environmentally relevant global impacts, such as obesity and coffee issues. While the industry bears the brunt of the blame for some major sustainability problems and can be directly punished if not seen to be actively dealing with them, actually doing something tangible involves interfacing with many other players in public partnerships and coalitions. This is an activity that the industry is not yet adept at handling since it implies a new approach often radically different to tried and tested ways of doing business.

2.3 Stakeholder dynamics: promoting and deterring factions

The perceived visibility and significance of issues has a direct bearing on the extent to which stakeholders are demanding the industry either to resolve these issues or in some way to mitigate them using its weight and influence. Sustainability issues achieve their economic relevance in the corporate business arena primarily through the pressuring effects from the industry's stakeholders and the reward and punishment measures that they take to show satisfaction or otherwise with the industry's internalization of these issues into corporate strategy. Stakeholders that promote sustainability agendas maintain companies in their Smart Zone, preventing sustainability projects from crossing into corporate oblivion.

Since many global F&B companies are moving out of direct sourcing, the F&B value chain is becoming ever longer and more complex, and there are significant associated risks. At the end-user side, particularly when it concerns a health risk for consumers, there is pressure for full traceability of products from food industry customers (retailers) and legislators. The move of the major players in the industry out of direct sourcing comes at a time when pressures to ensure transparency in the supply chain are strongest. This means that close supplier relationships, carefully monitored and measured, have become much more of a priority for global companies. This has an added buffer impact of giving a new business rationale to supplying companies – including SMEs – to behave in a more sustainable manner.

Managers perceive NGOs as very proactive stakeholders. They have become more streamlined, strategic and professional in recent years, and they drive the corporate sustainability agenda increasingly by adopting a political lobbying stance. However, NGOs struggle to leverage action in F&B companies when not supported by consumers, retailers and shareholders. Although partnerships and platforms with NGOs are more common now than even ten years ago, managers remain sceptical – and sometimes cynical – about NGOs, especially their potential to undermine hard-won stellar global brands and corporate reputation. The media, used by NGOs and others as a willing transmission agent for and amplifier of their concerns, are perceived by business managers as conveyers of bad news who ignore the good stories that can be told about positive action taken. Managers regret that industry is not given more credit by non-business stakeholders for fulfilling their primary responsibility of achieving profits, with the positive externalities their economic activities trigger.

Companies are rapidly learning what their own weaknesses are when confronted with activist pressure, and they have been rectifying these quite effectively. The ensuing learning process has brought very positive developments in terms of bringing sustainability to the global negotiation table. Although the issues are so complex that no one company – no one industry in fact – can deal with them in isolation, the current increased drive towards coalitions and public–private partnerships conveys hope for the sustainability agenda in the mid-term.

However, there are limits to the BCS in the sector unless substantial external political and economic pressure is applied to the industry. It is currently simply not in the immediate economic interest of companies to move towards sustainability in more than incremental steps leading, granted, to continuous improvement but on a scale far below academic expectations of breakthrough innovation and new business models and far lower than that required for truly sustainable development in the short to medium term. It is likely that there will be increased legislative pressures on companies in Europe, particularly on labelling efforts, but no 'quantum leap' effects will ultimately make the difference to the BCS in the short to medium term.

Retailers move in a cut-throat, competitive environment themselves, and 'squeezed' F&B companies try to find no-cost solutions for their sustainability efforts. The most prevalent reason is that, apart from a niche market, consumers will not pay for sustainable products unless they also perceive a direct benefit for themselves. A rising wave of hard-discounters in Europe, have not been quick in introducing more responsible sustainable sourcing policies, since they perceive this as increasing costs. However, of late (2006 to 2007), some important players in the retail sector (Wal-Mart, Tesco and others) have begun to more actively promote the sustainability agenda and their actions are starting to make a real difference in food supply chains. What we see emerging therefore is a 'race to the bottom' at the same time as a 'race to the top'. It is still not clear which side will conquer; the jury is still out.

Consumers are perceived by managers as the least proactive of all in pushing a sustainability agenda. Although the niche of aware consumers is growing (particularly in view of recent intense exposure of issues related to climate change), many are still 'head in the sand' or just simply ignorant about sustainable development. With the current weak standards of product labelling, it is very difficult to point the finger at consumers for choosing products that are not sustainable. Yet, sustained push from customers and consumers is the single factor that can make most difference to the BCS in that they can influence all strategic business decisions in the industry. Since retailers are under extreme pressure from their own competitors, and because the consumer is not 'voting with his wallet' by paying for more sustainable products, significant change may continue to be halting. Recent increases in food prices worldwide owing to shortfalls in world markets as subsidized cereals are switched to biofuel production may also not help the situation.

National governments, careful about the whims of their electorates, do not put companies under significant pressure and in the absence of a 'level playing field' very much take things step by step also so as not to jeopardize national competitiveness in the global markets. Neither do investors and shareholders currently push the sustainability agenda of F&B companies significantly enough, because of a short-term results focus which is counter to a strategic long-term perspective required for an effective sustainability agenda. The perspective from shareholders is veering towards ever more short-term, not only because of the structure of our capitalist model, but also because of the exclusion of social and environmental risks from the materiality issues affecting stocks. There are positive indicators that socially and environmentally responsible investment funds are on the increase, but trends have not yet entered the mainstream. The corporate drive to feature on new sustainability indices is really a mantra of major global players, leaving a substantial part of the industry uninvolved. Nevertheless, trends at the consumer level – and experience with the evolution of the obesity issue, in particular – should indicate to the financial services industry that it needs to have its 'ear more firmly pinned to the wall', so as to identify and monitor impending environmental and social risks more rigourously than currently.

So, owing to lack of pressure from the most relevant stakeholders, leaders in the industry will either continue to seek sustainable 'no extra cost' approaches to resolving key issues, or look for tangible ways in which sustainability can back up an added-value proposition using the brand and allowing the charge of a sustainability premium. The bottom line is that, it does not pay (yet) for companies in the F&B industry to be entirely sustainable and the result is that business models are being evolved cautiously at the margins. It is hard to blame companies; to do any differently would put them at risk and 'up for grabs'.

2.4 Sustainability's contribution to corporate value drivers

Leading global F&B companies have moved beyond the more straight-forward cost-saving approach to sustainability (picking the low-hanging fruits of easily attainable pay-offs through, for example, increased eco-efficiency or Health and Safety (H&S) performance). They have evolved towards more elaborate business logic for sustainability. Given the industry's front-line exposure to consumers, the identified value constructs of reputation, brand and licence to operate have become strong drivers of the BCS in these companies.

Profit margins are low for this industry and it does not offer lucrative remuneration rewards to staff compared with others. However, it is increasing its scientific base to produce ever more sophisticated food options, with health benefits, for example. This requires highly trained and competent staff. The contribution of corporate sustainability actions to attracting and retaining talent is increasingly providing a BCS to the industry in European countries in general and Nordic countries in particular.

CSM's contribution to key value drivers through the strengthening of reputation and brand value seem strong enough to convince the progressive thinkers in the industry to give more than lip service to sustainability. The industry sustainability leaders say that they are not involved in sustainability programmes for monetary purposes only, but because it is the 'right thing to do', primarily because they present an opportunity for their companies to establish leadership positions in the industry. But while this is laudable, there are dangers in adopting an entirely normative as opposed to strategic approach, as the support systems are weaker and alignment cannot be guaranteed, especially in the ranks of influential managers that turn over rather quickly. The rigour of the classical economics paradigm, with its profits maximization and economic efficiency principles, becomes more nuanced when it comes to business logic behind sustainability actions. The BCS is strongest if measured by a dual approach, drawing on aspects that are both validated and non-validated by measurement.

Leading companies believe that, by lobbying hard within the industry and showing by example, laggards will eventually follow, thus reducing risk of competitive disadvantage. However, neither can the leaders sacrifice their competitive position in the meantime. Hence, investments in sustainability are heavily weighted against other activities. Although interesting and promising coalitions have been developed with a view to testing and eventually mainstreaming sustainability concepts, we did not find significant examples of sustainable agriculture pilot projects hitting the mainstream. This, in itself, reveals the conservative, no-risk industry approach and the still relatively weak position of the BCS against the prospect of shorter-term gain.

To assure that sustainability projects do not remain in the pilot ranks for as long as they seem to, sustainability officers need to continue pushing the frontiers of quantification, and developing the business logic on a multidimensional basis. The fact that the BCS is primarily focused on soft, complex and intangible value constructs poses a significant problem in that managers are accustomed to hard figures and tangible outputs.

Cost savings based on eco-efficiency and H&S performance are relatively easy to quantify, and accounting systems are already equipped for tracking the ensuing financial benefits and reaping the 'low hanging fruits' first. On the other hand, brand value or licence to operate drivers are heavily influenced by a host of other, non-sustainability related factors, such as political agendas or, indeed, market performance. The constructs themselves have to be leveraged in order to increase financial performance. There is a cascading effect that makes the business logic complicated; for example, sustainability actions contribute to increased brand recognition, which in turn contributes to higher market shares. Increased licence to operate leads to fewer workplace disruptions and accelerates permit authorizations implying cost reductions overall. Retaining talent through improved employee welfare leads to improved industrial relations and therefore fewer strikes, and reduced training costs through lower staff turnover. Isolating the corporate sustainability contribution to these constructs is considered so time-consuming and expensive an exercise as to make the task undesirable from a business logic standpoint. Sustainability officers tend to still dream about a more quantified case, as they would welcome any opportunity to build a stronger BCS. While this is particularly true for laggards, as clearly it is easier to present tangibles than intangibles to sceptics, even sustainability officers at progressive companies found that the potential for quantification had far from been exhausted.

Owing largely to a conservative stance within the industry, managers do not generally perceive sustainability as an opportunity to innovate, although with some of the major players, this thinking has finally changed in the last two to three years. This value construct is probably undervalued, both in terms of product and process innovations, and in terms of radical innovation for new markets. Too many managers still perceive sustainability projects as being the remit of 'the sustainability or corporate responsibility people' rather than something for Research and Development (R&D), marketing and business managers to take on. However, F&B companies must seek new businesses and new marketplaces in order to remain profitable. Innovation through sustainability may be able to contribute to building up critical mass in the markets of tomorrow. Also, by creating high quality, added-value products, we suggested that brand values and consumer trust might eventually be used in marketing and selling products. New aspects of managing the marketing value of a brand that are different to traditional approaches might emerge as a result. Solid arguments based on scientific fact are convincing but these must be qualified by a communicating absolute benefits that consumers value. It follows that if a company's initiatives are successfully communicated to consumers, building not only on consumers emotions, while assuring them of quality and personal benefits, confidence in the company's food supply chain will increase, ultimately affecting profitability.

A more robust case for sustainability can probably be built right here and now by each and every sustainability officer in the F&B industry. Strategic corporate frameworks can, and should, incorporate parameters that are less fixed, since industries are moving in a dynamic environment where all elements; consumer behaviour, legislation, technology, economies and competitive features are changing and, indeed, expected to change.

3 Exploiting the business case

We found many areas where the industry was still either in an experimental stage with sustainability concepts and principles, or at the beginning of stakeholder engagement processes that will assure corporate learning about new angles on environmental and social issues. Currently, F&B companies do not comprehensively address the sustainability issues that are of economic, and thus strategic, importance to them, although the leaders in the industry have a high awareness of what those issues are and have initiated action. Better access to the economic reasoning behind adopting internalization of the sustainability issue as part of business strategy appears to be lacking, given that many managers had not actually thought about such a rationale until asked at our interviews.

Even sustainability leaders had not managed the difficult process of assuring organizational alignment behind relatively well-worked out sustainability principles. For this reason, strategies are in danger of not being implemented by key business functions and a diluting effect can take hold, which means that key messages about corporate sustainability strategies are not transmitted up and down through value chain as far as suppliers and consumers. The industry can most probably achieve significant progress with designing and applying sustainability strategies by opting for a more comprehensive and structured approach.

3.1 Promoting factors and barriers to roll out

While on the one hand, the rationale for the BCS is very definitely sector-specific, based on its own sets of issues, stakeholders and value drivers, on the other hand its application and interpretation are often culturally based. Open and transparent national cultures, such as those of the Nordic countries, are the ones that lend themselves best to the bottom-up processes that best promote corporate sustainability.

The decentralized nature of the F&B industry is currently perceived as a barrier to implementation of sustainability objectives, but we suggest that this could be converted to an opportunity if sustainability becomes one of the essential 'glue' elements that hold global companies together – such as by reinforcing tenuous corporate cultures in a global environment, and allowing access to much needed skilled and talented personnel.

While sustainability officers see top management commitment as an essential prerequisite to promoting the BCS both internally and externally, neither do they believe that this criterion is sufficient to assure success. Along with the top management commitment, an organizational commitment to integration of sustainability strategy into business strategy is essential. The identification of informal networks of sustainability champions positioned in key strategic areas throughout companies has proved in some companies to be a substantial contributor to success, and engagement of the 'second layer' of senior decision-makers is essential.

Overcoming internal constraints to rollout of a sustainability strategy presents the most immediate potential for further exploitation of the business case that sustainability offers within organizations. Mindset of managers, lack of knowledge and organizational culture are the most significant perceived barriers, but these are also areas that are entirely within the corporation's direct sphere of influence. The potential for further exploitation of the business case is therefore substantial, as managerial and staff development is within the competence and control of each and every organization.

A major inherent difficulty is the fact that, pushed by investors and customers, managers in business and industry look to the short-term business result, while sustainability benefits are undisputedly long-term. The F&B industry is far from being alone in this respect (Steger, 2004). We found that the 'right' language must be used to convince decision-makers in the industry of the benefits of more long-term business planning in the short-term.

The industry is nevertheless moving, albeit relatively slowly, in the direction of taking more of a long-term view into account, but such considerable change will not happen overnight. A major strategic challenge is that key companies in the industry join forces both in spirit and in action, and share experiences in order to create new industry standards and benchmarks. Despite a proliferation of Environmental Management System (EMS) tools and various standards available to managers, they still require help to manage the increasingly complex business environment within which they operate.

Major companies have a policy of not holding a sustainability function but are working instead on integrating sustainability across the organization. In progressive companies, cross-functional teams fulfil the need for an effective and much needed feedback process. There is nevertheless room for better coordination across units and departments in organizations, with scope for increased collaboration between sustainability officers and other functional units within organizations.

Hard-line sceptics in companies who are sometimes at senior management must be reached, – particularly at decision-making level. Key marketing and sales managers are largely left out of the sustainability equation at present and, because of this, product development, greatly influenced by marketing managers, is also strongly affected. Indeed, engaging sales and marketing staff at an early stage of development of a sustainability strategy – for example, by including them in strategic coordination committees, task forces or issue groups – would greatly contribute to breaking down the lack of knowledge that prevents these managers from exploiting the concept of sustainability to its fullest extent. Finding the right language for communicating with consumers about sustainability is a major challenge that marketing managers (conservative by nature and with ever more short-term targets) are unwilling to take on, and indeed they currently lack the skills for so doing. Relatively little has as yet been attempted by the industry to change the dynamics between the industry and the consumer. We identified some key players that are seeking breakthroughs through linking sustainability with other more personal benefits to consumers, thus using sustainability as a driver to enhance the brand, and trying to prove that sustainability does, in fact, sell.

So currently, there are cut-off points that ensure that companies cannot go all the way with their sustainability strategies. In general, more building of awareness and internal education on sustainable development could eventually change the way F&B companies relate to the consumer, as this would change mindsets over time. More radical innovation than today, based on sustainability concepts, could go beyond experimental projects as a result. Today, support frameworks for such a move are still lacking.

Managers in global F&B companies regard stakeholder interaction as part and parcel of today's business model, and are in a learning process in this regard. There are some excellent, successful and leading examples of partnerships with stakeholders. Companies are still feeling the ground in this respect, but to varying degrees and depending on the company-specific business case for doing so. We have confidence that the learning processes that the industry has engaged in will bear fruit for a more robust business case in the future.

Problems with alignment are, in fact, largely due to the absence of comprehensive integration of sustainability strategies into organizational processes. We identified large gaps in the incentives programmes to stir managers to action. What is encouraging is that leading companies seem to be aware of such gaps. They intend to address them – eventually. But it was clear that, in the current very competitive economic climate, urgency was lacking.

3.2 Effectiveness of approaches used to exploit the BCS in companies

To create a robust BCS, leading companies are focusing on enhancing activities where an impact can be made and where a direct link can be made to the business product, and then on communicating these 'early wins' internally. Being able to share and exploit better practice and win-win success stories and, in the words of one manager, 'communicate,

communicate, communicate'; these are key components of both building and promoting a BCS.

Sustainable agriculture pilot projects focus on opportunities to create value in areas of strategic business concern, and introduce measurable indicators of sustainability performance, thus linking business performance and improved sustainability performance. The creation of value in these areas can contribute in turn to product differentiation, eventually enabling companies to demand a product price premium or access increased brand loyalty. It remains to be seen whether experimental practices in the industry will move into the mainstream. Currently, too many pilot projects remain in the wings, with no one company willing to go out on a limb and mainstream on its own: the competitive disadvantages involved are still far too great.

The price of raw materials is small compared with the processing and marketing costs of final products. Although efforts related to the BCS in leading companies are currently focused upstream – on the supply chain – there is substantial potential to work on downstream efforts and any current initiatives are very much in their infancy. Raising awareness in the company that sustainability can be about gaining major reputation and brand value benefits from little or no additional investment needs to be a key part of the communication strategy around the BCS. As sustainability is an essential prerequisite for the long-term security of the supply chain, progressive managers feel that it should ultimately be possible to sell the concept to consumers. However, first, a much stronger and tangible link needs to be made between the growing niche of consumers that have a broader concern for environmental and social issues, and the application of their principles to their buying habits.

4 So what's the bottom line?

So is corporate sustainability just a buzzword in the F&B industry or is it bringing the triple bottom line 'win-win-win' solutions that some of the hype around the concept suggests? To this question, one of the managers we interviewed responded:

> *Maybe corporate sustainability is not 'the next big thing' – but that is probably good because for me, 'next big thing' is consultancy-speak for the next thing that will be forgotten.* (BCS47 – Business manager, Supply chain)

We identified enough enterprising initiatives to show that sustainability is firmly on the agenda of major companies and it is there to stay on corporate agendas of the future. Several pioneering companies are taking on the complexities and challenges of sustainability and pushing the boundaries of environmental and social business improvements. But the BCS clearly has its limits under prevailing economic conditions. For a quantum leap forward, leaders in the industry will have to join with trade initiatives to support changes to the economic and political framework within which the industry is operating. The industry would also do well to support more mainstreamed labelling initiatives and the establishment of a 'level playing field' through regulation that makes sense. This view is encompassed in these rather disenchanted comments; one from a stakeholder, one from a business manager:

The economic case will have its limits – even with the best resource scarcity arguments, and cost savings and any other economic justifications to impress the financial managers, there is a limit of 5 per cent plus or minus of overall company turnover that can be influenced by CSR. The rest is the daily grind of business and maximizing shareholder value. (BCSBM10 – Senior policy director, WWF)

If there was a really robust business case for sustainability, there wouldn't be need for so many publications. It is a real case of 'the lady doth protest too much'. (BCS40 – Senior sustainability officer)

While CSM's contributions to corporate reputation, brand value and attracting and retaining talent are stronger drivers for the BCS in the F&B industry than in most other industries, the level of this contribution is still unlikely to be sufficiently strong to drive the business case as far throughout organizations as is necessary for truly sustainable development. Food industry experts were not optimistic:

Current moves are on such a small scale that it's difficult to see a quantum leap taking place. There are many vested interests in maintaining the current system. I'm not optimistic that the current corporate control of food can be successfully challenged. The scales need to fall from the eyes of the industry. No single major company has reinvented itself throughout to fundamentally challenge the status quo. We need tougher incremental change. (BCSBM6 – Food industry expert)

However, we observed over the period of research that there was an evolution in awareness in the industry about the relevance of sustainability concepts to business. We met managers who perceived potential for large, global companies to make a difference mid-term:

> *If large companies change, then the markets will change. It will progressively become clear that all the work in the supply chain will only get so far and the consumption side of the equation will have to kick in. I see a huge change, not in the next five years maybe, but certainly within a five to ten year perspective.* (BCS43 – Senior business manager, Marketing)

Any research is but a snapshot of an existing state of affairs. Already in 2007, it seemed that there was a shift in the issues that were 'top of mind' for the global players in the industry. According to a recent published industry survey of food industry executives,[1] corporate social responsibility (CSR) is now one of their major stated preoccupations, prompted mainly by a surge of interest in health and climate change issues in 2006/07. However, complacency would be misplaced; our research clearly showed that there is often a gap between attitudes and positive actions. Moreover, change overnight is unfeasible as the issues are both controversial and complex and resistance in the ranks of managers needs to be dealt with. To be able to take more 'giant steps', the focus of the F&B industry BCS in the future must turn to addressing the gap between consumer awareness and the positive steps that some companies are making.

In the current unprecedented context of high fuel prices, shifts of cereal production to bio-fuels provoking the highest food prices in decades, emerging economies vying with developed countries for resources from energy to metals to food, and uncertain global economic and social stability, it is by no means a foregone conclusion that corporate action in the F&B industry will substantially accelerate the cause of sustainable development in the short or even medium term. But let's not underrate the power of marginal improvements that companies tend to opt for in this environment. Such changes will at least be long-lasting.

Our research conclusions are very much 'out of the horses mouth'; we allowed F&B managers to articulate their perceptions of the BCS in the industry. So we leave the last word to a visionary CEO of one of the companies involved in our research:

> *The questions are: Is there a consumer who recognizes and is prepared to buy sustainable products? Will there be a market to allow companies to have a decent return on their investment? Using reputation management*

as a driver of sustainability is not a viable business strategy. Things have to change – biodiversity is important. If the industry doesn't change – this is a dead end road. (BCS39 – Top management, CEO)

Note

1   CIES – the Food Business Forum; Top of Mind 2007.

Part I
Building the Business Logic

1
Introduction

We live in the golden age of the internet, the mobile phone and the constant and unrelenting exchanging of information across vast distances from one end of the world to the other. For this reason, only the most 'head in the sand' person nowadays will have missed the increasing attention devoted to sustainable development, particularly with the recent unprecedented focus on climate change in Europe and the United States. To read the press, it seems that everyone, from non-governmental organizations (NGOs) to governments to companies, is 'on the bandwagon', and must be seen to be doing at least something about sustainable development.[1] But does the rhetoric match reality or much of it a matter of hype?

In this volume we do not pretend to present a complete answer to this question, given that our focus is on the global company, and at that, global companies in the food and beverage (F&B) industry. Our purpose here is to show how global corporations in this particular sector, as primarily economic entities, take action on social and environmental issues *beyond compliance* only if clearly defined business logic to justify such actions is identified, and as we do so, we will understand the extent to which the reality meets the hype at least for the F&B industry.

We present the results of a research project incorporating data collected over five years on the perceived economic rationale – or 'business case' – for including environmental and social sustainability programmes and agendas in business strategy in F&B companies, and on the extent to which such programmes are strategically integrated. Many quantitative and qualitative empirical results contributing to this research were collected in the context of a more extensive research initiative covering nine industry sectors by the Forum for Corporate Sustainability Management (Forum for CSM), a research platform at the International Institute for

3

Management Development (IMD) business school in Switzerland during 2001–04: 'Building a Robust Business Case for Corporate Sustainability' – 'the BCS project' (Steger, 2004). Qualitative research continued during the period 2004 to mid-2007 and included additional benchmarking interviews with consumer organizations, supply chain managers, participants in corporate sustainability partnerships and other F&B industry stakeholders. The aim of the BCS project research was threefold:

- To identify and describe the perceived business and economic rationale used by managers in global corporations for integrating environmental and social criteria into business strategy – the business case for sustainability (BCS)
- To understand how the perceived business and economic rationale for implementing action on environmental and social problems or issues differs from industry to industry, to analyze the extent to which companies in different industries have exhausted its potential, and to identify reasons preventing companies from exploiting the potential of the BCS
- To design a set of diagnostic tools for each sector, using the empirical findings of the research as a basis for tool development, thus increasing its relevance and assisting companies to understand and build their individual BCS.[2]

1 Background: the conundrum

The concept of sustainable development was born out of a pressing need for making trade-offs between economic activities and the quality and sustainability of the natural environment. In 1987, the World Commission for Environment and Development – the Brundtland Commission – came up with what became the most widely adopted definition of this concept:

> *Sustainable development is any development which meets the needs of the present without compromising the ability of future generations to meet their needs.* (World Commission on Environment and Development, 1987)

The commission recognized that unconstrained economic growth, consumption and social injustice would ultimately lead to environmental destruction and poverty. The 'new twist' of the Brundtland definition at the time was the link that it made between current and future needs of humankind with environmental and resource bases, while at the same time incorporating the notion of equity within and across geographical zones as well as across generations. Thus, sustainable development came to encompass the full range of human and natural systems including ecological, economic and socio-cultural aspects; the three so-called 'pillars of sustainability'.

This had significant implications not only for governments and policy makers, but also business and industry. The commission recognized the potential to leverage the increasing power of global corporations to promote sustainable development. As a net contributor to unsustainable behaviour through its intense use of natural and human resources and the impacts of production and consumption patterns, industry would also have to be brought into the foray.

Since then, there has been growing momentum behind the idea that companies have broader societal responsibilities, particularly during a more recent period of growing privatization of functions and processes formerly under governmental responsibility. This has coincided with a period of unprecedented growth in size of the modern corporation and at the same time, a proliferation of NGOs and not to be forgotten, a highly active anti-globalization movement.

The list of corporate governance scandals in recent years, such as those surrounding Enron, WorldCom, Ahold, Parmalat, and Adecco leading to massive loss of investor savings (and prompting the establishment of the Sarbanes–Oxley Act to assure more transparency and accuracy in corporate financial reporting), focused media and public attention not only on corporate governance and reputation issues but also on business social responsibility, while at the same time increasing public cynicism about corporations.

As we shall explore in this volume, modern day industrialized food systems cause significant social and environmental impacts. F&B corporate behaviour in the environmental and social domain has, as predicted by many eminent academics, increasingly become part of the public's criteria for judging companies (Carroll, 1979), but in spite of this we find survey reporting that only one third of European consumers believe that global companies act in the interests of society at least some of the time (Bonini *et al.*, 2006). The extent of distrust of European consumers about the F&B industry, for example, has been heavily impacted by numerous food scandals (see Chapter 3). The full extent of public mistrust of the industry is demonstrated by a study released by Tate & Lyle in 2005 which shows that as many as 65 per cent of consumers agree with the statement that 'often brands that claim to be healthy aren't healthy at all' (Sleep, 2005).

But, as with all additional complexity, external social expectations of companies increase both corporate risks and opportunities. This book will also explore these dynamics in the context of the food and beverage industry.

2 Conceptual framework

The Forum for CSM is a membership-driven research initiative. In May 2001, a representative of one of its member companies, a fast moving consumer goods (FMCG) company, wrote:

> *Our senior management takes a compliance driven view of environment, health and safety. This creates a dilemma for me when trying to deal with corporate social responsibility. They are not against, they just do not understand. I need to defend everything that my group does outside of compliance. Can you provide robust arguments about the contribution to shareholder value of 'sustainability' management? I need pragmatic, defensible information that cannot be challenged as being 'contrived' or biased towards an 'environmentalist' philosophy.*

This request typifies the dilemma often faced by those trying to promote the BCS in today's corporate environment. It contains some of the principle ingredients of what promoters of sustainability are often up against in their organizations; a sceptical management demonstrating a pragmatic 'what's in it for us' approach, a demand for as 'quantified' a business case as possible, with indisputable proof that sustainability positively impacts the corporate bottom line.

The correlation between sustainability and economic performance leading to a U shaped distribution curve has been used by several researchers as a model for promoting the case for 'win-win' BCS solutions (Lankowski, 2000; Steger, 2004). Steger refers to the positioning of a company on the curve as the search for the 'Smart Zone' (Steger, 2004), where companies can 'kill three birds with one stone' and create additional economic value by improving environmental and social performance (see Figure 1.1).

The most profitable sustainability projects are likely to be carried out first by companies (low hanging fruits), and moving along the curve, the company will finally reach a 'crossover point' where the investment becomes unprofitable. Allocating capital to projects that are not

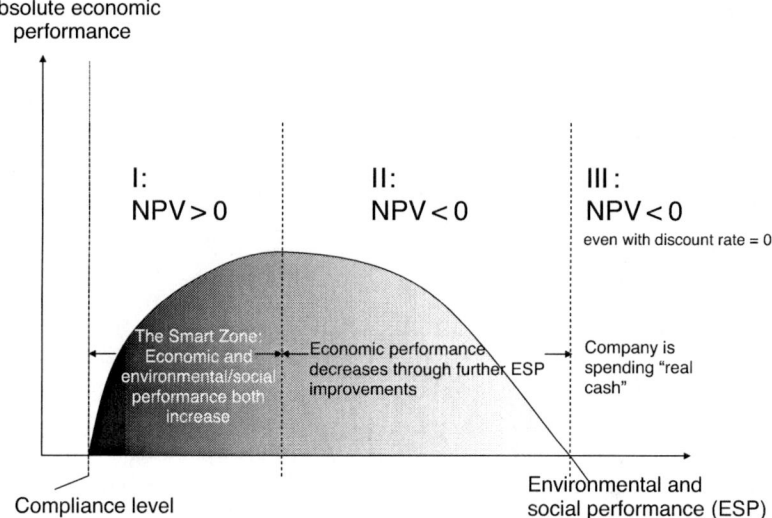

Figure 1.1 Relationship between economic and environmental/social performance beyond compliance – the 'Smart Zone'

as profitable as other competing projects then becomes a dilemma since corporate decision-makers weigh up the benefits and drawbacks of each and every project brought to their attention. Thus, the BCS must draw on as many elements as possible in order to make it robust and watertight. This book is intended to provide robust 'Smart Zone' arguments to managers in the F&B industry.

Members of the Forum for CSM felt that the question of whether the business case differs across industries is hardly ever addressed in research, although there are researchers that have identified the need for an industry or even company-specific business case.[3] The Forum for CSM therefore elected to approach the issue on a sector-specific basis so as to provide research perspectives and conclusions offering a more detailed and representative insight on the BCS across industries.

2.1 The BCS project

The BCS project was designed in partnership with the World Wide Fund for Nature (WWF) and was endorsed by the European Academy for Business in Society (EABIS). The project covered nine industries: chemical, pharmaceutical, automotive, technology, utilities, oil and gas, aviation, financial services and, last but not least, the industry that is the subject of this study, the F&B industry. The nine industry sectors were chosen based on their significant economic relevance and social and environmental impacts, and included a diversity of industries that had both similarities and differences.

The BCS project team acted within a solid framework of support and peer review from various entities; IMD itself, the members of the Forum for CSM, the project team, and an appointed Advisory Council that included representatives of the Forum for CSM member companies, the World Business Council for Sustainable Development (WBCSD) and WWF.

3 Research questions and objectives

For the sector-specific study on the F&B industry, we formulated several research questions based on a number of assumptions:

> **Research question 1:**
> *What is the perceived economic rationale behind the business case for sustainability in the F&B industry?*

Here, we seek arguments to constitute as robust a business case as possible. We aim to evaluate the extent to which managers are or are not convinced that by integrating sustainability issues into business strategy and focusing on the business opportunities they bring, F&B companies can better create economic value. In this way, we can assess the strength of the business case in the industry and its application. After all, when it comes to such value-loaded concepts, perception represents reality. Also, if managers are not convinced of the value of a proposition, then it is unlikely that they will act effectively upon it. We propose looking specifically at four areas and therefore formulate four sub-questions:

Research question 1a: *What is the competitive framework within which the industry is operating and how does this influence the sustainability agenda?*

Research question 1b: *What are the key social and environmental issues of economic relevance to the industry and why are they relevant?*

Research question 1c: *What stakeholder dynamics influence the business case for sustainability in the F&B industry; in particular, to what extent do different stakeholder groups promote or deter progress on application of a business case for sustainability in the industry?*

Research question 1d: *What are the value drivers prompting the industry to take action on sustainability issues and how are they currently operating?*

> **Research question 2:**
> *Is the F&B industry currently fully exploiting its business case for sustainability?*

Even if a robust business case is identified for the industry, we cannot assume that it is automatically integrated into industry business strategies, and adequately and efficiently rolled out. In order to understand the future potential of the economic argument, we describe the status of exploitation of the business case internally within F&B companies at the time of our research. It was our view that a reasonably accurate current assessment could only be obtained by talking to managers in their own contexts. There are two main sub-questions linked to the question of rollout of sustainability strategies that we wish to address:

Research question 2a: *What are the primary internal promoting factors and barriers influencing the rollout of the business case for sustainability in the F&B industry?*

Research question 2b: *What are the tools, instruments, methods and approaches currently being used to exploit the business case for sustainability in the F&B industry and how effective are they?*

4   Terminology

The concepts of sustainable development and hence corporate sustainability are complex and thus may seem abstract to managers. Indeed, we discovered a wide variety of definitions and interpretations of the term 'corporate sustainability' within the F&B industry. In order to better focus our research, we defined it as 'the corporate effort to improve social and environmental performance in areas not required by law without compromising financial performance'. To clarify our meaning, we supplied the following definition of the BCS to managers interviewed:

> *The business case for sustainability focuses on opportunities that companies can take to create economic value by improving environmental performance (such as increasing efficiency or reducing pollution) and social performance (for example, by engaging in community development) beyond compliance.*

In our study, all management tasks implicated in applying the concept of sustainability to business operations are referred to as 'corporate sustainability management' (CSM). We define CSM as:

> *a strategic corporate approach (based on a profit-driven agenda) to dealing with environmental and social externalities caused by corporate activities and operations.*

To simplify matters and to avoid confusion, we have used the term 'sustainability officer' as a generic term to refer to all managers with a heightened awareness of sustainability and who are dealing directly with sustainability matters and promoting the BCS for their companies internally and externally. However, it should be noted that most F&B companies have not defined the function under this name as sustainability tends to be addressed in different ways by different companies. All other managers, other than sustainability officers as defined above, are hereinafter referred to as 'business managers'.

5   Research instruments

We carried out both surveys and interviews, but looked also comprehensively at case studies, and other research, including empirical research related to both the industry and sustainability or corporate social responsibility (CSR). The research instruments – the survey and interview guidelines – can be consulted on the following website: www.imd.ch/research/centers/csm. We analyzed company reports and other data supplied by interviewees to complement our findings. We also reviewed media and press reports in the course of the research.

5.1   Survey results

Two complementary surveys were designed, one for sustainability officers and another for business managers. Certain questions included were devised specifically for the sustainability officer questionnaire in order to capitalize on the specific expertise and knowledge of sustainability officers. However, the majority of questions were in both questionnaires, allowing comparison of attitudes and perceptions between sustainability professionals and business managers.

Given that our research is based on managers' perceptions of issues that are sometimes sensitive, we expected to find a degree of bias towards 'social desirability'. Since volunteers to complete such surveys are often those who naturally have most interest in and motivation related to the topic of the survey, this is a significant source of positive bias in our study. Also, as is often experienced with similar management surveys and studies, the sample is male gender-biased.

Questionnaires were distributed:

- by e-mail to the companies participating in the research, for distribution as they felt appropriate
- by personal distribution to executives attending management courses at IMD
- via the BCS project website: www.businesscaseforsustainability.com to food and business managers encountered in the course of carrying out the research or doing business with the *Forum for CSM*.

A total of 123 surveys were collected from sustainability officers across sectors. Of these 19 were from the F&B industry (17 per cent of all responses) received, and was the second highest response from sustainability officers across all nine industries.

- The CSM research team collected 945 questionnaires from business managers in all industry sectors, of which 116 were completed by managers in a variety of management functions in the F&B sector.

5.2 Interviews with corporate executives and stakeholders

To triangulate our results, overcome any risks of subjective analysis and to assure credibility, extensive interviews with sustainability officers, business managers and stakeholders were carried out up to mid-2007. This also allowed us to establish causation as well as to benchmark the survey data over the period of research. This again also prevented bias or self-delusion, always a risk with qualitative research, with a chain of evidence assured using multiple data sources. Face-to-face semi-structured interviews were chosen as the best method to encourage sustainability officers and corporate executives to talk frankly about their views on the economic rationale and business logic for the BCS in the F&B industry. Also, since our approach would mainly be focused on 'if', 'why' and 'how' companies integrate or do not integrate sustainability into their business strategies, we felt that this could be best achieved in personal interviews. This helped to circumvent the bias towards social desirability to some extent and create an informal setting where executives would be less guarded and more willing to share attitudes and convictions. The interviews were not taped as, with some of the sensitive issues that had been thrown into the sustainability 'Pandora's Box', it was felt that this might inhibit managers.

We conducted a total of 53 personal interviews with sustainability and mostly senior business managers at 17 leading F&B companies. Extensive notes were taken and within 24 hours the content was summarized in a set format. In most cases, transcribed notes were sent to interviewees to ensure their accuracy and to invite additional clarification.

To continuously benchmark the research over time and incorporate views of relevant stakeholders, we carried out a total of 55 relevant interviews with F&B industry stakeholders, a further 60 hours of interview time. The interviews carried out were mostly informal benchmarking either in person or on the telephone.

5.3 Participating companies

Our sample includes large, globally active companies (multinationals), with more than 10,000 employees and activities in Europe, the Americas and Asia and with a home base primarily in Europe. The 17 F&B companies that engaged in the interview research were: Aarhus United, Cadbury Schweppes, Chiquita, the Coca Cola Company, Coca-Cola HBC (Switzerland), Danisco, Danone, Diageo, DSM, H.J. Heinz, Kraft International, Nespresso, Nestlé, Nutreco, Procter & Gamble (P&G), Scottish and Newcastle (S&N), and Unilever (see Figure 1.2).

The top five European Union (EU) F&B manufacturers, ranked by turnover, are Nestlé, Unilever, Diageo, Danone and Cadbury Schweppes, all of whom are included in our sample, lending considerable credibility to our research. In 2007, Nestlé, Unilever, Kraft and Danone alone accounted for more than 50 per cent of the global market capitalization of the top 30 global food companies.

Companies that choose voluntarily to participate in research of this nature tend either to be leaders in corporate sustainability or

Figure 1.2 Food and beverage companies involved in the BCS food and beverage interview research

are striving to become so. For obvious reasons, our research was unlikely to appeal to corporate laggards; the study therefore enables us to provide a snapshot of industry benchmarks on CSM better practices and capitalize on a deep understanding amongst managers of barriers and promoting factors for the BCS within the sector.

6 The roadmap

A preliminary literature review revealed that research so far has not succeeded in *empirically* identifying the key economic arguments that managers require to push the business case for sustainability through the decision-making structures and align their organizations behind it. An overview of the literature is presented online at www.imd.ch/research/centers/csm and is enlightening.

In Chapter 2, we carry out a brief industry analysis of the F&B industry, relating current trends in competitiveness in the industry to threats and opportunities presented by sustainability objectives. Chapter 3 assesses the economic relevance of issues of most importance to managers in the F&B sector based on empirical data and reveals how stakeholders and the media transmit these issues onto the sustainability agenda of companies (stakeholder transmission belts). In Chapter 4, we identify the principal stakeholders perceived by managers as deterring or promoting sustainable performance in the F&B value chain and assess external pressures on the industry to act on sustainability issues. Chapter 5 examines the key value drivers for sustainability identified by managers and relate these to competitiveness and financial performance of F&B multinationals. We will summarize the approach of leading F&B companies to sustainability management and exploitation of the BCS in Chapter 6, and scrutinize the principal factors and functions impeding or promoting rollout of sustainability objectives within F&B corporations. We also scrutinize industry better-practice examples of implementation of the BCS in food supply chains.

The executive summary provided at the beginning of this book provides an overview of the current exploitation and potential for exploitation of the BCS within the sector. In it, we identify why and in what circumstances corporate sustainability matters to corporate competitiveness within the F&B industry. We describe how companies are exploiting the BCS and outline factors limiting a more comprehensive exploitation of opportunities that sustainability might present to the industry.

Notes

1 See *The Economist*, 2004e.
2 See www.imd.ch/research/centers/csm for access to the reports and toolsets.
3 See Henriques and Sadorsky, 1996 and Lankowski, 2000.

2
Industry and Competitive Analysis

1 Introduction

Competition drives the very need for a company to be strategic. As Kenichi Ohmae, Japanese business writer and McKinsey consultant once pointed out:

> *Without competitors there would be no need for strategy, for the sole purpose of strategic planning is to enable the company to gain, as effectively as possible, a sustainable edge over its competitors.* (Ohmae, 1983)

One of the original meanings of the word 'strategy' was 'to create an advantage' – usually military – which implied the existence of competition. Our study is concerned with questions related to if, why and how F&B companies integrate social and environmental programmes or actions into business strategy in order to create a sustainable comparative business advantage.

To formulate their business strategies, companies first gather data to understand their macro business environment and the forces that determine their position within the markets they serve. Various dimensions require attention: governmental, socio-cultural, economic and competitive. This forms the basis for a corporate strategic plan and long-term vision that is grounded in a company's own economic reality, allowing the development of a product/market portfolio that places the company in an optimum position of comparative advantage. Indeed, since corporate strategy is very much related to the relationship between the company and society in general, our competitive analysis provides a suitable framework within which to consider sustainability in later chapters.

Following this logic, we consider that an understanding of the motives behind consumer trends, the competitive environment and the relationship between supply and demand within the F&B industry will inform our research on a BCS within that industry, allow us better to understand the economic rationale for including appropriate sustainability strategies in overall business strategy, and set the context for our subsequent analysis of our empirical results and discussion.

2 Industry definition and profile

There is no all-encompassing definition of the F&B industry. Given the diversity of this industry segment, it is difficult to set boundaries that apply globally. For the purpose of this study, the F&B industry will be defined principally by its role as secondary or final processors of agricultural raw materials into food and beverage products.

Rabobank expands on the *raison d'être* of companies in the sector:

Food and beverage companies in the world's food markets provide low, middle and high income populations with basic and special foods, with fresh and long life products, packaged and unpackaged foods, bulk and added value products. (Baas *et al.*, 1999)

The F&B industry is a highly visible and important part of the world economy. Today, an estimated US$ 4,300 billion is spent on food worldwide and of this, the developed markets of Europe and the USA account for almost 60 per cent. In Europe, the F&B manufacturing sector's economic influence is substantial (CIAA, 2006). It is:

- Europe's largest manufacturing sector (13.6 per cent of the total with over €836 billion of production).
- the European Union's third largest industrial employer with over 3.8 million employees Through its activities, the sector creates a myriad of additional jobs for retailers, suppliers and other business partners.
- made up of some 282,600 companies. Since dominated by SMEs, it is a fragmented industry with a relatively low concentration but it is important nevertheless to note that the 0.9 per cent represented by global companies produces a little over 50 per cent of the total turnover.

- widely diversified, covering both first stage as well as second stage processing.
- a leading exporting sector with a positive trade balance of some €4 billion.
- a transformer of more than 70 per cent of the agricultural raw materials produced in the EU.

Overall, the sector has little cyclicality and assures consistent returns based on steady growth. In 2002 – at the outset of our research – it had held its own despite a difficult economic climate in Europe, and had even registered a slight growth. Some researchers describe the sector as recession proof,[1] since while consumers may be able to do without other material goods, they will always need to eat and drink. For this reason, it is popular with investment buyers, and attracts institutional investors with diversified portfolios (the relevance of capital markets to sustainability is explored in Chapter 4). While F&B companies went through a difficult period in the late 1990s, seeing their market value decline, with investors steering towards technology, media and tele-communications companies, the sector is now increasingly attracting the attention of private equity buyers as a result of the bust of technology stocks and the trend towards consolidation.

Of the total budget annually spent on food worldwide, approx-imately two-thirds is spent on food in retail outlets and one-third in food service establishments. For this reason, we include a discussion not only on the competitiveness of the food manufacturing sector and its relevance to sustainability, but also the dynamics of the power pulls between retail outlets and food service establishments that affect the ability of F&B manufacturers to sustain and gain market share in both domestic or foreign markets, and also, and very importantly for this study, their capacity to integrate and implement sustainability objectives.

3 Demographics, consumption trends and markets

Between 1960 and 2007, world population grew from 3 to over 6.5 billion people – the staggering rapidity of increase is unprecedented in the history of human society. This trend will almost certainly con-tinue, to reach a level of at least 9 to 10 billion people at the end of the twenty-first century. About 60 per cent of this population growth will occur in the currently low income group in underdeveloped countries (Baas *et al.*, 1999). This fact provides substantial 'food for thought' when it comes to the question of the nature of the industry's future markets.

At the turn of the century, 16 of the top 30 food companies were still obtaining more than 70 per cent of their turnover in their home markets (Baas *et al.*, 1999). As we go to press in 2008, the industry is undergoing major change in its markets. Most managers in the industry agree that very little or zero growth will be experienced in the future in the high-income markets of the USA, Europe and Japan. Instead, middle-income markets, such as some countries in Asia, will be the primary targets for F&B companies as these are the areas where new future high-income consumers will be found. Countries such as China, for example, have been experiencing the most buoyant growth in recent years (GreenBiz.com, 2006; CIAA, 2006), and F&B companies are increasingly but cautiously looking in this direction, acquiring local brands and adapting products for these markets (Chang, 2004).

However, whereas customers in Europe spend only 20 per cent of their weekly budget on food, alcohol and tobacco, people in middle-income markets spend anything between 35 and 40 per cent. Price is thus a primary decisive factor in purchasing in these markets. This is significant in terms of our later discussions in Chapter 4 on consumer 'willingness to pay' for more sustainable products.

Given recent histories of financial crises, political unrest and even civil wars, developing markets also imply a fair share of risk for F&B, as well as other companies (just-food.com, 2004a). Danone's bitter 2007 battles in China and India with local business partners is a case to consider. Despite the risks, because of their immense future market potential these markets cannot be ignored (*The Economist*, 2004c).

Furthermore, demographic growth is tending towards zero in the rich developed countries where most of the market is currently focused, and the post-war 'baby boom' populations that reached a peak in the developed world in the 1960s and early 1970s are aging, implying substantial changes to future consumer bases in these countries. Industry pundits generally agree that F&B companies will increasingly have to cater for the old and infirm in Europe, Japan and the United States; this will greatly influence product portfolios in those regions.

Given the dependency of the human organism on food and drink for survival, demographics and the socio-economic circumstances of people are fundamentally important to F&B industry competitiveness. Relationships with food can be very different around the globe depending on population demographics (numbers, age), national culture and economics (relative wealth). One of the indicators of wealth of a society is observed evolution of food consumption patterns and food related behaviour. As personal income increases, consumers move away from commodity products such as grains and cereals and increasingly opt for more value-added convenience products involving complex processing steps for manufacturers and reduction of overall consumer preparation time. As they move along the spectrum of wealth creation, people also begin eating not only to satisfy basic nutrition needs, but also for pleasure – so called 'indulgence eating' – and in more sophisticated markets, increasingly for health benefits. It seems that little will change the trend amongst consumers in the United States and in Europe to opt for convenience and indulgence in their food consumption (OECD, 1998). In currently defined middle-income markets, we can expect similar trends to those currently observed in high income markets; an increasing popularity of fast, processed and indulgence food and more diversified consumption.

In developed countries, women have moved to working more outside the home, and there is also a significant and ongoing rise in single parent families. The average Western consumer today expects to spend no more than 30 minutes in preparing, eating and cleaning up after a meal and food products are increasingly more complex and highly processed (frozen or pre-prepared) to cater for this demand. Studies even show that cooking in the USA is trending to become more of a hobby than a practical everyday requirement and family meals have often become the domain of the more affluent members of society, having been replaced by a snacking culture – or 'grazing' as it is often now termed, with large numbers of consumers unused to preparing meals from basic ingredients. According to US government statistics, almost half of all food in the USA is now eaten outside the home and, as with many US trends, Europeans are rapidly following suit. This has led to a gradual but steady rise in importance of the food service sector over the last few decades as a key part of the competition equation for the F&B industry.

In Europe, there has been a gradual convergence in taste and diet. Research even indicates a trend towards convergence in demand amongst consumers worldwide. Manufacturers have been leveraging their strong worldwide positions and ensuring maximum profitability by adopting global strategies but adapting to local market conditions where necessary. Competition between firms is absolutely fierce, not only between the multinationals themselves but also between multinationals and rapidly expanding local groups (in Asia for example) that have a cultural and political knowledge of their markets way sometimes beyond that of multinationals (Ashcroft and Goldberg, 1996). We shall examine in later chapters whether corporate sustainability management can contribute to closing this gap.

However, while convenience is the main dominant factor in the USA, Rabobank reports that European consumers consider convenience as only one of several factors such as freshness, price, quality, health and so on. Partly due to the fact that populations are aging, consumers are starting to seek healthy options in their diet; this is also confirmed by industry market research (Baas *et al.*, 1999; just-food.com, 2004d). Indeed, health and safety in eating is becoming a major focus of certain niches of consumers in the developed world, leading to a growing interest in local food access and organic markets with emphasis on direct contact between consumers and farmers. A 'slow food' movement has also gathered momentum, aiming to cultivate common cultural interests of food social utility.[2]

4   Competitive analysis

Porter's model of the five forces of industry competition (Porter, 1980) is a standard tool for analysis of competitiveness. Briefly, here is how Porter describes these forces:

- Intensity of rivalry among the producers themselves within a specific industry, cutthroat competition, oligopoly, dispersion and so on.
- Threat that other products or services could be substituted, thereby placing the industry in a weaker position.
- Power of suppliers to ask for, and receive, higher prices in their sales negotiations.
- Power of buyers to obtain better deals through comparison shopping, threat of desertion, or other ways of weakening producers' bargaining power.
- Barriers to entry preventing new firms from competing and weakening the position of existing firms.

In the following sections, we elaborate on these forces and how they affect the F&B competitive environment, outlining important sustainability dimensions.

4.1 Degree of rivalry

F&B manufacturing industry mainly comprises three types of corporate entity:

- Global multinationals, such as those researched in this study, with turnovers measured in billions of euro and with significant exports.
- Large companies with turnovers in tens or hundreds of millions of euro, supplying a limited range of national brands and increasingly supplying private label products to retailers, but not exporting significantly.
- SMEs, often family owned, mostly supplying local or specialist markets – the most common category, but also increasingly exporting in niche markets.

According to a report in 2001 by Bank Sarasin on the F&B industry (Fawer-Wasser *et al.*, 2001), there were about 1,000 listed F&B companies coming into this century. Owing to a period of intense mergers and acquisitions that has gone on for over the last two decades, the sector comprises an increasingly smaller number of global international players but is still largely fragmented. Under considerable competitive pressure, companies have been using mergers and acquisitions to align themselves to their corporate strategies, and buy technology or brands. There is a confirmed Europeanization among the larger food manufacturers. Companies in Europe have also been consolidating to take advantage of the single market. The result is that today, a few large firms with similar market share and that produce well known brands globally dominate the top end of the market, with the top four players in the industry accounting for more than 50 per cent of the global market capitalization of the top 30 global food companies. The world's top 30 companies have food sales of just under €580 billion, and the top ten have sales sometimes well in excess of €20 billion each. In the future, multi-site processors will probably strategically reduce numbers of sites, while smaller and larger companies will still merge with others to create economies of scale in the face of continuing price pressure from consumers. These trends are typical of what Porter (1985) refers to as a 'wealth driven economy'.

Amongst the top players, there is a significant struggle for market leadership, with intense rivalry in the marketplace. Companies strive to take market share away from competitors in saturated markets in developed countries in the USA and Europe, where overall food spending has been reaching a plateau and opportunities for growth are limited. To offset this situation, larger companies are also devoting considerable resources and energy to increasing their market share in the developing countries, their main opportunity for growth. Acquisitions are often the most efficient way to penetrate such markets.

Leaders in the industry are using options such as product differentiation, creative use of distribution channels and exploitation of relationships with suppliers in order to move away from a commodity type market where no competing firm has a differentiation advantage. Our book explores whether this presents an opportunity for sustainable development to feature more in future strategy-making in the industry.

4.2 Barriers to entry

The vast number of start-ups, small and medium-sized companies in the market is an indication that there are low barriers to entry to F&B markets, at least on a local level. Producing food on a small scale does not involve the investment of large capital resources and assets can be utilized to produce a variety of different products, again leading to economies of scale. The push from retailers for new and innovative products, so that they themselves can gain competitive edge, provides opportunities not only for new entrants to the market, but also for growth opportunities and development of existing manufacturers. In Chapter 5 we examine whether this is also an opportunity for sustainability to take more of a strategic hold in companies.

However, at the global level barriers to entry are significantly higher, in that companies have achieved very significant economies of scale over small firms. They have also been in the market place for a long time and can thus exploit their experience, established assets and know-how. They also work hard at increasing product differentiation through branding. Investing capital in building a brand name is a risky business for start-ups and has become so capital-intense that even the major players balk at introducing new brands.

Food safety regulation lowers barriers to entry for new entrants, in that standards for product testing impose substantial lead times that raise capital costs and also give rivals access to information about new products not as yet launched, affording them time to plan a retaliatory strategy. One might therefore assume that it is in the industry's best interest to be ahead of regulation and to foresee areas where regulation may become a competitive disadvantage. We discuss regulators as 'promoting' stakeholders for corporate sustainability in Chapter 4.

4.3 Threat of substitutes

The relatively widespread availability of close substitutes for F&B products is a considerable competitive threat for the industry. In addition, the costs to retailers of switching to a substitute product are often low, unless the manufacturer has a brand advantage. The threat of substitutes typically impacts an industry through price competition. This makes it difficult for other companies in the sector to raise prices, except where there is a product differentiation advantage. It also leaves the sector, as a whole, much less profitable than other sectors. Thus, major companies are reducing these threats mostly by focusing on product differentiation through perceived brand value and product repositioning, with the expectation that this will lead to surges in demand and sustained growth. Moreover, by establishing brand loyalty, leading companies in the industry can increase barriers to entry, making it more difficult for retailers to switch to new competing products or to establish their own brands. Again, in Chapter 5, we explore whether this constitutes an opportunity to move sustainability further up the company agenda.

4.4 Supplier power

The negotiating power of producers for the industry is generally low, mainly owing to a fragmented source of supply, with elongated and complex supply chains that are extremely variable depending on the commodity in question. In general; the more complex the supply chain, the less influence suppliers have over companies. The overcapacity of some commodities in developing countries is a good example of these forces in operation, where there are significant implications for sustainable development in the developing countries that produce the commodities, as producers working in fragile economies are at the mercy of the fluctuations of volatile commodity markets (see Chapter 3). The switching costs of changing from one primary producer to another are low for the concentrated group of global companies, thus increasing the vulnerability of producers. However, companies in the industry trend away from vertical integration (and are shedding ownership of commodity production) which works better for multi-crop per year horticultural production facilities; for commodities, there are too few crops per year to hedge risk. This does mean that there is greater risk for companies that do not have robust supplier relationships.

4.5 Buyer power

In less mature markets, food is either produced for subsistence or is sold, unprocessed or requiring minimal processing, direct to the consumer. However, in mature markets, the food retail sector and the food service sector are the final links in the supply chain, and it is through these sectors that the food manufacturer interfaces with the end consumer. Hence, the role of these two sectors in influencing manufacturing activities, including the sustainable development agenda in companies, is primordial.

4.5.1 Retailers

Retailers are veritable gatekeepers controlling the direction of the modern food system. This is reflected in a growing share of profits of the food chain. They are up against similar challenges to the manufacturing sector: changes in economic factors, demographic changes, consumer concerns and behaviour and, in Europe, the convergence in demand patterns, taste and diet.

Retailers purchase a significant proportion of output from the F&B industry and buy in volume. To be in Europe's top ten grocers requires annual sales of more than 25 billion euros (Blake 2003); competition is fierce since F&B products provide a relatively low profit margin. There are two possibilities to enhance the bottom line for retail companies: finding economies of scale or creating a captive market. This increased power and concentration has often been at the expense of small and medium-sized – so called 'mom and pop' – retail stores, an evolution that certainly has sustainability dimensions on a social level. There is an identifiable and ongoing trend towards consolidation of the retail sector through mergers, takeovers and strategic alliances, and collective purchasing – bulk buying. As one NGO observer points out:

> *It is not unrealistic to imagine global markets in which food retail is controlled by four to five global firms, with a handful of regional and national companies, and in which food manufacture is dominated by some ten companies using only about 25 brand names.* (Tickell, 2004)

The trends give significant power to the previously fragmented retail sector over both the product and its price. Traditionally, when the retail sector was more fragmented, the balance of power swayed in favour of the food manufacturer (Baas *et al.*, 1998, p. 38). But the roles have evolved significantly in the last ten years, and a much more ambiguous relationship has emerged. On the one hand, there is mutual dependence involved and a great deal is to be gained through working together (see Unilever, 2005 for an example). We acknowledge, for example, the emergence and increasing importance of initiatives such as 'Efficient Consumer Response' (ECR),[3] a voluntary and industry-wide effort by the whole F&B industry, including manufacturers, suppliers and retailers to provide increased quality and service to consumers at reduced prices through cost control, automatic replenishment of shelf stock and minimizing inefficiencies. On the other hand, in a mature purchase environment the retailer has evolved as a purchase channel of increasingly more sophisticated consumers expecting retailers to meet their requirements. The retailer transmits this pressure to the manufacturing sector. Retailers and manufacturers can gain from working together on aspects such as product range composition, promotional activities and product development, in terms of cost savings, for example. If they do not, they risk not being able to meet the increasingly changing expectations of the consumer.

With concentration, retailers have started to 'brand' themselves by developing special images for quality, variety or value for money, and are also exerting power over manufacturers through the provision of private label options to consumers. Private brands can either be cheap alternatives to existing brands, items that limit quality characteristics while maintaining a price advantage, or they can be brands that compete fully with major brands in terms of quality and innovation (Baas *et al.*, 1998). Retailers use their own private labels as a positioning tool and as an opportunity to achieve higher margins (Quelch and Harding, 1996). Catering for private label brands that lack a public identity neutralizes the strength of the processor's brand in overcoming the strong buyer power to which manufacturers are subjected. Therefore, rather than produce private brands for retailers, leading manufacturers trend more to strengthen their own brands to overcome the push–pull dilemma and reach out directly to consumers.

The existence of private labels transforms the retailer into both a buyer and, to some extent, a competitor of the branded manufacturing industry in an ever intensifying 'rat-race'. The marketing and advertising associated with branding is an expensive endeavour, possibly more than 15 per cent of the final price of a food product (Giampietro, 1997). It is an activity that commercially applies itself most effectively on a global level, where the manufacturer can achieve both economies of scale and a more powerful position, minimizing or – at least reducing – threats of new entrants to markets. Indeed, if food manufacturer branding is successful, it makes retailers question whether a private brand endeavour will be worthwhile.

Globalization of the F&B industry has led in many cases to instant brand recognition around the world. The fact that consumers demand their preferred brands globally obliges retailers to stock them. Customers in emerging markets often know the strong recognizable brands well in advance of the arrival of F&B multinationals, and demand these brands as they move towards matching their aspirations to a better standard of living. When this happens, negotiating power transfers to the manufacturer. Thus, the manufacturers try to build up consumer loyalty carefully by producing appealing and successful brands, and the retailers try to create similar loyalty to their stores by manufacturing private labels, thus undermining the global brand loyalty built up by manufacturers.

In low technology products, retailers can shop around to obtain the lowest price, especially when raw material costs are a high percentage of total costs, as in fresh foods. Retailers have alternative sources of supply depending on the complexity of the product. This leads to a significant trend to discount at retail level. The costs of switching to other products can be low provided the product does not require advanced technology for production. Often, the lower the level of technology incorporated in a food product, the higher the private label share of total sales, and the greater the risk of switching. Thus, leading manufacturing companies are increasingly moving even further along the spectrum of added value, producing, for example, 'functional foods'; foods that require costly development and are oriented towards specific consumer requirements, such as providing health or medical benefits, or preventing illness.

In developing countries, buyer power tends to be weaker as retailers are generally more fragmented, although this is also gradually changing as European retail companies move to expand into these areas. The significance of retailers in deterring the promotion of a BCS is discussed further in Chapter 4.

4.5.2   Food service operators

Food manufacturers recognize the new potential for food service operators to innovate and will be increasingly looking to them in order to diversify their customer base and escape the power pulls of large retail chains. The food service sector includes fast-food restaurants, standard restaurants and catering firms, and is extremely diverse. Indeed, it is difficult to define succinctly as there are so many types of operation in this area.[4] The food service sector is also engaged in a process of consolidation and globalization. Apart from mergers, acquisitions and joint ventures, what characterizes the food service is its success in developing global networks of franchisees such as McDonald's, Pizza Hut and Burger King. Known the world over, these companies have successfully built up strong brands to differentiate themselves in the global market.

There is fierce competition between retailers and food service operators to gain what the industry refers to as 'share of stomach'. Retailers regard the food service sector as a threat to their own market share and have innovated to compete (such as by producing 'ready' and chilled meals). Retailers strive to build their positions in local markets in advance of the arrival of food service competitors. Once the food service operators arrive, they target customer loyalty based on a number of intangibles such as convenience and reputation.

Considering the direct interface between food service operators and the consumer, sustainability issues that arise with food service operators are bound to also be of relevance to the food manufacturer. In the remainder of our study, we have therefore taken account in our analysis of the impact of some of these issues on the F&B sector when relevant and appropriate.

5 Synthesis

The competitive environment within which the manufacturing sector of the F&B industry operates is in continuous flux, since global megatrends are constantly creating entirely new dimensions to the competitive relationships within the industry. Globalization has led to a breakdown in boundaries, increases in competition and, thus, rivalry. Markets, technologies, regulation regimes, consumer behaviour and geopolitics as a whole subject the industry to an array of discontinuities. No doubt about it; the business environment for the F&B global multinational is complex and challenging.

The socio-cultural, ecological and economic factors influenced by, and influencing, relevant mega-trends lead to a startling range of social responsibility implications for F&B companies. We suggest that balancing the social, environmental and economic position is perhaps even more challenging for front-runners such as the F&B industry than for industries that are more removed from the 'front line', such as the technology sector. F&B companies that wish to do well and be profitable have to keep an ever closer eye on developments outside the factory gates. Our next chapter will show how sustainable development is an integral part of this picture.

Notes

1 An example: the sector was less affected than other industries by the economic crisis following terrorist attacks in the United States on 11 September 2001.
2 See www.slowfood.com
3 See www.fmi.org
4 See Rabobank's 'The World of Foodservice' (market study, December, 1998), p. 10.

3
The Economic Relevance of Sustainability Issues

1 Introduction

The primary and secondary activities of companies can be linked to social or environmental externalities. Externalities are either positive or negative impacts on any entity not involved in a given economic transaction. They are non-market forces and occur when decisions cause costs or benefits to third party stakeholders, often, though not always, through use of a public good.[1] Moreover, participants in the transaction do not bear its full costs or indeed reap all of its benefits.

Environmental or social externalities may be directly traced to a specific corporate operational activity – such as the local pollution of a river system. However, other externalities are less directly attributable – such as the impacts of supplier behaviour upstream of company operations when, for example, child labour is used in production of raw material. Externalities – global, regional or local environmental or social problems – convert to what we refer to in this chapter as *sustainability issues* for companies when there is pressure to integrate them as part of a company strategic agenda either because regulation requires the company to address them, or because of increased pressure or expected increased pressure from stakeholders such as NGOs, customers and regulators. It is the latter case that we are considering in our search for the BCS.

Since the days of the industrial revolution, there is somewhat of an expectation in Europe that social issues such as health and safety (H&S) and social security (pushed onto company agendas by both unions and legislators) are dealt with appropriately by companies. The focus by companies was thus initially squarely on H&S as well as employee rights issues 'inside the factory gates'. While environmental destruction and the usurping of non-renewable resources ultimately also has a social impact, development of the environmental dimension to the BCS, both in academic theory as well as in corporate practice, has been in rapid evolution only since the latter part of the twentieth century. This was primarily due to increasing pressure on natural resources, the failure of governments to police industrial impacts efficiently and increasing public interest in these issues. The already mentioned phenomenal increase in the political and public influence of NGOs[2] had a first knock-on effect of increasing focus by managers precisely on managing environmental externalities, again as they related to daily operations.

What follows in this chapter will show that the focus of stakeholders has irrevocably changed to also focus on 'outside the factory gates', for a variety of reasons, creating a great number of relatively new, complex and challenging dilemmas for companies, some of which are of increasing strategic significance for the sector. We assess awareness of F&B managers to sustainable development issues and their perception of the level of integration of sustainability issues to corporate strategy during the period of research. We identify the issues perceived as economically relevant by managers and analyze the forces that work to call a specific corporate behaviour into question around certain issues, in some cases threatening the economic *raison d'être* of companies.

2 Industry awareness of sustainable development and issues

Several managers we interviewed commented on the personal nature of food and the emotion surrounding the topic that made their industry vulnerable to public appraisal and changing dynamics:

> *There is a lot of emotion involved with food. Even though we have an agenda, there will be issues for which our company is not prepared. Points of view are varied on the issues and it is difficult to ascertain who will get it right. Multinationals and large companies are under more scrutiny than smaller companies.* (BCS46 – Senior regional business unit manager, Marketing and sales)

Indeed, people generally feel strongly about what they consume; we can deduce this from public reactions when issues concerning food hit the headlines and in today's world, this happens uncomfortably often for F&B companies. From bird flu and foot and mouth to obesity and the plight of poverty stricken farmers in developing countries, in consulting the daily press during the period of our research, there was virtually no day when a F&B sustainability related issue was not featured either directly or indirectly. The fact that F&B products have their direct origins in the natural environment brings an added complexity to the framework within which F&B companies operate. A mass of diverse sustainability issues related to F&B can potentially hit corporate radar screens, because the personal nature of food has a myriad of social and environmental dimensions.

At the outset of our research, some 45 per cent of managers from diverse business functions in global companies in the F&B sector considered themselves to be very familiar with the concept of sustainable development. This indicated relatively high estimation of awareness within the industry since the average of all industries surveyed in the BCS project was at a level of only 27 per cent (see comparative Figures 3.1 and 3.2). Even taking social desirability bias into account, it is evident that given the frontline nature of the industry, and most probably the publicity that F&B sustainability related events generate, managers have probably gained more familiarity with the concept of sustainable development than managers in other industries.

Interestingly, and probably for very similar reasons, a large majority of business managers surveyed (84 per cent) felt that the concept of sustainable development would grow in importance in the future.

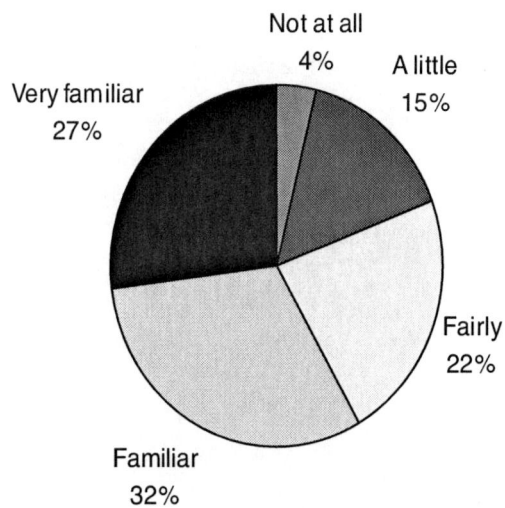

Figure 3.1   Managers' familiarity with sustainable development: all industries

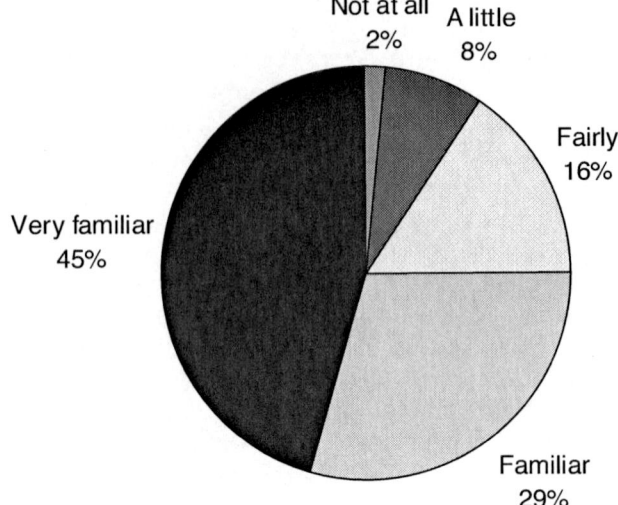

Figure 3.2 Managers' familiarity with sustainable development: food and beverage industry

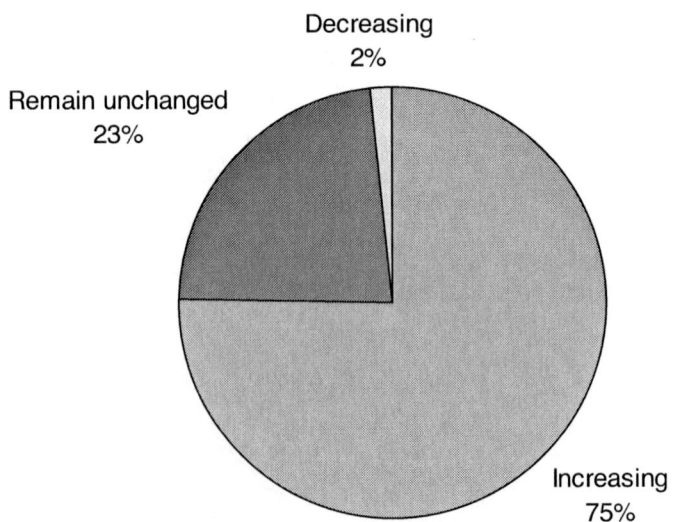

Figure 3.3 Business managers' view on whether SD as a concept would grow in the future: all sectors

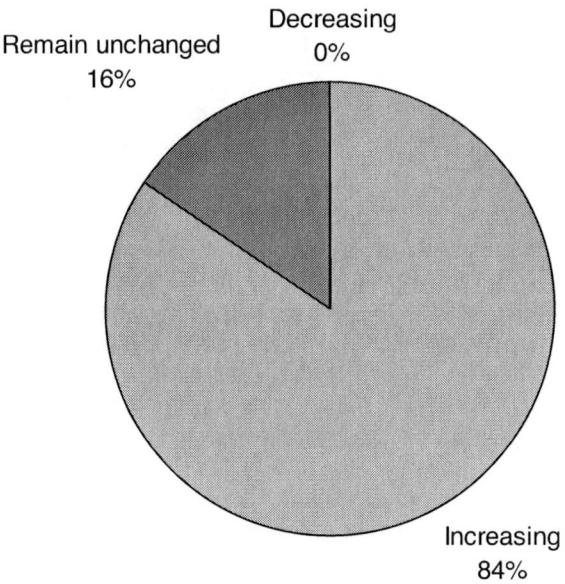

Remain unchanged
16%

Decreasing
0%

Increasing
84%

Figure 3.4 Business managers' view on whether SD as a concept would grow in the future: F&B industry only

A lower (but nevertheless large) average percentage of managers in other industries also believed this (75 per cent) (compare Figures 3.3 and 3.4). Certainly, the depth of conviction in the F&B industry was striking.

Without exception, our interviewees also felt that the importance of sustainability would increase significantly for F&B corporations of the future. In fact, business managers appeared convinced of the permanence of sustainability on their corporate agendas:

There are clear messages that the sustainability agenda is not going to go away and is too big to ignore. (BCS47a, Business manager, Supply chain)

This being the case, one could expect that the record for actual performance in social and environmental issue integration into business strategy would be somewhat better than average. However, research carried out by Oekom[3] examined the extent to which 32 major players in the F&B industry were responding to the environmental, social and cultural challenges confronting them (Reinery, 2004). The industry scored only average performance in social and environmental sustainability, with Unilever, Nestlé and Danisco achieving the best results. In a grading system on a scale from A+ to D–, only one company, Unilever, received a score above the average (B–). A slightly later study by Aon, an insurance broker, on how F&B companies were addressing social and environmental risk produced similar conclusions (Aon, 2005).

As a further benchmark, our own survey offers some endorsement of these independent survey findings. The sample of sustainability officers we surveyed was convinced that, compared to other industries, the F&B industry was mostly only an average performer (where sustainable practices are concerned) – see Figure 3.5 – suggesting that in these managers' perceptions, there was still ample room for improvement. This is in spite of the fact that 61 per cent of the same officers rated their own companies as being out-performers as compared to other F&B companies in their industry.

Much of this chapter, as well as Chapters 4 and 5 are devoted to looking at and understanding the dynamics that pushes sustainability onto the company radar screen, and also why it is sometimes difficult for companies to integrate such issues.

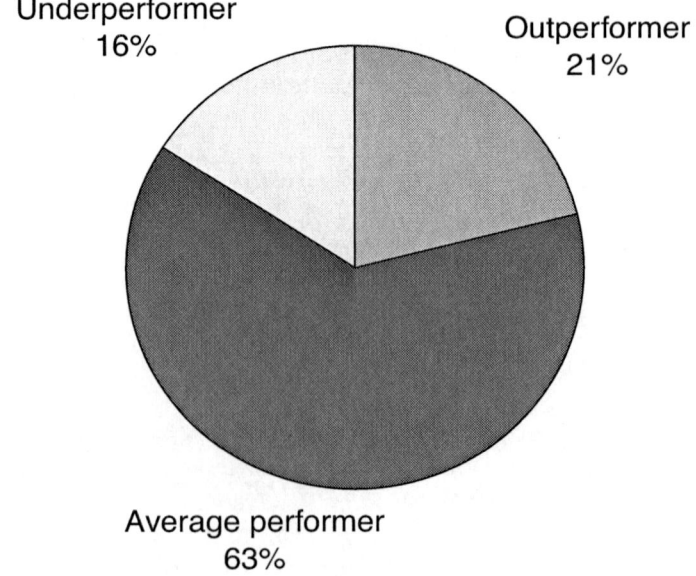

Figure 3.5 Industry progress in adopting more sustainable business practices

Managers were sceptical about the food industry sustainability leadership position:

If investor relations look to the food industry for sustainability leadership (...) it does not have a very impressive record. (BCS11 – Senior business manager, Investor relations)

The food industry is not head of the field on sustainability issues; there is not much clear thinking about these issues and there are not enough companies in the lead. (BCS03 – Senior sustainability officer)

The F&B industry produced a report on collaboration with United Nations Environmental Program (UNEP) as a contribution to the United Nations World Summit on Sustainable Development in Johannesburg, South Africa (CIAA, 2002). The report stated that:

much has already been achieved and (...) in many cases the food and drink industry has been at the forefront of the development. (p.5)

However, views of managers within the F&B industry during the period of research did not correspond to this public statement of the industry view of itself:

The food industry is broadcasting the fact that everything is under control. Yet it is not paying enough attention to emerging issues and doesn't see the challenges or problems. For example, the sector lobbied to be exempt from the IPPC directive.[4] *Clearly, the industry finds it difficult to link production of food to environmental degradation.* (BCS47a – Business manager, Supply chain)

External stakeholders we interviewed were also sceptical about the sustainability record of the industry:

The food industry is lagging behind other sectors. The environmental impacts of branded companies are dire. Food companies have an opportunity of being at the vanguard of sustainability; instead, they have an extremely narrow perspective. (BCSBM6 – Food industry expert)

The F&B industry reminds me of how the tobacco industry was 30 years ago. Large parts of the industry are in denial. When challenged, responses are reactionary. The industry is not acting on the problems. (BCSBM7 – Food industry expert)

What, then, might be stopping F&B companies from moving forward with a strategic and efficiently operational sustainability agenda? The reasons are complex and relate to both the building of the BCS and its implementation. To start with, we look here in detail at the dynamics of how and why issues hit the corporate radar screen and the challenges that companies have in dealing with them.

3 The food and beverage value chain

Michael Porter's concept of the industry or business value chain (1980) is cited as a centrepiece of business strategy by management theorists and practitioners in recent years. Rather than describe business as a set of sequential manufacturing based operations, the value chain concept encompasses a set of processes involving numerous actors (suppliers, business partners, alliances, customers) working together to produce value for customers.

The value chain of the supply of food materials from farm to supermarket (leading to popular jargon terms such as 'farm to fork' or from 'stable to table') is ever longer and more complex. As we can see from Figure 3.6, the food industry is 'sandwiched' between its suppliers and its customers, and is at least one step removed from the end consumer. As a consequence, the issues that affect its suppliers and its immediate customers (the retailers) can also be relevant for the processing industry.

Commodities or other ingredients undergo a complex process of production, processing and distribution as they are transformed into a processed food product for consumption. A single product may have ingredients from many different locations, and may have undergone several stages of processing in different countries. Indeed, the total distance travelled by the average food item has more than doubled in the

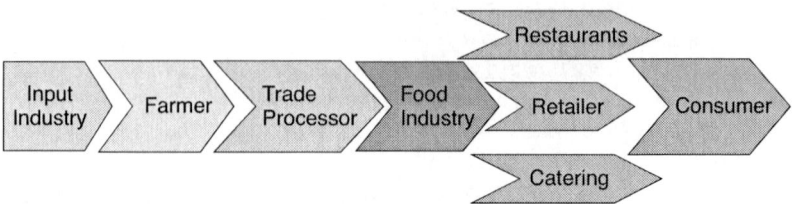

Figure 3.6   Food and beverage industry value chain

last ten years, and it is still growing. At each stage in the chain, there are sustainability issues; in fact, so many – both environmental and social – that several sustainability managers told us that it is a significant challenge for companies to identify those that are economically relevant to their company and to establish a coherent sustainability agenda around them:

> *There is a difficulty in creating a sustainability agenda in an organization. There are too many issues that can be boxed as 'sustainability'. It is difficult to tie down a prioritized agenda and thus also difficult to create a clear message.* (BCS03 – Senior sustainability officer)

> *There are so many initiatives going on that integrating sustainability into one management model is a challenge.* (BCS47a – Business manager, Supply chain)

4   What are the issues?

When business managers were asked to identify from a multiple choice list the nature of the issues that affect their business units, there was a significant degree of non-response (54 per cent). There was

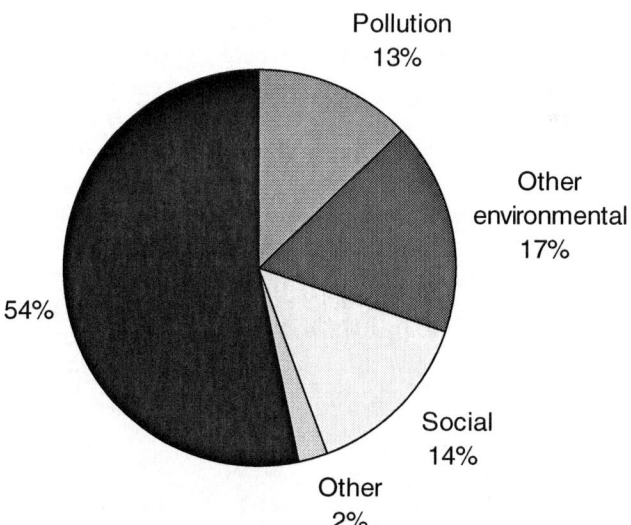

Figure 3.7   Nature of issues identified by business managers

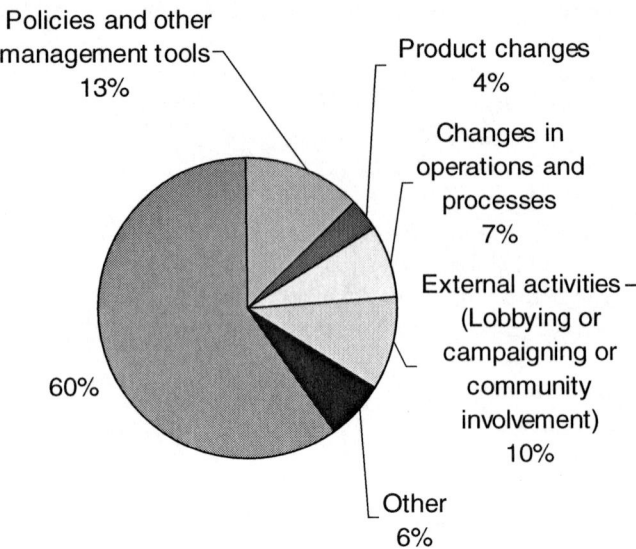

Figure 3.8   How business units respond to issues

an even higher degree of non-response (60 per cent) when the same managers were asked how their business unit responds to the issues (see Figures 3.7 and 3.8).

This result reflected levels of discomfort amongst managers about the nature of issues affecting their business and also about how they might deal with them. This might seem surprising considering the earlier mentioned self-proclaimed familiarity with sustainable development. It may indicate that managers had simply not reflected on the sustainability issues relevant to their own specific circumstances.

Apart from the multiplicity of issues, sustainability officers we interviewed also mentioned the interconnectivity and complexity of issues that made it challenging and therefore all the more imperative to formulate an integrated strategic agenda:

> *There is a problem with the complexity of sustainability issues....and business people dislike complexity.* (BCS47a – Business manager, Supply chain)

> *Individual issues have been addressed by isolated parts of the organization for a long time. However, everything is interconnected. The issues are interdependent.* (BCS35 – Top management, Operations)

Business should be modest. Issues of environmental and social policy are complex and some issues are more important for the business than others. (BCS44 – Top management, Board member)

The 19 sustainability officers surveyed were asked to identify the three most important sustainability issues for them. The results, while by no means comprehensive given our reduced sample (19 respondents), gave at least a good indication of the sheer diversity and fragmentation of the issues facing managers in the industry. Interestingly, we found that issues were relatively incoherently interpreted across even this well-informed group. We concluded that sustainability issues are not only very fragmented by nature, but also that different terminology can be used to refer to more or less the same issue (this was also confirmed during interviews).

Business managers we spoke to in interviews were also not always clear on what a relevant issue might be to them. To add to the complexity, issues that are economically relevant to the company may occur at any stage in the corporate value chain. Figure 3.9 illustrates how relevant issues might occur at various stages in the chain (the lists are not exhaustive, but include many of the potential issues we came across in our research).

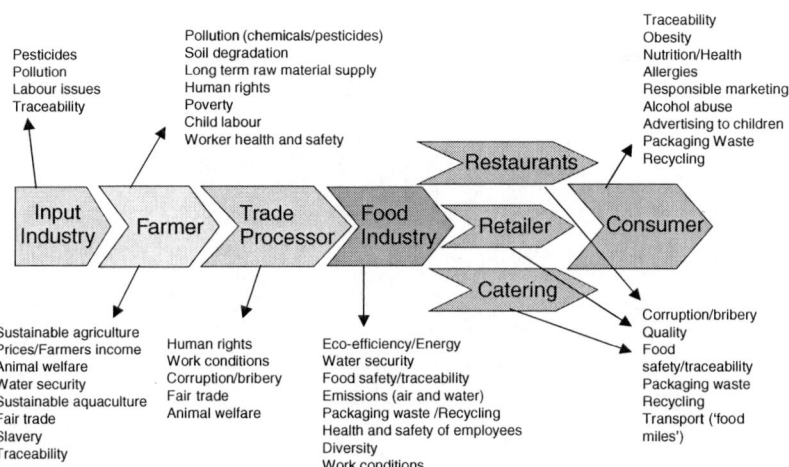

Figure 3.9   Issues in the food and beverage value chain

The results of our surveys were also informative about managerial perception of relevant issues. We asked the following questions in our survey of business managers:

- *To what extent is the business unit you work in affected by environmental issues?*
- *To what extent is the business unit you work in affected by social issues?*

Interestingly, although many of the interviews with sustainability officers indicated that the principle impact of the F&B industry was environmental, business managers indicated that social issues touched them marginally more (see Figure 3.10).

Externalities more directly attributable to corporate activities tend to be more on the radar screen of individual managers. Hence, the perception of relevance of an issue is directly affected by managers' direct experience of it in their everyday work. Managers are in general greatly impacted by human resources and internal health and safety considerations, mainly perceived as social issues by managers. Also, if short-, mid- and long-term effects of an externality are more measurable, and thus more tangible, then managers are more likely to attune to the related sustainability issue more easily. We remarked during our

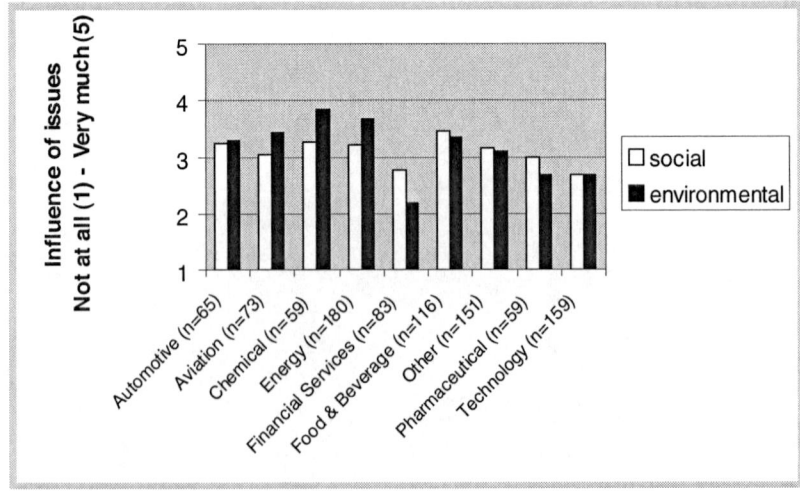

Figure 3.10   Manager's perception of influence of social versus environmental issues in business units/functions

interviews that manager's perception of issue relevance is very much related to:

- the extent to which awareness about an issue has been raised throughout the corporation
- the integration of issues to corporate strategy building, allowing issues to be more visible (in corporate documents such as the sustainability report, or even the annual report), and
- personal world view (as we shall see in Chapter 6, this is by no means an insignificant consideration).

Our interviews allowed us to refine the most important issues and to establish causality. The following sections throw light on the economic relevance of the main issues identified by managers interviewed for our research, and include many of their own perspectives as well as those of stakeholders we spoke to. We refer to case studies and other research material to illustrate the materiality of economic impacts. We also draw extensively on media material to illustrate the power of what we call stakeholder transmission belts. By 'transmission belts', we mean the processes and approaches used by stakeholders to induce pressure upon companies to internalize relevant issues (we address this even more comprehensively in Chapter 4). We look first at issues in the supply chain upstream of F&B corporate operations, then at sustainability issues touching operations, and finally we address issues that occur downstream. We include only issues mentioned by managers in interviews as being economically relevant.

5 Upstream

5.1 Raw materials and natural resource depletion

The demographic explosion we described in Chapter 2 brings market challenges, but it also poses a major sustainability challenge for F&B producers. The fact that worldwide nutrition requirements are expected to double by 2025 (OECD, 1998) will place significant demands on future agricultural productivity (GreenBiz.com, 2006). As the world's population increasingly moves to live in urban areas – two out of three people will live in a city by 2025 – fewer people are producing food for themselves. Thus there will be increasing reliance on F&B companies for sustenance and increased demand for diversity of F&B products including more meat, dairy and processed products. Providing these consumer choices necessitates livestock rearing, perceived by many scientists, researchers and NGOs as an inefficient and inequitable use of grain supplies.

The world's food production system is already struggling to meet the needs of these ever-growing levels of population, but there is an imbalanced picture; security of food supply is a major challenge in developing countries where food is the most costly household budget item, while in developed countries the public perceives food supply as unlimited and also cheap. In 2007, we had the first indicators of a potential worsening of this imbalance, with food prices increasing owing to cereal shortages as major quantities of (mainly US) cereal production previously destined for food production switched over to production of bio fuels; this will mainly impact poorer countries in the first instance.

Up to some 50 years ago, the area of land used to produce more food was simply expanded when more food was required. Today, land available for conversion to agricultural production is less rich and less plentiful (see Figure 3.11). Since production and productivity increases are nevertheless essential in order to ensure future global food requirements, the industry is faced with a significant dilemma.

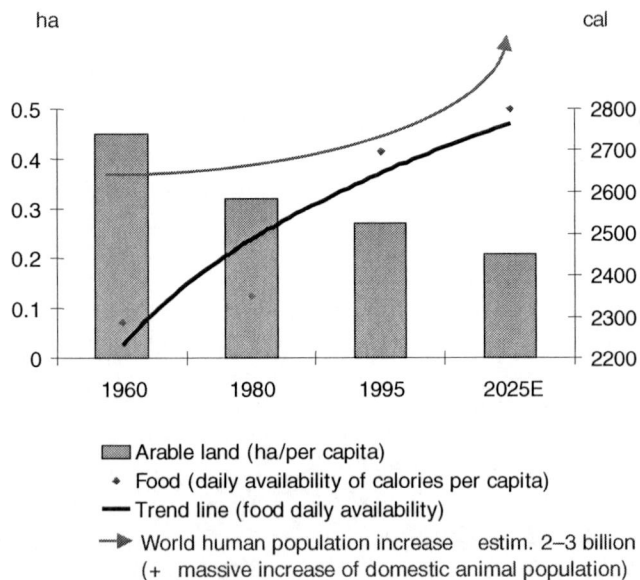

ha   cal

Arable land (ha/per capita)
* Food (daily availability of calories per capita)
— Trend line (food daily availability)
→ World human population increase   estim. 2–3 billion
    (+ massive increase of domestic animal population)

Figure 3.11 World trends indicating land and food availability and population increase[5]

To manufacture processed F&B products, the industry is dependent on a constant and long-term supply of high quality agricultural raw materials. Yet every global trend is moving in the opposite direction to guaranteeing this security (Loh and Wackernagel, 2004). Renewable resources such as forests, soils, water and fisheries are being pushed to their limits by overpopulation and industrial development. Managers suggested that the immediate threats to natural resources (and therefore the raw material base of the industry), have potential for major economic impact on their companies:

The whole of the business case for sustainability for the food industry rests on long-term access to key natural resources upon which the business is dependent. The key driver is ensuring long-term supply of raw materials. (BCS49 – Senior manager, Manufacturing and supply chain technology)

Principle environmental effects occur in agricultural systems further up the supply chain rather than in manufacturing operations *per se:* negative impacts of erosion, soil degradation and loss of biodiversity and organic matter, abandonment and expansion into other areas of natural habitat, deforestation, groundwater pollution and increased residues due to accumulated pesticides and the use of agrochemicals. Even though the industry is largely not vertically integrated (with its own raw material production facilities), companies are under growing pressure from regulators, NGOs, retailers and consumers to interface with, and influence, the agricultural methods that their suppliers use to grow raw materials for food products.

The following sections elaborate on three cases; global fish stocks, water supply and organic farming. These cases illustrate the complex related dilemmas with which companies are confronted and serve to emphasize the actual and potential significance of related economic implications for industry.

5.1.1 Case study: the fish dilemma

Fish is of primary importance to humanity. Many people, particularly in developing countries, rely on fish as a source of protein. However, scientific experts have been ringing alarm bells for some considerable time: catch rates have been far exceeding supply. In late 2006, they proclaimed that one-third of all fishing stocks worldwide have collapsed to less than 10 per cent of their maximum observed stock, and that if current trends continue all fish stocks worldwide will collapse to the same level within 50 years.

What led to this situation? By the end of the 1990s, the fishing industry had begun using sophisticated means of locating and capturing large numbers of fish including satellites, sonar devices and other military technologies on ever-larger factory boats and trawlers. This ever-increasing capacity enabled an unprecedented 'scraping' of the ocean fish resources. The WWF points out that this increasing capacity was largely due to government subsidies that even today still amount to some US$ 15 billion per year worldwide.[6] WWF is working to eliminate subsidies by persuading the World Trade Organization (WTO) to establish new rules that penalize states that subsidize their fleets and contribute to over-fishing.

Since the 1990s, WWF has been suggesting what it sees as the only feasible solution:

> *Only a series of fundamental reforms of contemporary management, coupled with heightened public interest and powerful economic incentives, will bring chronic over-fishing to a halt and shift the paradigm of fishery management from development and exploitation to conservation and sustainability.* (WWF, 1996)

The fish crisis is both an ecological and social dilemma; ecological, of course, in terms of the possible imminent disappearance of a potentially renewable resource and a resulting marked reduction in marine biodiversity. However, from a social standpoint, fisheries have sustained many coastal communities for centuries. There have been substantial job losses and breakdown of social structures as a result of the decline of fish stocks; for example, as a result of increased EU legislation leading to massive cuts in catches while stocks recover (Aroq Ltd., 2003a). To deal with over-fishing problems, the main world fisheries have introduced a precautionary approach and Harvest Control Rule (HCR) management principles and a Traffic Light colour convention introducing sets of rules based on certain criteria. The Marine Stewardship council (MSC), set up initially by WWF and Unilever (at the time, the world's largest buyer of seafood) in 1999 to find a solution to the over-fishing dilemma, is today an independent, global, non-profit organization whose role is to recognize, via a certification programme, well-managed fisheries and to harness consumer preference for seafood products bearing the MSC label of approval. As of January 2007, some 22 fisheries had been independently assessed and certified to MSC standards, with almost 500 products sold by retailers in 25 countries around the world.[7]

But the fish issue gives 'food for thought' when it comes to other raw material issues. A supply chain manager commented:

> *Disappearing fish stocks are an extreme example of a diminishing resources dilemma and a wake-up call for the industry as it contemplates the sustainability implications of even bigger bottom line effects such as agriculture.* (BCS42 – Senior sustainability officer)

Pressure on the natural resources constituting its raw material base can potentially affect the long-term (and, in the case of fish, short- to medium-term) economic sustainability of the industry as a whole. And although incomes worldwide are rising, promising more disposable income (thus, good news for companies), continued growth along current trends of consumption will place even more pressure on natural resources. One fish business manager publicly expressed the critical nature of the threat to the business (see also World Bank, 2004):

> *Put simply, if our supply of raw materials runs out, we cannot produce anymore, and cannot sell anything to anyone – no matter how good our branding.*[8]

This kind of black and white 'no resource = no business' argument implies that it is critical to the food industry to ensure long-term security of the supply chain. Increasingly, scientists and academics point out that progress on sustainable development in agriculture is a matter of 'necessity and not choice' (Mason, 2004). But to move forward with this goal is more than challenging in a competitive environment and goes beyond the remit of even a handful of powerful companies (although this is an excellent lever), or indeed the corporate world as a whole (we explore these challenges in Chapter 6).

5.1.2 Case study: water scarcity and climate change

Many academics and scientists consider that water will be one of the most significant economic issues for the foreseeable future. It is not out of the question that in tomorrow's world, a struggle for access to water resources may even evolve and compare to the fight for oil that has propelled the world economy since the industrial revolution. Indeed, prominent organizations such as UNEP see water as a potential reason for future major socio-political conflict. Certainly, insufficient freshwater is likely to be the most challenging problem of the developing world in the next decade, as agricultural, commercial and residential uses increase. Some managers were aware of the 'seething' nature of the issue:

> *Water has the makings of being the most important and universal initiative – it is used for manufacturing and it is front-line in terms of consumer perception.* (BCS46 – Senior regional business unit manager, Marketing and sales)

A World Water Forum[9] in 2000 signalled the critical need for a platform to engage all key stakeholders in discussions and decisions regarding the world water situation (World Water Council, 2000). Multinational companies are involving themselves closely in these discussions since. It is not difficult to see why. Businesses simply cannot survive in a thirsty, water deficient world. The dilemma is outlined in the 'World Water and Food to 2025' report produced by the International Food Policy Research Institute:

> *In the coming decades, the world's farmers will need to produce enough food to feed many millions more people, yet there are virtually no untapped, cost-effective sources of water for them to draw on as they face this challenge.* (Rosegrant *et al.*, 2002)

Water tables are being drawn down at an alarming rate and, in the last decade, unsustainable water use has accelerated particularly in heavily polluted nations such as China and India; precisely the areas where there is greatest economic growth potential for the F&B industry (refer to Chapter 2).

Although only some of the companies involved in our research were directly involved in the water business, clearly all companies are impacted by this issue in one way or another. Apart from urgent needs in the agricultural supply chain, there are operational and consumption issues linked to water affecting the industry. Wastewater generated by F&B companies is extremely polluting although it does not tend to be toxic, but disposing of it is becoming difficult and in Europe water utilities are now becoming costly. The industry uses large quantities of water as a product ingredient, as a heat transfer mechanism and for cleaning and sanitation. Water consumption in operations is intense: cooling and heating systems and washing in F&B processing plants require vast amounts of reliable and high quality water supplies.

Moreover, almost all products in the industry are manufactured, conserved and eventually prepared using water.

In spite of this, it may be surprising to the reader that in manufacturing processes, even a company as large as Nestlé uses no more than 0.005 per cent of total global freshwater withdrawal. The industry impact is mainly upstream in the supply chain where agriculture, which provides most of the raw materials for the F&B industry, accounts for 70 per cent of all global freshwater used each year; only 20 per cent is used by manufacturing industries and 10 per cent for domestic purposes. (Nestlé, 2003a, p. 11)

The impact of climate change on agriculture in developing countries with already relative scarcity of water has compounded the problems. According to a report by IIASA prepared for the Johannesburg 2002 World Summit on Sustainable Development (Fischer *et al.*, 2002), developed countries in temperate zones gain in agricultural production due to climate change while many developing countries in the tropics lose out, ultimately leading to extensive food insecurity in these areas.

Growing water dilemmas will ultimately drive up food prices worldwide. According to the 'World Water and Food to 2025' report, there is a possibility of food prices nearly doubling in the medium term, as world cereal production slumps to 270 million metric tons less in 2025 than in 2002 unless sustainable water use policies are adopted (Rosegrant *et al.*, 2002). And the increasing risk around water implies that most of the other agricultural raw materials for the F&B industry are also at risk.

We also identified some looming issues related to water on the consumer side. One manager pointed out that in the developed world, people buy water for perceived health benefits, while in developing countries, they buy it in the absence of any other uncontaminated source. Since municipal water authorities do not deliver, companies fill the market void that they leave:

> *Water producers are accused of taking advantage of this situation, taking water, cleaning it and charging a huge premium. NGOs accuse companies of creating an elite product for the elite, and insist that water should be free, or very cheap, as a human right. Water is potentially a business with a bad reputation. It's a simmering issue that could explode if NGOs take it on like Oxfam did with coffee. I am convinced it will be the next media issue.* (BCS34 – Business manager, Communications)

Can companies be complacent about this? The industry has a vested interest in maintaining a secure and sustainable water supply throughout its value chain. In the future, critical water issues will affect the F&B sector in terms of both risks and opportunities. But the water debate once again illustrates the interconnectivity, complexity and uncertainties of sustainability issues as a whole.

5.1.3   Case study: organic farming as an alternative to conventional agriculture

Organic foods are grown without artificial pesticides and fertilizers, and are perceived by consumers as more natural than non-organic or conventional foods. Organic farming activities were marginal to activities in the F&B industry until the 1980s, when environmental issues were increasingly entering the public limelight (Aroq Ltd, 2003b). According to Foodwatch[10] (a German NGO), a major contributing factor to the growing popularity of organic food in the late 1980s and 1990s was the lack of trust of niche consumers in the food industry, and increased consumer awareness about environmental, animal welfare, food safety and quality issues. Managers concurred:

> *GMOs – labelled 'Frankenfoods' by a journalist – created a horror in the public mind of farming methods adopted to retain competitiveness. The result in the UK is a swing toward organic food.* (BCS44 – Top management, Board member)

In developed industrialized countries today, there is ever-increasing interest in organic foods, as niches of consumers perceive their added value in terms of environmental, livestock farming, food safety and food quality benefits. Contrary perhaps to beliefs in some quarters, empirical research assessing the mass market for organic products indicates that consumers are primarily pursuing the latter two aspects (and thus personal benefits for the consumer) and that fewer consumers buy organic foods based on environmental or ethical grounds.

In the 1990s, the increase in consumer demand for organic produce led to a corresponding rise in organic farmland. Conversion to organic farming was promoted by national and regional support programmes; the European Commission began to provide subsidies to organic farmers, and European farmers were encouraged to convert to organic agriculture. Sales in organic food and beverages have been undergoing spectacular growth in mature markets since then. This is of particular interest since overall global sales of food stagnated or greatly slowed down in mature markets over this period. For a time, markets such as the UK were showing growth rates at 20 per cent per annum – by any standards, incredible – and more recently, they still showed healthy annual growth rates at a level of 10 per cent. In Europe, the total area under organic management is currently highest out of all continents, at a level of 23.8 per cent compared to North America's 5.5 per cent. Trade in organic foodstuffs has become a global agribusiness in spite of considerable differences between countries and with the European market constituting over half of global revenues.

But now there is evidence emerging that the majority of consumers are not willing to pay the premium for organic food (Urry, 2001); high prices are limiting the demand, and the impressive initial market growth rates are slowing down. In other words, the market niche has been filled. Consider Germany, for example: a consumer organization representative told us in 2006 that the organic market had virtually stagnated in that country.

Managers perceived that an inherently more expensive product (between 20 and 30 per cent higher than conventional foods) brings with it considerable marketing challenges; the higher price is a key barrier to more widespread consumer acceptance of organic food. To assure growth, marketers have quite a selling job to do. Educating non-'niche' consumers on the benefits of organic food and beverages to both their own health and to the environment at large is vital to success.

In spite of these challenges, certain organic retailers, such as Whole Foods Market[11] in the US, continue to have phenomenal growth rates (Murray, 2004a). Such successes unsettle the mainstream industry. The increasing interest of supermarkets and food multinationals in the organic market is evidence of a restructuring of the organic food market overall. Some F&B companies jumped on the bandwagon of organic food's increasing popularity. As an example, in January 2003 (and following their announcement of huge losses for the last quarter of 2002) McDonald's stated that it would sell organic milk in its British restaurants (just-food.com, 2003a). Other mainstream food companies have also shown interest, as can be demonstrated by the acquisition in 2001 by Danone of a 40 per cent stake in Stonyfeld Farm (USA) so as to enter the organic yoghurt market, the acquisition by H.J. Heinz of Earth's Best, an organic baby-food manufacturer and more recently in 2005, Cadbury's acquisition of Green and Black's organic chocolate. While Ben & Jerry's is not an organic brand, it is a company with a reputation for social responsibility, and Unilever's acquisition of this company in 2002 was also an illustration of the industry's awareness of increasing importance of niche areas to consumers. Growth in the organic sales market has probably given a boost to the concept of more sustainable farming in general, since a growing sector of the public was making it clear that they wanted alternatives – but not necessarily more expensive alternatives – to industrial intensive food production. However, sceptics in the NGO community comment that the acquisition of organic businesses allows 'big food' to stifle competition. Managers perceived that the significant decrease in inputs on an organic farm leads to a natural decrease in production and revealed plenty of scepticism about whether the demands of an increasing world population could ever be met by organic farming. They did not see organic production growing beyond a niche market:

> *We do not want to go into niche markets. Our view is that buying organic would put a lot of people out of work as it is currently only two per cent of world volume.* (BCS27 – Senior business manager, Supply chain)

Managers also felt that an organic food premium would put off all important new consumers in emerging markets:

> *Underdeveloped countries are the source of future growth. If these countries were to eat organic – then a clear business case is there.* (BCS39 – Top management, CEO)

Thus F&B industry managers believe that the solution has to be found in a more sustainable approach to more conventional methods. But an NGO representative interviewed was unimpressed with efforts so far:

> *Because of a lack of economic and political pressure, F&B companies are simply not seeking the alternatives to conventional agriculture that they must seek in order to ensure sustainable development.*

5.2   Social impacts

In rural areas in developing countries, an F&B company may be the only viable means of employment. On the other hand, if a company depends on that rural area for its own economic progress, it is in its long-term interest to promote a sustainable local economy. This involves stewardship of both environmental and social issues. A number of significant social issues relate to traceability in the F&B supply chain, especially in emerging economies; child labour, slavery and employee rights (such as health issues related to pesticide use) are examples. In this context, managers referred to the 'ethical sourcing' of agricultural raw materials. In a globalized world, with raw material production in holdings many thousands of miles away from the corporate or consumer home base, where wages are low and working conditions in the producer countries often primitive, companies are under particular pressure to prove to the public and media that no exploitation or child labour is used in the complex labour-intensive supply chain loops of the F&B industry. Initially companies resisted such challenges, but consumers started to insist through boycotts and so on, that they focus on these externalities (Smith, 2003).

An example: In 2002, a study was completed by the International Institute of Tropical Agriculture (IITA) and national research collaborators in Cameroon, Côte d'Ivoire, Ghana, Guinea and Nigeria, with the support of the United States Agency for International Development (USAID), the US Department of Labor, the World Cocoa Foundation, the International Labour Organization (ILO) and various governments (IITA, 2002). It found that about 284,000 child labourers worked in hazardous conditions on the cocoa farms of West Africa, thus exposing themselves to pesticides without protection and hard labour such as clearing undergrowth with machetes. Moreover, the study found that many children are trafficked as slaves to work in the region's plantations.

Once the problem was identified and quantified, multinational companies could move towards developing an industry strategy to deal with it. The International Cocoa Initiative was set up in Geneva to eliminate abusive child labour practices in cocoa cultivation and processing (Ethical Performance, 2002; Peel, 2004). Along the way, companies realized that the problem is more complex than simply eliminating child labour altogether. Many children have no alternative but to work in the fields as they are sometimes refused access to limited places in schools. Farming families can also depend heavily on children's help and/or income. The tradition of having children work on family farms (contributing to the harvest, for example) is an activity that is still maintained even in developed countries in Europe. Multinationals struggle with dealing with these problems fairly (for example, by sometimes accepting that children work on farms that ultimately supply them as long as they are also in full-time schooling), while keeping public image intact at the same time:

It is important to adopt a thinking approach – take (Company X) – they reviewed their product policy on with regard to child labour. They went to

Asia and redeveloped their suppliers. They did not cut off the income immediately. This made a lot of sense. (BCS41 – Senior sustainability officer)

The child labour issue is tricky. When I did cocoa crop forecasting, I spent half my time on plantations. Families come in agriculture as a package – if children are on the farm they are not necessarily labouring. How can you know whether children are working or not? (BCS25 – Senior regional business unit manager, Purchasing)

The social and economic complexity of the child labour issue in agriculture is greater than most consumers in Europe, eager for a 'black and white' solution, tend to realize.

5.3 Market distortions

Public policy aimed at protecting industry from competition can result in negative effects: social and environmental costs, economic and international market distortions and trade policy disputes. The CAP (EU Common Agricultural Policy), for example, was introduced by General Agreement on Tariffs and Trade (GATT) in the 1960s. While on one hand, the creation of a single European market relieved tariffs and non-tariff barriers throughout the EU, intensified competition and gave opportunities to companies willing to 'go international', on the other hand, the CAP has had a considerable negative effect on the functioning and operational efficiency of the European food industry and food chain. Having introduced price and income support measures to achieve a farm income goal, the results have been much criticized. The UK Food Group (a network of nongovernmental organizations from a broad range of development, farming, consumer and environmental organizations)[12] point to a multitude of negative effects: farm income objectives were in any case not reached, inappropriate support and regulation means were used, structural development was hindered, inequalities between regions and member states were worsened, negative environmental externalities were created, and excessive costs were imposed on citizens through high consumer prices and taxpayer costs (UK Food Group and Sustain, 2002a, 2002b, 2002c).

The EU has now moved towards reviewing these impacts and introducing measures to rebalance the CAP equation (*The Economist*, 2005a). But there is still a long way to go. NGOs we interviewed tended to say 'too little, too late' and insist that current protectionist agricultural policies of developed countries (for example, trade barriers and subsidies) require more serious and immediate global reform, since they are detrimental to agricultural progress in developing countries (Vorley, 2003; Oxfam, 2004a and 2004b). Effectively, subsidies stop thousands of farmers in developing countries from exporting their produce to developed countries (even if it has sometimes been more efficiently produced), promote the dumping of cheap produce in the developing countries thus further undermining agricultural systems in these countries. The NGOs complain that this simply protects the interests of relatively few companies and farmers in the developed world and insist that only a massive overhaul of taxes, trade incentives, subsidies and market barriers in the farming sector would make a substantial difference in terms of promoting sustainable development in the food and agriculture sector as a whole. Business managers wholeheartedly agreed, but the important point they made was that public policy was greatly undermining the BCS within the industry:

Governments need to change the way they subsidize agriculture. If subsidies were lifted, farming would become more productive, African countries would not need so much aid, people in developing countries would be more prosperous and there would be more buying power overall. (BCS44 – Top management, Board member)

Whatever we might do on sustainable agriculture, the effect pales in comparison with what could be achieved by abolishing subsidies to agriculture. (BCS45 – Business Manager, Corporate economist)

So leading F&B companies openly speak out for the elimination of these trade barriers:

A significant reduction in tariffs on farm products and the ultimate phasing out of farms subsidies and protection of the rich countries would offer third world countries real benefits. (Peter Brabeck-Letmathe, CEO of Nestlé, *The Guardian*, 8 September 2003)

Inter-governmental organizations (IGOs) and multinationals have been discussing the social and environmental impacts of trade distortions (IUF, UITA, and IUL, 2002; WTO, 2004), but the complexity of the problem is apparent in every discussion (CSR Europe, 2003b), and has not been assisted by intermittent breakdowns of discussions on world trade and the lengthy processes involved (*The Economist*, 2003f):

> *The failure of governments to reach any substantive agreement (...) is a bitter disappointment. It is outrageous that rich countries' farm subsidies are greater than Africa's gross domestic product and indefensible that the EU and the US government should continue to defend such trade distorting practices.* (Niall Fitzgerald, ex-CEO of Unilever)[13]

The problem of subsidization touches on the issue of local versus non-local produce and is linked to transport issues (increased transport costs). It is also linked to trade liberalization issues and the potential for social destabilization in Europe (destruction of traditional farming sectors). In short, these complex issues will involve the efforts of several constituencies to resolve, and this must include the F&B manufacturing sector contribution.

5.4 Power of multinationals

In Chapter 2, we mentioned the growing concentration in industries that trade, process, manufacture and sell food and beverages. Critics such as the UK Food Group have pointed the finger at major multinationals for undermining food security worldwide and presenting a global threat through their control of a large proportion of the world's food production, processing, and even retail systems (UK Food Group, 1999). Christian Aid, for example, accuses global companies of issuing sustainability policies and not abiding by them, and calls for more legislation as an alternative to voluntary approaches. This NGO rejects voluntary mechanisms as unworkable since, in their view, companies will always act in their own self interest no matter what is transmitted in social and environmental reports (Christian Aid, 2004). This uneasy struggle between corporate power and anti-corporate activism is captured in a popular book ('No logo') by journalist Naomi Klein (2001), resulting from a comprehensive study based on hundreds of interviews with young activists, advertising executives, union leaders and corporate directors. Most of the focus is on branded companies. This book had huge impact and, ironically perhaps, has practically become a brand in its own right.[14]

The purchasing policies of companies in the F&B sector and their potential and real effects on the pricing and sourcing of raw materials are issues of deep concern to NGOs working with rural communities in developing countries. Most global companies procure their raw materials from the global commodities markets. Although companies can benefit in the short term from cheap commodities, the enormous fluctuations in prices of raw materials and the effects of low prices on production (given the social problems this causes) constitute a significant mid- to long-term business risk for the sector:

> *The incentive for us in caring about our suppliers is the assurance of future raw materials. We also need to make sure that all effort in developing our supplier base is not wasted. We are looking for longevity. If you do not look at the issues, you will lose the supplier because the system will not be able to sustain itself.* (BCS25 – Senior regional business unit manager, Purchasing)

Activists complain that the savings accrued from paying suppliers below competitive levels are either kept by multinationals or passed on to consumers to gain market share, thus transferring value from the rural producer to urban consumers and from commodity producing countries (usually in the developing world) to consuming countries in the industrialized world. Aware consumers and activists want local communities to receive a much fairer share of the economic benefits of the food they produce and exert considerable pressure on the industry to change its approach to sourcing.[15] There is no commodity that illustrates these global tensions and their economic implications more provocatively than that of coffee, given the massive global appeal of this product. The issue was at its hottest during the earlier period of our research; it was informative to observe the gradual surging of the issue as – much like a tsunami – it gained momentum, broke over the industry and then quickly lost momentum again.

5.4.1 Case study: Global coffee dilemmas

As we entered the new millennium, coffee prices were at a historically low level. The slump was due to factors related to market supply and demand, and the simple equation that applies in capitalist economies: when there is oversupply, prices paid to suppliers go down. The supplier base for coffee is exceedingly fragmented, with millions of farmers producing the quantity of coffee required. This has significant business implications:

> *We are not always sure where the beans are coming from. With coffee, it is too ambitious to expect to know all suppliers. It is simply too costly*

a proposition and I am not sure that the consumer 'willingness to pay' is there. (BCS26 – Senior regional business unit manager, Purchasing)

A manager told us that only 50 per cent of existing coffee stocks at the time of our interview were required for annual worldwide consumption. Running down these stocks was contributing to the problems:

When prices were high in the late 1990s, many farmers in developing countries switched to coffee farming, and simultaneously, new players such as Vietnam entered the market while technological improvements led to reduction of the cost of producing coffee, thus encouraging still more farmers to start growing coffee. (BCS31 – Business manager, Supply chain, Purchasing)

In the last decade, when coffee prices have been high, this has unsurprisingly resulted in overproduction in the market. However, when prices are low, overproduction nevertheless continued. Agricultural commodities consistently trend towards overproduction and prices that are under the price of production. This irrationality of the market is characteristic of the agricultural sector and contrasts sharply with other sectors. As prices fall, farmers in developing countries, with little income to invest in alternatives, simply produce more of the same commodity (often using unsustainable techniques) in an effort to maintain a stable income and to retain their place in the marketplace. Even in developed countries, the traditional nature of farming, added to the long lead-time required for conversion to alternative crops, implies that gluts are a common feature of agricultural production in the marketplace.

While traditionally the coffee industry was regulated by national coffee organizations, new trends towards liberalizing the market and the inefficiency of the organizations themselves collapsed this system making producers much more dependent on the open, free market. Managers pointed to the increasing volatility of prices after liberalization.

We have to learn how to address boom and bust cycles in the future. The days of international commodity agreements controlling price through restrictive production are gone. (BCS26 – Senior regional business unit manager, Purchasing)

Behind the already less than simple economics, there is an environmental and social reality. Environmental destruction often results from grim social realities. The low prices due to oversupply of mainly low-grade coffee in 2002–03 led to extreme poverty and other social ills, and a risk of farmers diversifying into coca or illegal logging. This is of great concern to NGOs whether in the social or environmental arena,[16] since these forces engage the entire food system in a 'race to the bottom', an evolutionary trend gravitating to the 'lowest common denominator' that challenges our mental models of investment in global businesses. The 'race to the bottom' is based on market economy principles (of seeking ever-increasing efficiency at lower costs) but evidently has negative as well as positive consequences. NGOs point out that only 10 per cent of coffee retail value is retained in producing countries and that, in spite of lower prices for coffee as a commodity, the multinationals that dominate 50 to 60 per cent of the market do not reduce their prices for end-consumers.

During our research, after one of our interviews, we encountered a large group of activists led by José Bové,[17] the French activist at the front entrance of the corporate headquarters of a food company. This group proceeded to break into the reception area, smash windows and heckle the management of the company for its perceived inaction on precisely this issue. This kind of direct action by NGOs, with the risk of impacts on corporate reputation and image (the event was all over local newspapers the following day), is not uncommon[18] and forces economic relevance onto the corporate agenda in a particularly virulent manner. And companies can be caught unawares. According to one interviewee:

> *The business case comes home to roost with activists demonstrating at your gates and climbing over the factory walls. When this happened to us, three directors had to be involved in deciding what to do – so it was impossible to make a quick decision. Our reputation was up for grabs in the meantime.* (BCS50 – Senior regional business unit manager, Marketing and sales)

Coffee companies point out that if coffee farmers were paid more than market prices, this in itself would tantamount to a subsidy, which would encourage farmers to increase coffee production still further, distorting supply and demand even more and further depressing green coffee prices:

> *Everything has a cost. For coffee, we want to pay a fair price, but we should not pay a premium for mainstream coffee.* (BCS31 – Business manager, Purchasing)

A niche market has been growing for Fair Trade coffee such as Max Havelaar[19] targeted at consumers who wish, through purchasing action, to promote fair prices to small farmers in developing countries (just-food.com, 2004b). Fair trade is a principle whereby support (through increased product prices) is given by food retailers to small farmers in developing countries so that they can access an acceptable standard of living and more equitable distribution of wealth and income. Fair Trade also works towards establishing fair production and trade structures in developing countries and on the global market.[20] Business managers we interviewed felt that supply for commodities such as coffee is so fragmented and quality so potentially variable under the Fair Trade system that it is not a feasible alternative in the long run, especially considering the volumes required and the uncertainties in producing countries:

> *We are in some volatile countries. And with the volume of coffee we require, we have to assure continuous supply. Sustainable sources can contribute to speciality coffees and special premium brands. To introduce the concept to mainstream would be impossible. There would not be enough sustainable coffee to go around. In fact, it is difficult to say if coffee can ever be completely sustainable. I do not think that is achievable.* (BCS31 – Business manager, Purchasing)

As an experiment, Starbucks introduced fair trade coffee options and found for example that demand is relatively flat and that there were difficulties in consistency of quality and volume.

Nestlé suggests a three-pronged strategy as an alternative to Fair Trade:

- Increase consumption of coffee worldwide
- Encourage farmers to engage in niche markets, such as speciality coffees requiring higher quality coffee
- Reduce over-dependence of developing country communities on coffee by finding new sources of income, be they alternative crops or other activities (Nestlé, 2003b).

But as already indicated, it is not an easy matter for third world farmers to switch to new crops. In addition, the farm subsidies and other trade barriers in developed world markets mentioned earlier may not allow access to major markets.

The coffee companies have worked on finding other solutions to resolve, or at least relieve, the economic and social stress provoked by this issue (Technoserve and McKinsey & Company, 2003), and created the Common Code for the Coffee Community Association (4C Association), an independent, open and non-profit membership association, based on multi-stakeholder participation. Its members are coffee producers, coffee trade and industry, civil society organizations and associate members. The goal is to increase levels of sustainability in the mainstream coffee sector.

At the time of writing, the coffee issue was again at a lull, as prices had improved:

> *Coffee declined as an issue because the price went up. This lowered supply. Vietnam then came on board and glutted the market. It took a time for the supply and demand to be sorted out. The prices are on a steady growth pattern now.* (BCS34 – Business manager, Communications)

And NGOs, with more pressing concerns, had largely moved their focus to other issues.

This brief overview of the coffee crisis – which gathered momentum and reached break point during our early research – brings us a deeper understanding of the interconnectivity and complexity of associated sustainability issues. Indeed, the number of social, industrial and political actors required to resolve the coffee issue is striking.

6 Operations and downstream

6.1 Manufacturing operations

Looking across industries, the F&B industry could not be classed as one of the 'big sinner' polluters or social rights abusers within its own operations although because of its front-line and visible profile, the sector has regulatory, visibility and image factors to consider. However, when one takes into consideration the industry sustainability risks upstream discussed in this chapter, managers admitted that F&B companies devote a disproportionate allocation of time and effort to controlling the environmental impacts of the industry's own operations. The graph in Figure 3.12 was produced by a sustainability manager to illustrate to decision-makers that 80 per cent of corporate efforts on social and environmental issues were focusing on only 20 per cent of their total risk.

Executives pointed to climate change as an economically relevant issue for the sector in general, often due to impending legislation on emissions. The sector is under European legislative pressure to focus strongly on issues that relate to input–output ratio, (emissions into the air, water and soil, energy intensity, recycling and waste management)

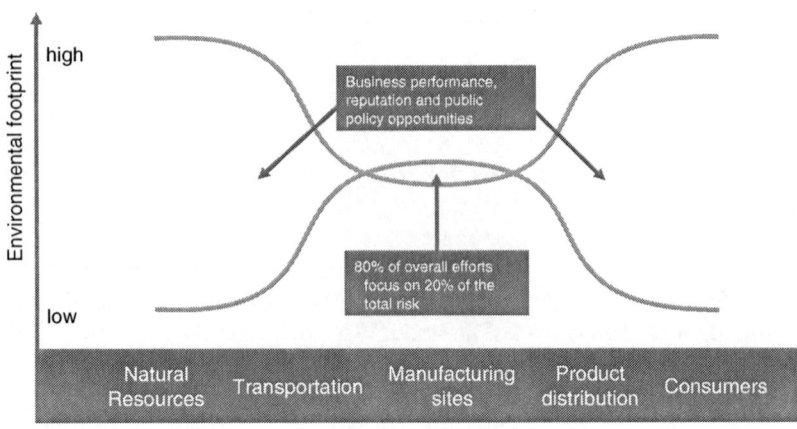

Figure 3.12   Potential risks and opportunities along the F&B product chain

but has the potential to reduce waste to a minimum. Regulation as a driver of 'beyond compliance' sustainability measures is discussed further in Chapter 4.

Companies lend significant importance to packaging and recycling primarily due to the visibility of packaging and potential to affect company image and reputation. Initial activist pressure on food companies was certainly directed at this issue[21] and, since the 1970s, there has been significant legislation introduced regarding recycling (of glass, for example). But in the 'beyond compliance' arena, companies are still learning. In 2006, Nestlé learnt its lesson the hard way when it changed the packaging of its Cailler chocolate bars to bulky 'designer' style clear plastic packaging, discarding the previous compactable paper solution. Swiss consumers reacted negatively since there is high awareness and personal responsibility for disposing of waste efficiently in the Swiss market. Not only did Nestlé get negative publicity on this issue, but it lost a large percentage of the domestic Swiss chocolate market to competitors, and finally opted to redesign the packaging.

Notwithstanding such cases, although packaging waste is one of the most visible impacts of the industry to its consumers, it is by far not one of the major environmental impacts of the industry and pales in comparison to its upstream impacts discussed above. But because of close relationships between packaging and the all important brand, managers still consider optimization of packaging as one of their key environmental challenges.

Interestingly, the industry's safety record is not without its imperfections; there are similar rates in the F&B industry as in the global energy and mining sectors (Goldman Sachs, 2007b), and lost time injuries are even more for the F&B industry than for global mining, steel and energy industries. This may seem surprising, but is in part owing to the location of operations in emerging markets where there are more risks to human life even on an employee commute and poor health and safety training for low wage workers. Numbers of fatalities and injuries is a very visible indicator of health and safety performance, carrying with it much reputation risk.

Transport eco-efficiency in distributing products is growing in importance as an issue, according to managers interviewed. Since the distances 'from farm to fork' (now popularly referred to as 'food miles') are ever greater, there are corresponding risks. Very little research has as yet been carried out on this topic, although some country-specific studies are available (Quist, 2000). Increased media attention on climate change in 2007 has created a rebound focus on food miles as consumers start asking for (and getting) more 'carbon footprint' information about the how food travels from farm to fork.[22] There is increasing concern in the industry that the reliance on transport, and also a corresponding reliance on refrigeration, not only massively increases the dependence of the industry on limitless cheap energy but also threatens food security:

The current system creates gridlock and environmental problems. This issue has the potential for a new kind of protectionism – where governments will try to protect local products. The multi-model way of transporting is not competitive. (BCS32 – Senior sustainability officer)

There is no capacity to handle increasing transport needs. We will have to become more local, unless there is uplift through private investment or government. We have three to four factories producing the same product. It is tempting to move this to one factory but with the cost of transport going up, we would not like to have all our eggs in one basket. Even if production sites that supply Western Europe move, our main consumer base will still remain in Western Europe. If strong limitations come for transport, this may give more opportunity to smaller companies. (BCS – Senior regional business unit manager, Purchasing)

The relevance of the sustainability impact of transport on the industry also comes to light in 'foot and mouth' and 'mad cow' scares as diseases can spread from one country to another through transport of cattle (*The Economist*, 2003c).

NGOs support the use of locally sourced raw materials, where possible substitutes are available, as a potential way of alleviating this impact. One result of these concerns is the growing movement of Community Supported Agriculture (CSA) farms that have begun to spread in Europe and the United States. The innovative strategy of the CSA movement is to 'put a face' on farming by connecting local farmers with local consumers, developing a regional food supply and strong local economy while maintaining a sense of community, encouraging land stewardship, and valuing the knowledge and experience of growers and producers working with small- to medium-sized farms.[23] The issue of food miles is complex since it is important to consider energy use over the entire life cycle of products. These are not easy concepts to convey to consumers through labelling.

6.2   Traceability and health

A few new age realities are summed up by Douglas Adams in *The Hitchhiker's Guide to the Galaxy* (1979):

> *Nothing travels faster than the speed of light with the possible exception of bad news, which obeys its own special laws.*

The F&B industry has learnt this lesson the hard way. Globalization of world trade, and its impact on the way in which companies move goods and services around the globe, has demonstrated the vulnerability of the food industry to risks of various food scares and public suspicion (*The Economist*, 2003b). With global telecommunications systems, reputations of companies in many industries are more exposed to risk; the internet is also an increasingly powerful tool used by activists to reach global audiences.

Moreover, a new type of consumer is emerging and today, F&B companies face intense stakeholder demands for total transparency.

> *Consumers are changing quicker than in the whole history of mankind. They are well informed, with access to the internet and media – more information than ever. The numbers of people caring about these issues will increase.*
> (BCS30 – Senior regional business unit manager, Purchasing)

The media eagerly target F&B companies on the emergence of consumer health and safety issues related to F&B products (*The Observer*,

2004). This sells newspapers and makes for good headlines given that most people feel personally affected by food scandals. Consumer health and safety considerations (including contamination of food) are the primary issues pushing the sector into the headlines, and the focus is often on food preparation and factory processing methods. Given the severe impact of such media attention on companies' public image and reputation, assuring health, safety and traceability are vital issues for the sector. For this reason, global companies tend to voluntarily go way beyond compliance requirements in this area. The food processing industry has been lending increasing importance to monitoring and recording the use of critical additives, such as flavourings and colour enhancers, to maintain traceability. At the operations level, this is one area where the food industry has taken sustainability on board primarily because of strong consumer pressure, and also because of a threat of even stricter legislative requirements.

Foods scares also sell books; a plethora of popular tomes on the subject written in the late 1990s are not only proof of the fact that there is a lucrative market for such publications but also a demonstration of a public concern about food scares almost verging on paranoia. Even if companies are not found to be directly responsible for incidences, NGOs and the media nevertheless often hold them accountable for the consequences of food scares:

> *Traceability is a real issue. Up to what and down to where? We need to bear in mind why we are tracing; are the reasons ethical, geographical, intellectual property related? After scandals, traceability takes another hit – the bird flu issue, for example, has impacted our company and others.*
> (BCS31 – Business manager, Purchasing)

With increasing food chain complexity, it is more challenging for companies to guarantee levels of product safety and traceability than even 20 years ago. Business managers seemed convinced that there is now more transparency and higher quality than ever before:

> *Stakeholder pressure overall has lead to more transparency. The information available is 10 times more than 10 years ago.* (BCS34 – Business manager, Communications)

> *It is basically wrong to say that the quality of food has never been worse. The fact of the matter is that it has never been better – there is loads of*

data around this fact. (BCSBM3 – Business manager, Strategy, Agribusiness company)

However, NGOs beg to disagree; in their perception, the increased flow of goods had simply led to less transparency, not more. We often found such divergences in opinion between NGOs and business managers in our interviews.

The sector has experienced many crises in the last few years related to food scares; the Coca-Cola dioxin scandal in Belgium was one such example (Steger, Lehmann *et al.*, 2001). Animal production has become an increasingly high-tech industry, and large-scale production of meat has led to consumer concerns both with animal welfare and the emergence of serious meat production problems indicating either full or partial potential of disease to cross the species barrier from wild animals to humans. Antibiotic residue in meat products is also of major concern to consumers. Each incident experienced by the public in the last few years has brought its own immediate, and sometimes catastrophic, set of economic consequences for the industry. In the following sections, we look at two more extreme examples that stand out for their significant and dramatic effects on the economic frameworks of many companies in the F&B industry.

6.2.1 Case study: the BSE crisis

Bovine spongiform encephalopathy (BSE), referred to more commonly by the public as 'mad-cow' disease, is a fatal, neurodegenerative disease in cattle that causes a spongy degeneration in the brain and spinal cord. BSE was not widely known to the public until the 1990s. Scientists suspect that BSE disease can be passed on to humans through consumption of infected meat, resulting in the incurable brain-wasting disease Variant Creutzfeldt-Jakob Disease (vCJD),[24] caused by ingestion of tissue containing abnormal variants of brain cell proteins – prions – capable not only of multiplying but also of destroying healthy brain cells.

But what caused BSE? With the development of intensive agriculture to maximize productivity, a system of mass cattle-feeding with rendered meat and bone meal products was widely adopted by farmers in the 1960s and 1970s. This practice was later identified as the trigger for the disease. In 1986, Britain had its first confirmed case of BSE in cattle; by the end of the century, some 180,000 cases had been registered and 4.4 million were killed as a precautionary measure. By June 2007, 165 people had died of vCJD in the United Kingdom, the country worst affected by the crisis. The total cost to British taxpayers has been estimated to be in the region of £4 billion.

The British government did not confirm the link between BSE and vCJD until March 1996. The subsequent banning of meat and bone meal in cattle feed did not prevent an increase of the disease in both animals and humans as the knock-on effects of early feeding regimes were felt. Outbreaks of the disease in humans resulted in massive consumer backlash against British beef in Europe. The spread of BSE initially provoked a US and Canadian ban on British meat products. As the disease made its way around Europe – first France, then Germany – the North American ban was later extended to the whole of Europe. This devastated beef markets in Europe in the late 1980s and early 1990s. The use of meat and bone meal in cattle feed is now banned worldwide.

The disease has pursued mankind into the twenty-first century. Japanese beef consumption dropped by 60 per cent and beef imports dropped by 30 per cent when a 'mad cow' was first discovered there in 2001. Although consumption climbed back by mid-2002 to within 10–15 per cent of normal levels, the impact hit the Japanese economy hard. Previous experience has led to public paranoia about this disease; a single case of BSE found in Canada in May 2003 led to massive beef trade restrictions against the country, severely impacting Canada's beef industry. Each instance of mad cow disease began to be treated 'as a harbinger of a British-style epidemic' (Jenkins, 2004). In December 2003, the US discovered its first case of mad cow disease, provoking grave concern at potential economic consequences. Although epidemics are now most unlikely, given the steps that had been taken to prevent brain tissue containing the dangerous prions identified as the cause of BSE from entering the human and cattle food chain, the disease still makes top headlines in the media.

The international community is far from convinced that 'mad cow' is a unique case and largely blames the ever-increasing intensity of farming techniques:

WHO experts said yesterday that diseases transmitted from animals to humans (zoonoses), such as bird flu, mondepox and 'mad cow' disease, posed an ever greater threat to public health, due mainly to changes in animal husbandry and international movement of both people and animals. (...) Though it was not possible to predict when and where the next new disease would emerge, existing diseases were expected to spread. (Williams, 2004)

The food markets have a habit of 'bouncing back' relatively rapidly from such scandals while stakeholders criticize the industry for its relative imperviousness:

> *Flare-ups over issues just fizzle out. The BSE crisis, for example, did not fundamentally change anything in the industry.* (Food industry expert, BCSBM7)

It is interesting that, by 1998, beef sales in Britain were virtually back to normal, demonstrating remarkable market resilience. Nevertheless, because of cases such as BSE, the once trusting European public had a rude awakening to what was for at the time, a relatively new reality: food had the potential of being devastatingly harmful to health. Worried consumers now demand food safety and quality and, above all, greater transparency. BSE also brought the greater debate about sustainable agriculture more into the limelight.

6.2.2   Case study: Genetically modified foods

Genetically modified (GM) foods are foodstuffs produced from genetically modified organisms (GMO) that have had their genome altered through genetic engineering. GM foods are derived mostly from plants such as soybean, corn, canola, cotton seed, and wheat and have been available since the 1990s. One of the most significant food controversies of past years involving the F&B manufacturing industry – and, as we shall see, one that has succeeded in stirring the industry in Europe to significant action – is that of GMOs and their as yet unproven and controversial environmental and health risks (*The Economist*, 2003g, 2003i; just-food.com, 2003c). The experience of Monsanto, a large US biotechnology multinational, in trying to launch GM products in Europe, is a classic illustration of the power of NGOs to incite the public to activism (Steger, Humm *et al.*, 2001), and of how a major company lost face and market share through mishandling of this issue.

European companies have since been on the receiving end of successful anti-GMO campaigns; the Greenpeace 'beanfeast' campaign against Unilever products is a good example (Thorpe, 2000). In the late 1990s, activists, public pressure groups and media began to refer to GM foods as 'Frankenfood', a term expressing the depth of their antagonism towards GMOs. An ongoing debate about GMOs, bio-diversity and human health impacts has contributed to growing public scepticism in Europe about the food processing industry. In 1999, a five-year moratorium on GM crops in Europe began, on the basis that there was inadequate scientific understanding of their environmental and health impacts. The controversy has not been resolved since; close to 150 governmental and/or industry-financed studies, and at least 47 peer reviewed articles in scientific journals have been published to attest to the safety of GM foods while consumer rights groups say that the risks of GM have not yet been adequately investigated and that there may be long term health or environmental risks that are not yet understood by modern science.

Companies got pressure to withdraw products owing to 'contamination' by GMOs (Elghamry, 2001). They were pressured by shareholders to go GM free (socialfunds.com, 2000) and many did so. Innovest concluded in 2003 that because of market rejection and contamination issues and effects on its corporate reputation, Monsanto was overvalued for mainly political reasons and that its GMO-focused strategy actually posed substantial and large risks to investors, consumers, the environment, and food manufacturers (Innovest, 2003). In 2004, under pressure from the wheat industry, Monsanto shelved its plans to commercialize genetically modified wheat in Europe. Consumer opposition to GM foods and the difficulty of segregating GM crops from normal crops increased the risk of an out-and-out ban on imports from any country that produced GM wheat (Sissell, 2004).

This created considerable trade tension between the USA and Europe, and with pro-GMO commodity producers in developing countries such as Brazil. The WTO has addressed the issue and determined that not allowing GMOs into countries unnecessarily obstructs global trade. Organizations such as Greenpeace recommended that F&B labels indicate the presence of genetically engineered ingredients and that genetically engineered crops be segregated from conventional crops.[25]

In the USA, public opinion appears more receptive to GMOs than in Europe, and companies there are not under the same intense pressure. This does not mean that activists in the USA are not also targeting companies on GMO related issues (just-food.com, 2003c). Activists we spoke to about the differences between the United States and the EU are quick to point out that US consumers are mostly ignorant to the fact that they are eating GM foods since the producing companies have successfully lobbied to suppress labelling requirements. A poll carried out by the Pew Initiative on Food and Biotechnology showed that only 25 per cent of US citizens actually believe that they have eaten GM foods at some stage in their lives, in spite of the fact that the majority of processed foods on the shop shelves contain GM ingredients.[26] Polls have also shown strong support for GMO labelling in the USA.

In 2004, Monsanto claimed that the F&B industry in Europe was showing renewed interest in selling GM foods, despite public scepticism (Mason and Firn, 2004). A new generation of GM products may also have consumer benefits, such as vegetable oils that help prevent heart disease. Although the European public's attitudes towards GM foods may shift, the strength of public opinion is still such that many European food manufacturers and retailers (with consumer preference in mind) have implemented policies to ensure that no genetically modified ingredients are used in their products. The reason for this is simply that the food-manufacturing industry is at the front line of complaints and potential boycotts related to GMOs, and has to carry the burden of legislation, segregation and recalls. This greatly increased the business case for excluding them from the supply chain. While we found during interviews that managers are often sympathetic to the possible advantages of genetically modified crops, they have definitively recognized the potential for profit losses that would result from not responding to consumer demand. In May 2004, the EU lifted its five-year moratorium on genetically modified food, but also stepped up the labelling requirements (*The Economist*, 2004a). NGOs were not happy about this:

> *Don't you worry; the big players in the food industry are in the corridors of Brussels heavily lobbying for the moratorium to end and also, without onerous labelling requirements – in the end of the day, they want GMOs!* (BCSBM11)

As pointed out by Lang and Heasman (2004), there is a veritable battle going on between two different paradigms of the production and supply of food to replace the industrial production model that has been dominant in the last century: life sciences (biotechnology-based) versus a more ecologically integrated approach, two biology-based approaches that differ fundamentally in their social and political understanding. The jury is still out on the outcome of this battle. However, a realistic economic supply and demand question remains: with rapidly increasing worldwide acreage of GM crops, it will also be increasingly hard to find non-GM sources, and a price premium may have to be requested in the future for non-GM sourced food, just as for organic foods. One F&B sector manager we spoke to predicted that the GMO issue would haunt the industry under a different guise in the future:

> *'GMO-free' will become a luxury. It will be a price issue as it is getting more difficult to source GMO-free. We ask suppliers to provide GMO-free if the price is right. But hard discounters will affect demand for GMO. In the future, GM products will simply be cheaper.* (BCS34 – Business manager, Communications)

The consumer will be asked to 'vote with his wallet'. As we will see in Chapter 4, this is not an optimistic scenario for keeping GMOs out of the mainstream in Europe.

In any case, as a result of crises – such as in the cases of BSE and GMOs – all indications are that, in the immediate future, consumers are likely to place even more pressure on F&B companies to label products in terms of ingredients, country of origin and even cultivation methods. Managers confirmed this.

The GMO issue is a good example of 'an issue that will not go away', and one that also demonstrates very well the tendency for F&B sustainability issues to 'ebb and flow':

> *Issues can change from month to month and are mainly based on media interest and scrutiny on certain subjects. The issues come in waves.'*
> BCS01 – Senior business unit manager, Sales

6.2.3 Case study: Obesity, a big issue for 'big food'

Owing to noticeable increases in levels of obesity,[27] alcoholism, diabetes, chronic dietary deficiencies and allergies to many of the common ingredients in processed foods, public health issues are now firmly on the sustainability agenda of F&B companies. The publication in 2000 of a World Health Organization report on preventing and managing obesity – now called a 'global epidemic' and popularly referred to as 'globesity' (*The Economist*, 2003a, 2003e) – was a clear indication that obesity was set to become a major global health issue. For example, more than 1 billion adults globally are overweight and at least 300 million are obese, with over 400,000 people per year dying of obesity related illnesses in the US alone. Interestingly, however, at the outset of our research, in March 2002, business and sustainability managers did not list obesity as a sustainability issue of primary economic relevance to their company. Later that year another 'tsunami' of stake-holder pressure broke over the industry in the form of extensive media exposure on this issue, the aftermath of which continues to this day. As we moved through the interview process, interviewees started placing the obesity issue as being of foremost significance to their business in relation to sustainability.

> *The obesity issue has come on the agenda mainly as a result of pressure from NGOs and media, but the issue has lots of relevance to the business – more than others.* (BCS09 – Sustainability officer)

The Worldwatch Institute points critically at the perceived misuse by the food industry of its position in the food chain:

> *To maximize revenues, food sellers invest heavily in the creation of a 'food environment' that makes unhealthy food and its promotion ubiquitous in modern life.* (Brown *et al.*, 2000, p. 67)

By producing processed foods that have more added-value (through enhanced packaging and product transformations), manufacturing industries charge more for their products and thus earn higher profits. Activists say that much of this revenue goes to fund expensive market-ing strategies around innutritious food products (with a disproportion-ate amount allocated to targeting children). Indeed, they criticize the huge budgets devoted to advertising by the food industry. In the United States, an estimated $30 billion is spent on food advertising every year, more than any other industry (Nestle, 2002, p. 12), and food is also a top advertisement category in several countries in Europe. Activists emphasize that consumers are often unaware of any additives in what they are eating, as nutritional labelling is often either nonexistent or misleading (just-food.com, 2004c). The activists reflect a growing concern – especially in mature Western European and North American markets, but increasingly also in Asia – about the contri-bution of the F&B industry to unhealthy levels of sugar and fat in diets worldwide, leading to global health problems such as obesity and diabetes (just-food.com, 2003e).

A report produced by the UK Food Standards Agency (FSA, 2003) comprehensively examines the way foods are promoted to children and found definite links between advertising and children's eating patterns. The contents of the report created intense media furore on this subject. The inadequacy and absence of labelling on high fat and low nutritional value products and of alcohol (in particular, 'alco-pops')[28] and the marketing of these products to children and young people by the F&B industry is under intense scrutiny (*The Economist*, 2005b). Advertising to children is already subject to a relatively strict code administered by an independent body in Europe; most companies support the Children's Advertising Review Unit (CARU) for example. Coca-Cola, McDonald's and a host of other food and beverage companies have come under pressure in both Europe (Steele, 2004) and the United States to stop advertising in schools. Companies are accused of trying to convert children to loyal consumers by using pernicious marketing techniques and of trapping poorly financed school boards into allowing companies behind the school gates with vending machines, or even influencing curriculum design (Hardy, 1999, p. 6). The popular British TV chef, Jamie Oliver, sparked a lively and ongoing public debate in the UK when in 2005 he became an active campaigner[29] against 'junk food' school dinners. The beverages industry is equally under pressure; in November 2003, seven alcoholic drinks manufacturers were sued in the USA for allegedly deliberately targeting under-age drinkers (Jones, 2003b).

In the future, it is likely that manufacturers' options may be limited by more restrictions on advertising to children and on using schools to make sales pitches. Legislators in the USA are looking at introducing bills requiring food service operators to display nutritional information on menus and product packaging. In the UK, there were suggestions of placing taxes on food with a high fat content in order to fight obesity (just-food.com, 2003d). The US Food and Drug Administration (FDA) is working on rules for including mandatory information about trans fat[30] content in nutrition labels on food packaging (just-food.com, 2003f) and some states have moved to prohibiting them from restaurants.

The evolution of public attention on McDonalds is an interesting demonstration of how sustainability risks can threaten business viability and reputation. Since the 1980s, this US fast-food giant has been working on environmental issues by, for example, reducing waste, phasing out animal growth antibiotics from its global supply chain and stopping the purchase of poultry treated with antibiotics. In partnership with Conservation International, it worked with big buyers of fish and with beef and potato producers to put incentives in place for suppliers that support sustainable practices.

In spite of this and because of the nature of its products and public perception of its employment and sourcing practices, McDonald's is seen by many as a symbol of global US-style extreme capitalism, and has been the supreme target of activists' attacks. This was tellingly evidenced in the longest legal case in British legal history, now termed 'McLibel'. In this case, McDonald's brought two people to court in 1990 for allegedly libelling the company in a leaflet entitled 'What's wrong with McDonald's?' What ensued led to a massive amount of negative publicity for McDonalds, as the media cashed in on the 'David versus Goliath' appeal of the case. A special website, which is still in existence, was even created to showcase the trial.[31]

In spite of the media exposure of this case, the 'rise and rise' of McDonald's was evident in its pervasive presence across the globe, leading Paul Hawken, author of the ground-breaking book *The Ecology of Commerce* (1994) to comment:

> *Does McDonald's want to see the rest of the world drink the equivalent of 597 cans of soda pop a year, as do Americans? Do they think every third global meal should be comprised of greasy meat, fries and caramelized sugar?* (Gunther, 2003)

In July 2002, Caesar Barber filed a lawsuit against several fast food chains including McDonald's. He claimed that eating food from these chains caused his heart disease and diabetes, alleged that fast-food is more dangerous than customers expect, and also that the pricing schemes in such restaurants employed 'predatory' pricing strategies by, for example, offering super-sized helpings for a small increment on price that forced consumers to make unhealthy choices (*The Economist*, 2002). This lawsuit was heavily criticized by McDonald's itself, as well as the National Council of Chain Restaurants, and was eventually thrown out of a US court in January 2003 (just-food.com, 2003h). The court ruled that the plaintiffs had not satisfactorily demonstrated that McDonald's products involve an unknown danger to the public.

And unsurprisingly, the McDonald's litigation spurred a number of 'copy cat' cases. At the end of 2002, Hans-Josef Brinkmann sued Coca-Cola and Masterfood (again, unsuccessfully) for the supposed role played by their products in causing his Type II diabetes.

In late 2002, a class action against McDonald's on behalf of several overweight children was brought to a US district court. This case and the accelerated nature of litigation developments led to restaurants in the USA demanding congressional protection from lawsuits over obesity, resulting in the so-called 'Cheeseburger Bill'.[32] Significantly though, this case also coincided with the year when McDonald's posted its first ever quarterly loss (just-food.com, 2003g). Economists and journalists attributed at least some of the apparent downfall to reputation loss:

> *Although it has long denied that its food is linked to obesity, McDonald's, a firm that is all about image, has finally twigged that it is under threat from its unhealthy reputation.* (*The Economist*, 2003d)

McDonald's image suffered a further beating in Morgan Spurlock's film *Super Size Me*, in which Spurlock, as the main protagonist, renders himself ill and gains 11 kg by eating only McDonald's food for 30 days (*The Economist*, 2004b).

In McDonald's case, the reputation impacts of these specific incidents were not the only reason for its woes, although consumption of its products was clearly affected primarily in the developed world. Other issues looming at the same time were the price war with competitors – business as usual – but also the growing popularity of healthy food in the context of the general obesity crisis, as well as outbreaks of BSE in Japan and Europe. All of these factors started to hit the company's share price.

The prospect of obesity lawsuits alarmed the food processing sector as a whole, and raised the spectre of the litigation challenges that have beleaguered the tobacco industry. Many in the industry recognized that this was a 'wake up call', potentially the beginning of a new and dangerous battle against 'big food' (Nestle, 2002; Wells, 2003). The media have a heyday with these issues, given their global, mass market appeal and the prevalence of related cover articles in well known magazines has increased exponentially. Best selling books such as Schlosser's *Fast Food Nation* (2002) have also drawn public attention to these issues, and more recently even more scientifically grounded books have also hit the bookshelves. Public pressure has built up around obesity on an unprecedented scale as the marketplace applied discipline to the industry. In the absence of action, government began to step in, calling on corporations to share responsibility with other stakeholders for finding solutions to what has become a global problem. The world's biggest food service companies have started to review menus, revise their business models and offer more healthy options while insisting that personal responsibility should not be overlooked as an important factor. Meanwhile, a handful of food and beverage processing companies are repositioning their brands in an increasingly health-conscious market.

Slow moves by governments in tackling this problem through action or policy has given the industry time to take self-regulatory steps, but for the first time in its history, the World Economic Forum had a discussion on the economic challenges of obesity in January 2004, a clear indicator that this issue had become a major global socio-economic, as well as a health issue.[33] Obesity had well and truly hit the world stage; and, by 2007, food companies were under the spotlight on this issue as never before.

7   Synthesis

The current food system can hardly be described as being sustainable; one that assures current and future quality of societal and environmental aspects. The theory of externalities explains why corporations, in general, are inextricably linked to their social and political context not only because of market mechanisms. Our analysis shows that F&B corporations can be pushed by stakeholders – be they the public, regulators, even individuals – to go beyond a focused corporate profit objective around their own operations, and to take responsibility for a host of negative consequences of economic decisions occurring as a result of actions elsewhere in the supply chain. In some cases, pressure to internalize these externalities is intense and the global players have reacted accordingly.

The industry insists that the F&B industry is not solely to blame for certain outcomes and claims that although the industry clearly does influence consumers through advertising, there are also lifestyle changes and work pattern fluctuations outside the control of the industry that have greatly influenced the eating habits of populations.

Whatever the reality, attention and resources of NGOs and media are focused on the world's food supply. Each issue described in this chapter provides a potential starting point for food industry critics to undermine consumer confidence in the F&B sector, as well as provoke processes leading to new layers of regulations. Whereas in 1993, a leading journalist with *The Economist*, wrote an overview of the key trends, competitive and influencing factors relevant to the food industry and did not mention a single associated sustainability issue, it is difficult to imagine that such an analysis would leave out sustainability considerations today. The modern press is clearly looking at food industry sustainability issues very differently. Accountability for companies is toughening and it is challenging the mental models of traditional business as a result.

These changes to the F&B business environment have all happened within an exceedingly short time span. On first glance one can ask how F&B companies can possibly ignore many of the issues we identified. The strategic importance and urgency of the issues may seem self evident to the reader. However, given the diversity, fragmentation and sheer number of issues that can hit the corporate radar screen, companies are actually challenged to develop a coherent sustainability agenda. With such value laden, intangible and relatively fuzzy concepts and in particular those related to social issues upstream or downstream, it is not surprising that managers are confused and unclear about sustainability issues, how they might be prioritized and applied to daily business operations, and what competitive advantage addressing them brings their company.

Although managers well know that economic decisions usually result in more than merely economic effects, predicting the positive and negative effects of economic decisions is difficult, and not always even feasible. We also would not wonder, in the midst of such confusion, that a measured and comprehensive corporate strategic response might pose a problem (see Chapter 6 for our full analysis). So by managers own admission, the industry is relatively slow to act on sustainability issues. The economic framework simply does not lend itself to accelerated action. No one company is willing to put itself out on a limb and jeopardize its own competitive position relative to others'. As one senior supply chain manager at a food company put it:

> The current policies of companies in the sector, even those of the leading companies, do not allow external costs to be allocated where they should be allocated. For example, if external costs were reflected in the cost of raw materials, the business case for sustainability in the supply chain would be greatly enhanced. (BCS49, Senior business manager, Manufacturing and supply chain)

Sustainability issues are often 'bigger than' the companies themselves; in other words, individual companies cannot simply take them on and resolve them on their own. By trying to do so the sector would render itself a 'David' faced with 'Goliath'-like dilemmas. The sector, arguably more so than other sectors, is at the centre of a complex number of interactions and relationships involving a multiplicity of interconnected factors, be they political, environmental, economic or social (see also Steger *et al.*, 2005).

Overall, there is an increasing need for all stakeholders in the chain to increase their awareness of what comes before and what comes after their own contribution, with every link in the chain delivering value for the consumer. To act on the issues, companies require involvement – primarily at a global level – from various other actors in the food system, such as governments, farmers, producers, distributors, retailers, consumers, scientists and so on. In our next chapter we evaluate the push–pull relationships between those stakeholders that promote a sustainability agenda (and thus the BCS), and those that, on the other hand, deter decision makers from taking faster action.

Notes

1 See Steger, 1998b for further discussion on externalities.
2 Today's conservation organizations (for example, WWF, Greenpeace and Friends of the Earth) have some of the world's most recognizable brands.
3 See www.oekom-research.de/index_english.html
4 The Integrated Pollution Prevention and Control directive (see: www.europa. eu.int/comm/environment/ippc).
5 *Source*: Sustainable Agriculture Initiative Nestlé (SAIN) presentation. *Original source*: National Council, CNIE, FAO, CGIAR.
6 See www.panda.org/about_wwf/what_we_do/marine/solutions/overfishing.cfm
7 Consult www.eng.msc.org
8 See www.unilever.com/environmentsociety/newsandspeeches
9 See www.worldwaterforum.org
10 See www.foodwatch.de
11 See www.wholefoodsmarket.com/
12 See www.ukfg.org.uk/
13 Speech at the London Business School in October 2003.
14 See www.nologo.org/
15 See Oxfam's purchasing policy at www.oxfam.org.uk
16 See www.fairtrade.net/sites/products/coffeewhy.htm
17 José Bové, founder of the Confédération Paysanne – a leftist farmers' union in France – is known for strident activism such as destroying farms growing genetically modified crops or in one instance, dismantling a McDonald's outlet.
18 Greenpeace is particularly renowned for intense forms of activism.
19 See www.maxhavelaar.com
20 See www.eftafairtrade.org
21 For example, when Schweppes introduced the concept of disposable containers for mixer drinks, in May 1971, Friends of the Earth initiated a major environmental pollution campaign against the company.
22 Companies working on putting carbon labels on products in 2007 are Coca-Cola, Scottish & Newcastle, Walkers and Tesco, though collaboration with The Carbon Trust.
23 See www.greenleaf.uncg.edu/community_supported_agriculture
24 See Winter and Steger (1998), pp. 151–68; and Schwartz (2003) for comprehensive discussions on the causes and subsequent evolution of the BSE crisis.

25 See www.greenpeace.org
26 See Pew Initiative on Food and Technology website: www.pewagbiotech. org/research/2003update/
27 More than 1 billion adults globally are overweight and at least 300 million are obese, with over 400,000 people dying of obesity related illnesses in the US alone.
28 Premixed bottled drinks containing spirits and mixer that have mass appeal to the younger age bracket.
29 See www.feedmebetter.com
30 Trans fats are artificially created through a chemical process of the hydrogenation of oils. This solidifies the oil and limits the body's ability to regulate cholesterol. These fats are considered to be the most harmful to health.
31 See http://www.mcspotlight.org
32 The 'Cheeseburger Bill' prevents frivolous lawsuits arising from obesity claims against food and beverage producers, and underlines personal responsibility for food and beverage consumption.
33 See www.edelman.com/events/WEF/transcript_w.asp for a transcript of this discussion.

4
The Pressure of Stakeholders

1 Introduction

Although the notion of companies serving broader interests than those of stockholders or shareholders has been around since the 1930s (Coase, 1937), the term 'stakeholder' first formally appeared with reference to business in a 1963 internal memorandum at the Stanford Research Institute. Researchers at the Institute postulated that instead of an exclusive focus on shareholders, corporations were also responsible for a wider range of entities or interest groups 'without whose support the corporation would cease to exist' (Freeman, 1998, p. 602). Society can call into question the right of companies' legitimacy to exist, that is; their 'licence to operate', should they not wield their power responsibly. If society grants legitimacy – and, hence, power – to business, what society giveth, society can equally take away...

Freeman popularized the 'stakeholder' concept in a groundbreaking book in 1984; Strategic Management: A Stakeholder Approach, and consolidated a strategic approach to stakeholder management. He refined the definition of the stakeholder:

> *any group or individual who can affect or is affected by the achievement of the project organization's objectives.* (Freeman, 1984, p. 46)

Since then, an energetic academic debate has arisen around stakeholder theory, which is not within the scope of this study to enter into. The rationale for stakeholder analysis is largely instrumental, that is; focused on theoretical links between stakeholder practices and firm performance. Our literature review found that the direct relationship between CSM and firm financial performance has proved elusive and this also applies to the relationship between stakeholder practices and financial performance.

A normative dimension also exists; corporations tend to pay most attention to those stakeholder groups that have power, urgency and legitimacy, since there is no other ordering principle that is equivalent to a price mechanism used by senior managers when determining the decisions that best generate shareholder value. Without such differentiation, the stakeholder concept would imply that companies have to think about the consequences of actions for virtually everyone with a legitimate interest in the corporation.

Empirical research on the F&B industry (Heugens, 2002) showed that stakeholder integration, through the development of mutually enforcing relationships with external parties, may result in both organizational learning and societal legitimacy. Effectively, managers we interviewed believed that managing stakeholders was an essential part of their mandate, and that there is certainly value-added in so doing. Overall, they appeared convinced that stakeholder management gives opportunities for learning and innovation that can impact longer-term business strategy and performance in indirect ways.

We observed in Chapter 3 that there is a strong link between economic relevance of issues and strength of stakeholder pressure to integrate externalities. Identifying stakeholder relationships regarded by managers as key influencers of company sustainability performance in the F&B industry, and benchmarking the views of stakeholders about these relationships, will therefore help us reach a better understanding of the BCS in the industry and to understand the economic, or 'Smart Zone' arguments for integration of negative externalities to core business strategy.

In this chapter we analyse the status-quo of stakeholder power in the F&B industry and the perceived added-value that managing these relationships brings according to managers. While strategic decisions concerning sustainability issues may require consideration of stakeholder interests, the decision as to which stakeholders to integrate and how rests very much with individual companies; thus, a deeper understanding of these decision-making processes in companies within the industry will also be of benefit.

2 Food and beverage industry stakeholders

Which stakeholders have a vested interest in the initiatives of F&B companies? The list is long: consumers, producers, wholesalers, retailers, suppliers, NGOs, community-based organizations, local agenda 21 groups, human communities impacted negatively by operations, fishing and farming communities, central and local governments, companies (in particular multinationals), shareholders, trade associations, employees and unions. In close association with the relevant sustainability issues, these different stakeholder groups intervene at different stages in the value chain, adding to an already complex business scenario.

The number of business stakeholders is potentially so extensive that some researchers suggest dichotomizing them into either primary or secondary stakeholders. A primary stakeholder group is 'one without whose continuing participation the corporation cannot survive as a going concern' (Clarkson, 1995, p. 106). Typically, these would be shareholders, investors, employees, customers and suppliers, and also the government and communities that provide either infrastructures or markets. Secondary groups are defined as 'those who influence or affect, or are influenced or affected by the corporation, but they are not engaged in transactions with the corporation and are not essential for its survival' (Clarkson, 1995, p. 106), an example being public pressure groups or NGOs.

The reality is that relatively little work has been done on identifying the stakeholders that really count to managers or on the stakeholder interests that should be attended to and what managers could do to address these interests. Such research could lead the way to allowing companies to adopt a more strategic approach to stakeholder management.

Managers we spoke to recognized the potential of stakeholders for accelerating change and changing perspectives within their organizations:

> *There many reasons why our company should change, but the sense of urgency can only be created by stakeholders, who are 'brought in' to assist the process.* (BCS47 – Business manager, Supply chain)

But to what extent are corporate stakeholders really pushing companies towards a more strategically integrated sustainability agenda? In the following section, we focus on those stakeholders that, according to our surveys and the managers we interviewed, play the most significant roles in deterring and promoting action on sustainability in companies.

2.1 Deterring stakeholders

Business and sustainability managers were very clear about which stakeholders were of most economic significance to them. Retailers came first, as customers of the industry, purchasers of manufacturing output and transmitters of consumer pressure and opinion. They were closely followed by shareholders, because of their significant influence on corporate revenue. Managers were highly aware of the fact that passivity and/or inaction of either group would certainly negatively influence progress on tackling sustainability issues in the sector.

In both of our surveys, we asked managers what they considered the most significant barriers to the success of social and environmental initiatives within their companies. In the business managers' survey, a large number (40 per cent) of managers did not respond to this question. This indicates a certain amount of uncertainty and perhaps also lack of knowledge amongst managers about what might be impeding

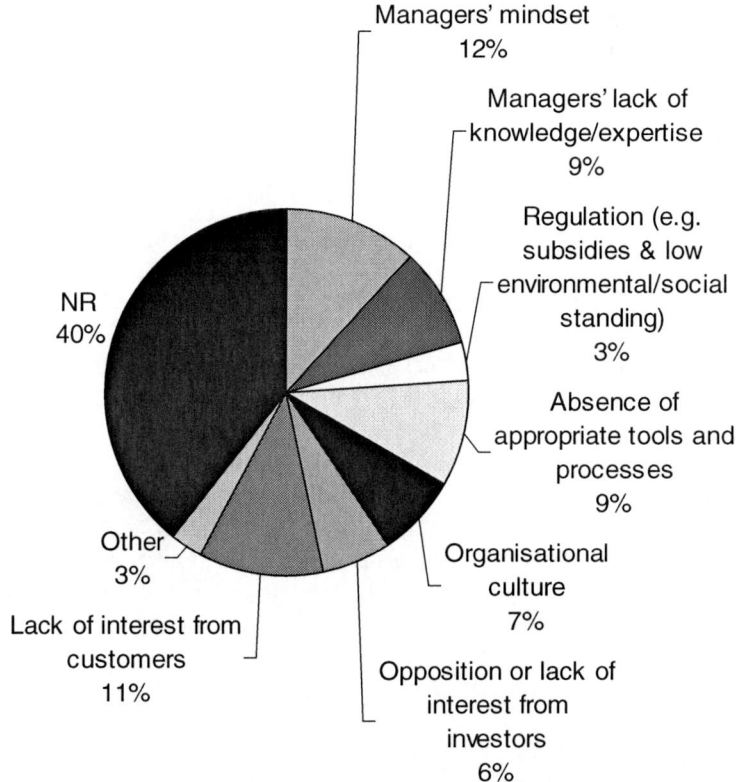

Figure 4.1 Main barriers to success with sustainability initiatives (business managers)

progress with sustainability objectives. According to both surveys, sustainability and business managers reported internal problems such as corporate mindset and organizational culture as the most significant barriers, and not lack of customer or investor interest. For results of the business manager's survey, see Figure 4.1. This may seem a somewhat surprising result, since investors were consistently mentioned in interviews as one of the most significant stakeholders deterring progress in sustainability activities within organizations. But our question about barriers and the choices given to respondents listed not only stakeholder barriers, but also several other potential barriers to implementation of sustainability objectives within companies. We thus found an overwhelming managerial conviction that the main problems are internal and related to organizational culture and mindset. With this in mind, we continue our analysis on stakeholders, but come back to this question in Chapter 6.

During our interviews, it was possible to go into much greater depth on the stakeholder hierarchies that managers perceive. The following sections elaborate on the significance of the stakeholders (retailers, consumers and shareholders) that, according to managers, deter progress on formulating a BCS for the sector.

2.1.1   Retailers and consumers

As far back as the late eighteenth century, Adam Smith had strong views on the importance of the consumer to industry based on an early capitalist model of free trade, competition and choice:

> *Consumption is the sole end and purpose of all production; and the interest of the producer ought to be attended to, only so far as it may be necessary for promoting that of the consumer.* (Smith, 1776)

The basic premise of capitalist economies has not changed. However, since the days of Smith, the dynamic between industry and consumers has evolved considerably and continues to do so. In more recent times, consumer self-awareness has greatly changed and increasingly activists are pressuring companies to take on the role of inducing consumers to change. At the start of the 1990s, Adams argued that concern for the environment, and the consumer's response in demanding environmentally friendly products, had actually generated a sense of consumer power. He forecast that consumers would increasingly use the power of the market to change it, thus making manufacturers and retailers respond to their concerns (Adams, 1990). Has this come to pass at least as regards food and food products?

Managers concurred that listening and responding to consumer needs was an essential part of their business:

Food companies should be ready for societal changes indicating increased demands for sustainability. We should recognize and respond to consumer changes as and when they occur. (BCS39 – Top management, CEO)

There is substantial independent research indicating that consumers will willingly say in surveys that they will pay more for more sustainable food (MORI, 2002a, 2002b). However, there are also abundant indicators that the consumer does not 'put her money where her mouth is' when standing in front of the supermarket shelves. Business managers also comment that consumers are confused about the numerous labelling schemes that already exist for 'green' products for example and that consolidation in this area is greatly needed (Salzmann *et al.*, 2004). However, our research did not indicate that consumers (other than an admittedly growing niche) are choosing to exert their power over companies:

Although a company's sustainability agenda is quality driven, it must also take account of what people are prepared to pay. If sustainable products are more expensive, consumers will not pay that premium, with the exception of a minority attracted to niche markets such as organic food. (BCS27 – Senior business manager, Supply chain)

I would love if someone could come and show me direct proof that consumers will buy our product instead of that of our competitors if they view our company as 'greener'. Consumers do not back up words with action. (BCS08 – Senior business manager, Communications)

Moreover, managers perceive retailers as the real gatekeepers of the modern food system, with substantial influence over consumer's purchase decisions, as is revealed in the following interview extracts:

Retailers squeeze us – companies like Wal-Mart basically tell processors what to do. They have the real power in the supply chain while we battle with other companies for shelf space. The trick is getting beyond the retailers through the brand. (BCS27 – Senior business manager, Supply chain)

Since the early 1980s , the proportion of what people in Europe spend on food has gone from 25 per cent of their income to some 17 per cent in 2006, and in the US, it even levelled off at about 10 per cent. The balance of supply versus demand in food has meant that until recently (with increasing shifts of cereal production to providing raw material for bio-fuels), it has been easier to sustain high prices in commodities other than food. To a large extent, this is because food is produced in a highly fragmented market as indicated in Chapter 2. But interestingly stagnation of wages and the establishment of large cheap workforces over this period has put pressure on the market to retain low food prices also. Managers we spoke with commented on the heavy pressure there was in the industry to sell products and that this pressure was augmented by the fact that there was 'always someone ready to sell cheaper'. And the consumer expects food to be, above all, cheap...

Would consumer behaviour change if people had more information when making a consumer choice? Industry stakeholders tended to believe so (see also Consumentenbond, 2002):

Beyond social and ecological aspects, labelling is a prerequisite for freedom of choice, but the food and beverage industry does not address this. (BCSBM11 – NGO)

We have proved that if you can adequately explain the value-added, consumers will pay more (between 15 and 20 per cent – and even more for some product groups) and these trends con be found not in several countries. (BCSBM13 – Retailer)

Managers were experiencing dilemmas with the 'state of affairs' in the industry as a whole, with perceived dichotomies and contradictions in industry models, which impeded moves toward more sustainable products:

There are two business models: one is the branded product companies with direct interface with its suppliers and retailers and the second is the fragmented model, with many interfaces between suppliers and companies, leading to retail discounting. The battle is between a model where everyone earns a living and another where everyone gets ripped off. The fragmented sector must be stopped... (BCS07 – Senior regional business unit manager, Marketing and sales)

It is an illusion to think that sustainable products will be at the same cost, or even cheaper. It is important and urgent to tell consumers this. Some companies are contradictory – on the one hand they say that they want to make their processes ecological and on the other, they say that they want to be cheaper in developing countries. In order to convince people of their commitment to sustainability, they need to put a strong message forward that sustainability comes at a price. (BCSBM13 – Retailer)

Retail managers had their concerns about profit margins and were feeling pressure from their competitors, but also from food processors:

Price is a huge issue. We have tiny margins and are constantly under threat from the discounters. You have to look at where the margins are between the different operators; for fresh products it is with the inter-mediary/distributor. By looking at the margin taken, you understand the dilemma. Food processors take the highest margin for their products; just look at the figures. (BCSBM36 – Top management, Retailer)

A German consumer organization representative we spoke to in 2006 felt strongly that consumers, other than those in a market niche, would not take sustainability on if a price tag were attached:

In the last 4 to 5 years, the most important buying factor has been price. Germany has the lowest supermarket prices in Europe. There was a period at the end of the '90s when ecology was high on the agenda. In the last ten years, because of economic problems, there has been a marked decrease in interest of German consumers. (BCSBM22 – Representative of a German consumer organization)

Research at IMD (Steger *et al.*, 2006) indicated that the push for corporate sustainability performance from consumer organizations appears to be increasing, but is still relatively weak, mainly because these organizations respond to their consumer clientele who, they reported, were themselves not pushing for more proactive moves. Consumer organizations also appeared to be severely under-resourced to cope with the complex issues surrounding sustainable consumption in an effective manner.

This state of affairs is not set to change overnight. In a 2003 report on a survey of retailing brands operating in the UK, results showed that 90 per cent of retailers with own brand goods produced in develop-ing countries either had no code of conduct, were developing one, or had one with no independent assurance of implementation (Young & Welford, 2003). This has often led to abuses in power and an engage-ment in practices that negatively influence supplier competitiveness.

Interestingly, an initiative ('Race to the Top') for benchmarking the performance of supermarkets across the whole of the UK sector was launched in 2000 by the International Institute for Environment and Development (IIED) to help major British supermarkets enhance their sustainability performance. The initiative had to be terminated in January 2004 because of lack of engagement from supermarket companies (Fox & Vorley, 2004). Key major players did not join the project, providing a disincentive for other supermarkets. Many others did not join because of a fear of provoking regulatory requirements for food retail, and the over-reliance in the project on voluntary reporting data without measurable indicators skewing comparability. Also, in a sector accustomed to 'squeezing' costs in order to stay competitive against discount stores, there was a general lack of willingness to dedicate resources to the project (Fox & Voley, 2004). These reasons reflect the highly competitive nature of the retail sector as well as a somewhat defensive stance when it comes to sustainability.

To sum up, retailers control distribution and marketing and have significant influence over the way consumers perceive a product. Manufacturers scramble and vie with each other for shelf space, but it is the retailer that ultimately decides whether a product lives or dies. Since the mainstream consumer is not voting with his wallet when it comes to sustainable products, retailers – the principle transmitters of consumer pressure to the industry – are, in their turn, not putting F&B companies under sufficient pressure to push the sustainability agenda. Nevertheless, the potential power of consumers to bring about radical moves in companies is demonstrated by the consumer and activist pressure on retailers, which led European companies to adopt their current positioning on GMOs and Monsanto to withdraw GM wheat from the market.

Ultimately, it is the consumer that dictates how the retailers push the sustainability agenda. While managers said that the consumer is the least proactive stakeholder, she is becoming more aware of product related sustainability, particularly taking into account the increased discussion around climate change in 2007. However, reaching a 'tipping point' in terms of personal behavioural change is probably still far off.

Also, in 2006 and 2007, retail companies such as Wal-Mart, Tesco, Marks & Spencer had become much more proactive. Starting in 2004, the powerful retailer Wal-Mart[1] reviewed its focus on the environment in partnerships with external stakeholders and this led to greater interest and participation in industry sustainability initiatives such as the Sustainable Food Lab and the Marine Stewardship Council. Managers reported that this evolution had the capacity to stimulate significant change in the dynamics around sustainability concepts and most importantly, for dramatic impact on supply chains of supplying companies. So will the 'race to the bottom' or the 'race to the top' win out? The jury is still out on this quesion. Also, it remains to be seen what the impact of increasing food prices worldwide as observed in 2007 will be on retailer and consumer behaviour in the short to mid-term. With this in mind, we turn our attention to the next least proactive stakeholder group – corporate shareholders.

2.1.2 Shareholders

The fact that CEOs of global multinationals are accountable to thousands of shareholders imposes both legal and other restrictions on them. If they do not deliver maximum value in the form of good shareholder returns in increasingly short-term time scales, either one of two things; their equity holders will remove them, or their companies will risk takeover or loss of access to capital markets.

So it is hardly surprising that leaders of multinational companies avoid erosion of shareholder value at all costs and their senior managers lend a willing ear to shareholders when it comes to corporate strategy. It is hardly surprising either that all aspects of strategy must create shareholder value and demonstrate the generation of tangible financial gains.

A survey carried out around the globe by PriceWaterhouseCoopers revealed that CEOs in general valued several social responsibility issues more highly than they thought the investors in their company did, the largest gaps being in terms of social factors and long-term issues such as workforce quality and retention, customer/client acquisition and retention, and innovation/research and development (PriceWaterhouseCoopers, 2003b). On the contrary, the CEOs felt that investors expect companies to shed employees, cut research spending and limit advertising to maintain earnings growth during economic crisis periods, possibly even to the long-term detriment of the company.

F&B managers are also well aware of the dilemma this creates for them:

Being a stock-listed company, shareholders scrutinize us. They expect that the business is being managed in an environmentally and socially sustainable manner, but they also expect an increase in share value.

Managing the conflict derived from this situation is the challenge. (BCS38 – Sustainability officer)

Our last chapter showed that the F&B sector is probably under more pressure than many other industries since it has been exposed to major issues affecting the stock market in recent years. When this happens, the business case for sustainability thus comes much more relevant, as was experienced by this company:

In January 2001, a damning BBC documentary impacted us badly – share price went down as a result – this gave us a clear business case for sustainability. (BCS37, Senior business manager, Communications)

Yet, the business managers surveyed generally did not perceive a strong role of capital markets in driving sustainability. According to our

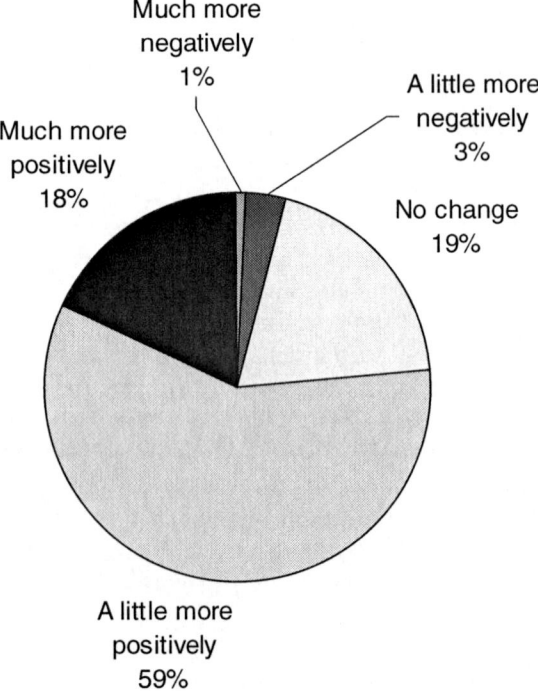

Figure 4.2 Expected reaction of capital markets to improved sustainability performance in the next five years (business managers, all sectors)

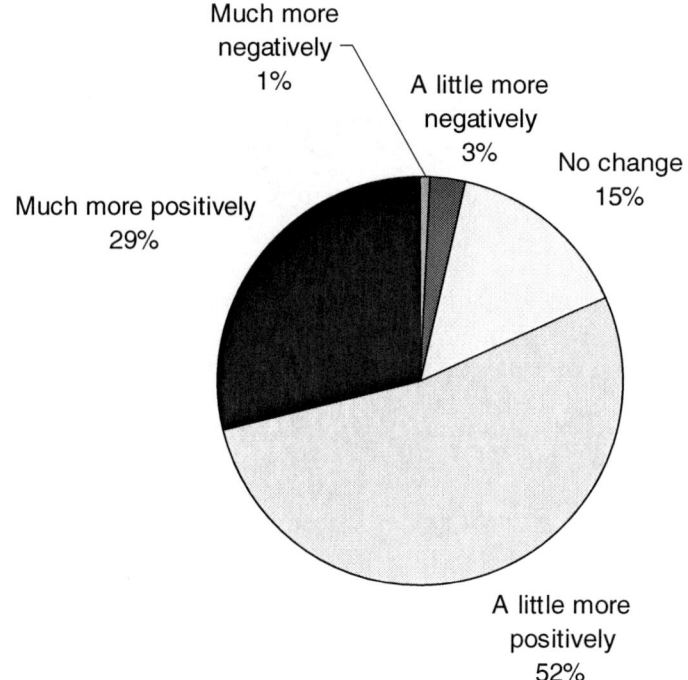

Figure 4.3 Expected reaction of sustainability performance in the next five years (business managers, food and beverage sector)

survey, only 29 per cent of managers considered that capital markets would react much more positively to improved social and environmental performance in the five years following our survey. However, at the time managers in the F&B industry showed considerably more optimism than the average opinion rating across all nine industries researched for the BCS project, which was only 18 per cent (see Figures 4.2 and 4.3).

However, the sample of 19 sustainability officers we surveyed tended to be considerably less optimistic than business managers (see Figure 4.4), with only 14 per cent indicating that they expect a very positive reaction from the capital markets over the following five years. This group, since more immersed in 'the business of sustainability' on a daily basis, may have tended to have a more pragmatic point of view.

Five years on, managers we spoke to recognized that more awareness was 'out there' in the financial markets, yet the model had not changed substantially.

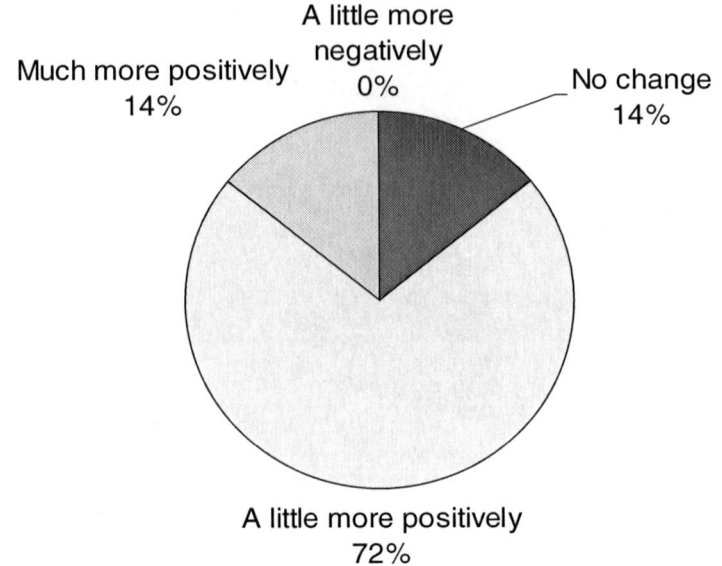

Figure 4.4 Expected reaction of capital markets to improvements in sustainability performance (sustainability officers, food and beverage sector)

Furthermore, when our 19 sustainability officer respondents were asked about their best possible argument for promoting the concept of sustainable development in their company, not one answered that they would use the argument that it improves access to capital.

Interviewees left us in no doubt about the strains that shareholder pressure places on companies:

> *If analysts, with one word, can damn a global company; they are the ones with the power. But this is the problem with the capitalist system as a whole.* (BCSBM33 – Senior representative of a food industry organization)

Most managers saw that the short term pressure to bring in shareholder returns greatly compromised the sustainability strategy:

> *The difficulty is always the 'short-term' that managers focus on – mid term is less important. The fact is that we are often in crisis mode due to market share considerations. If investors changed, we would have more innovation. The entire value chain could be re-evaluated. More overview*

over longer term would be possible. (BCS13 – Senior business manager, Innovation)

The quarterly focus is poison for sustainability policy. Stock exchanges dictate the strategy of a company. (BCSBM33 – Senior representative of a food industry organization)

While managers agreed that increased investor interest in sustainability would greatly enhance the BCS, they were also convinced that progress would be slow and halting, with no certainties, and largely dependent on a general framework of economic success:

> *The interest of institutional investors in sustainability had shifted positively over the last 10 years but now it has slowed down due to current economic difficulties – for me this is an indication that this trend has not as yet entered the mainstream.* (BCS16 – Senior business manager, Strategy)

One of the reasons why business managers are so pessimistic about shareholder pressure substantially influencing sustainability agendas is that mainstream investors do not yet consider sustainability as a core consideration in analysis. There are several reasons why this is so (see also EPA, 2000). Apart from short term focus already mentioned, and the non inclusion of the true economic costs of externalities in prices, corporations struggle with demonstrating, in a language that financial analysts understand, how current sustainability strategies relate to future financial returns. Staff with both financial and sustainability experiences is hard to come by, and in any case environmental and financial analysts do not have common reference frameworks.

According to a report in July 2003 from Innovest Strategic Value Advisors, a company that correlates sustainability ratings to corporate financial performance, sustainability leaders in the global food products sector outperformed industry laggards by 33 per cent over three years from April 2000 to June 2003. A later study in mid-2007, Goldman Sachs revealed that sustainability leaders in four sectors (including the F&B sector), had outperformed the MSCI world index[2] by an average of 25 per cent since August 2005. While this does appear to be positive news for sustainability in the industry, longitudinal studies are sorely lacking in this domain, and it is difficult to reach definitive conclusions. A 'chicken and egg' question can also be raised; do companies that do well have sustainability strategies or do companies with sustainability strategies do well? Overall managers were convinced that the overall performance of the indices has not given reason to believe that socially responsible investment (SRI) leads to out-performance:

Investors' interest would increase if there were a better business case showing that more sustainable companies give better payback. Overall ethical funds have not outperformed the market. Being included in the Dow Jones Sustainability Index[3] is important but needs to be quantified into value. (BCS11 – Senior business manager, Investor relations)

Interestingly, managers expressed frustration at the sheer number of questionnaires they received to fill in with relevant data for financial analysts. Although managers admitted that this trend did show an increased interest in these areas by the investment community (see also Bartolomeo *et al.*, 2003), they still insisted that the current dearth of shareholder interest constitutes a major barrier to getting issues on the strategic agenda:

There is a slow change in thinking of the investment community: they are beginning to recognise that businesses that take on sustainability have less long-term risk. Maybe in a few years' time... (BCS49, Senior manager, Manufacturing and supply chain)

During the Goldman Sachs 2007 study, the researchers complained that disclosure is a major issue; it remains extremely difficult to get data and that which is available is inconsistent. Since many companies report their accomplishments only in financial terms, a solution may be to increase reporting to investors on social and environmental aspects. When we interviewed a financial services authority regulator, we asked about the level of pressure to regulate where environmental and social reporting is concerned. He pointed to general lack of interest of investors in sustainability reporting:

I have been lobbied by interest groups/public pressure groups to include social/environmental disclosure requirements as listing criteria, and to move this from a voluntary to obligatory requirement. But issuers and investors have exercised no pressure whatsoever. Investors are, in the main, completely disinterested in sustainability and issuers are unlikely to beat on the door asking for rules. (BCSBM4 – Manager, Regulatory authority)

As with all areas of business, regulations can have considerable impact on accelerating sustainability agendas and the investment area is no exception. When the British Government for example started to require UK pension trustees to disclose how they take account of social, environmental and ethical factors in their investment decisions, leading pension funds in turn started to require more information from the firms they invested in. Companies listed on the main British stock exchange (FTSE) were thereby forced to produce information on their social and environmental performance. Thus impetus in this case did not come from the investors themselves, but rather from the regulator.

Winds, or should we rather say 'slight breezes' of change are also blowing as regards equity research; research departments of major financial institutions are starting to produce reports that analyse the material business risks and opportunities created by sustainability issues. We note the following comment, related to the obesity issue within the food industry, which is testimony to this trend amongst equity analysts:

> *We believe it is also crucial to take on board how pro-active the companies are to bring the right innovation to adapt their product portfolios and to adopt a sustainable socially responsible approach to the obesity issue.* (Morgan Stanley, 2003b)

While reputation risk is also gradually becoming more important in equity markets, managers we spoke to felt that tools are still lacking to analyse the social and environmental consequences and risks of competing investment alternatives even today. All indications from managers were that current communications between corporations and investors still do not reflect the full reality of business risks. Clearly, the more social and environmental risk factors are disclosed in the most transparent way possible, the more likely it is that investors will consider these factors. However, investors will be slow to demand information in the short to medium term:

> *The only thing investors care about is short- to medium-term financial impact. Because they can sell tomorrow, they don't care about long-term risks. That will be somebody else's problem in thirty years' time. And the market is becoming more and more short-term, because it is following the US model. Investors don't want to understand the risk. They want to go with the momentum. The investment community never operates together, they are equally competitive. There is nothing in it for them to get together and ask*

companies to disclose more information. (BCSBM34 – Stock exchange listing director)

Nevertheless, sustainability officers interviewed still believed that the potential for showing shareholders that the economic bottom line is enhanced by sustainability measures had not been fully exploited. Companies that are endeavouring to be progressive in the area of sustainability are aware of this and leading F&B companies are starting to communicate with shareholders more proactively. There are also increasing numbers of activists using shareholder resolutions to change company policy, targeting companies because of their size; for obvious reasons, activists tend to choose visible and large companies such as McDonalds, Nestlé or Coca-Cola. Annual general meetings have, in some instances, become an opportunity for minority groups, socially responsibility investors and NGOs to introduce resolutions for shareholder votes in order to change company practice and generate media attention for their cause against company policies. Although there are as yet few examples of success in this area, the motions often receive extensive media coverage.

To sum up, managers are simply not worried about shareholder pressure for CSM increasing and feel that they will not be punished by financial markets if they do not become more proactive on the sustainability front. However, it was evident during our research that senior managers at the leading F&B companies, aware of potential and evolving business risks, are nevertheless keeping a close eye on developments in this domain. They consider this to be in their enlightened self interest.

2.2 Promoting stakeholders

A range of other stakeholders exert pressure on the industry for increased CSM. In our study, we tried to understanding the extent to which these 'promoting' agents win out over the 'deterring' agents in the final analysis. According to our interviewees, key promoting agents include NGOs and also governments and regulators. Managers also viewed the potential of employees for influencing the corporate sustainability agenda as promising, since a major perceived economic driver for the BCS was also the contribution of CSM to attracting and retaining talent within the industry.

Our survey results allow us to compare the perceptions of sustainability officers versus those of business managers regarding the level of pro-activeness of certain key parties in promoting CSM. While, as previously mentioned, business managers regard the consumer as least proactive, public pressure groups such as NGOs are regarded as by far the most proactive, as is illustrated in Figure 4.5.

Our small sample of sustainability officers was even more emphatic about these differences (Figure 4.6).

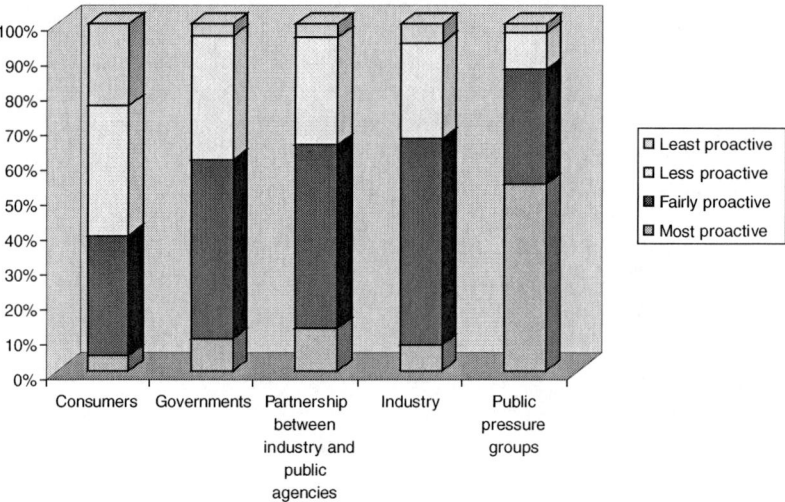

Figure 4.5 Pro-activeness of responsible parties in promoting sustainability (business managers)

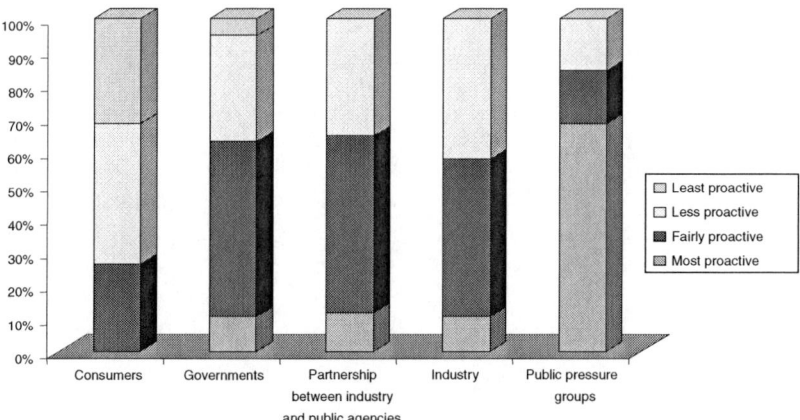

Figure 4.6 Pro-activeness of responsible parties in promoting sustainability (sustainability officers)

2.2.1 Public pressure groups

International NGOs have been growing in numbers in recent years and the numbers that qualify for this status have recently been estimated at some 25,000 organizations. Research has shown that in Europe, NGOs have a higher credibility rating than corporations; a survey for the World Economic Forum by Edelman PR Worldwide (2002) found that NGOs such as Amnesty International, the World Wide Fund for Nature and Greenpeace outstripped the highest-rated corporations in Europe such as Microsoft, Bayer, Ford and Coca-Cola by a considerable margin. A later survey carried out by SustainAbility reached similar conclusions (SustainAbility, Global Compact & UNEP, 2003). Interestingly around the same time, in America, the top places were still occupied by corporations (Coca-Cola and McDonalds being in the top three); however, the credibility of NGOs also rose sharply in the USA in the three years following the Edelman survey.

We found that European F&B business managers view the motives of NGOs with a certain degree of suspicion and scepticism. Views ranged from criticism and distrust of the 'extreme' and 'misinformed' nature of NGO positions, belief that NGOs will make 'their' point notwithstanding any economic rationale and without sufficient understanding of the corporate competitive environment, to a conviction in some cases that being more sustainable simply attracts more NGO attention and thus criticism:

> *We have sometimes improved nutritional benefits on our products and not advertised or broadcast this because it could attract unwelcome attention to our products. NGOs would start poking around and saying 'But if you are so good, what about this and that product...?' We do not want to create a combative environment....* (BCS20 – Senior business manager, Innovation)

Managers felt much maligned about the manner in which the corporate world was depicted by NGOs through the media:

> *Some NGOs and consumer organizations gain support by pointing the finger; they are hardly objective.* (BCS20 – Senior business manager, Innovation)

NGOs are generally critical of the free enterprise system and free market economy, and insist that major work needs to be done to achieve a workable economic system. However, the leading NGOs also believe that corporations are an important part of the solution. NGOs work hard on inciting the most important inactive corporate stakeholders, such as consumers, to action, and it can be difficult for companies to predict their strategies (Kong *et al.*, 2002).

The potential of NGOs to significantly influence public perception of companies is compellingly illustrated by the campaign against Nestlé's marketing of powdered milk formula for babies in the developing world (Prakesh Sethi, 1994). Beginning in the 1970s, campaigners claimed that artificial feeding promoted by Nestlé was responsible for infant deaths around the developing world, leading to a global boycott of Nestlé in 1977 and a smear on the company's image that has not entirely disappeared even today. This is in spite of the fact that the company has taken many steps to address these problems, including the adoption in 1981 of the World Health Organization and UNICEF's International Code of Marketing of Breast Milk Substitutes. The company lives with the legacy of these incidents; the aftershock felt in the company was evident in the number of times these events were referred to by even its youngest managers during interviews. The infant formula issue had virtually become part of the Nestlé corporate DNA.

As we have seen in Chapter 3, it was primarily pressure from NGOs such as Greenpeace that stirred the rejection of GMOs by the European public and the loss of billions of dollars in shareholder value for companies such as Monsanto. It was, again, to a large extent pressure from NGOs that forced multinationals to look seriously at the coffee issue and to put into place initiatives such as the Common Code for the Coffee Community (4Cs) initiative, for example.

The media tend to act as a transmitter of NGO preoccupations rather than demonstrate what companies are actually doing about sustainability issues, so lending significant additional power to the NGO movement, a power that the NGOs utilize to the maximum in order to leverage action within companies. However, we noted considerable bitterness in our interviews of managers at the fact that the media is so one-sided in its approach. Managers were extremely media-suspicious. They pointed to the sensationalist and biased nature of the press, and the focus on stories that 'sell most newspapers'. They criticized the press for not taking a more proactive role in educating the consumer based on facts and accurate reporting:

Trouble is, if a newspaper finds something wrong, and even if their information is wrong, a lot of harm can be done. We have been burnt so many times that we do not take risks anymore. And I don't see this changing fast.... (BCS20 – Senior business manager, Innovation)

Prominent F&B multinationals are considered strong strategic attack points by NGOs and they fully utilize the media in their battles. One NGO respondent told us:

What matters is the opportunity to draw an audience and heighten awareness about global dilemmas by attacking recognized brands. (BCSBM10 – NGO executive)

Our survey revealed that, according to managers in the F&B sector, NGOs or the media campaigns that supported them accounted jointly for 40 per cent of the cases that damaged their company reputation in the previous three years, whereas the average for all industrial sectors researched by the BCS team was at a level of 28 per cent (see Figure 4.7). If one adds to this the consumer boycotts also instigated largely by NGOs (10 per cent), NGO associated cases damaging F&B industry reputation would come to 50 per cent. Again, these results

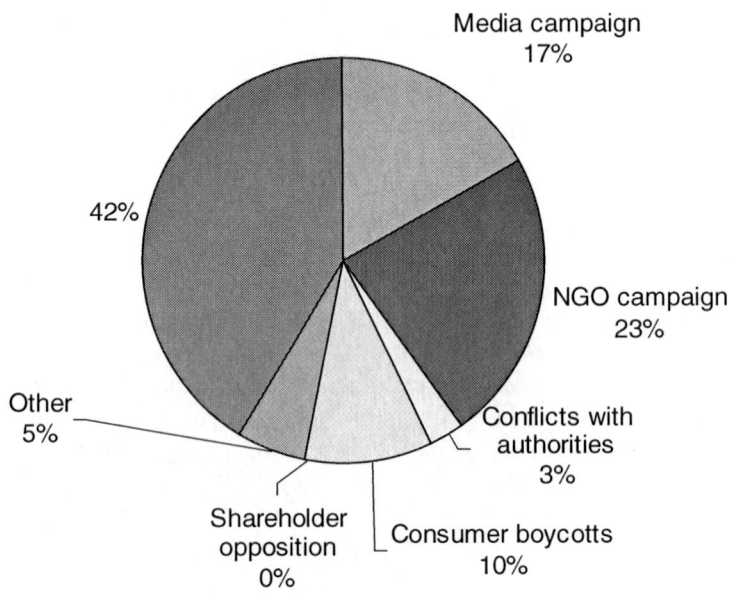

Figure 4.7 Causes of incidents damaging corporate reputation over the past three years (business managers)

also show the extent to which the industry is 'frontline' and vulnerable to attack.

Even though public pressure groups were viewed by managers as by far the most proactive stakeholders, our survey results and interviews demonstrated they were still not perceived as the most influential (see Figure 4.8) since the significance of impact was mostly considered slight for those that had experienced attacks.

Lewis carried out research on the perception of 255 F&B executives of the impact of food scares on consumer attitudes towards the food and drinks industry (Lewis, 2004). The impacts were largely considered to be short-term (71 per cent) rather than long-term (23 per cent). It would seem that the views of executives on the impact of NGO campaigns, which often use food scares as 'ammunition', extend to food scares in general. In our interview research, another sceptical manager illustrated his view that they had had a fairly marginal impact, even after a most extreme onslaught by NGOs on his company. He even pointed out that there had even been some unexpected benefits:

The impact on profitability of our most major scandal was marginal. There may even have been an unintended but ironic positive effect; the brand got recognized by consumers that otherwise would not necessarily

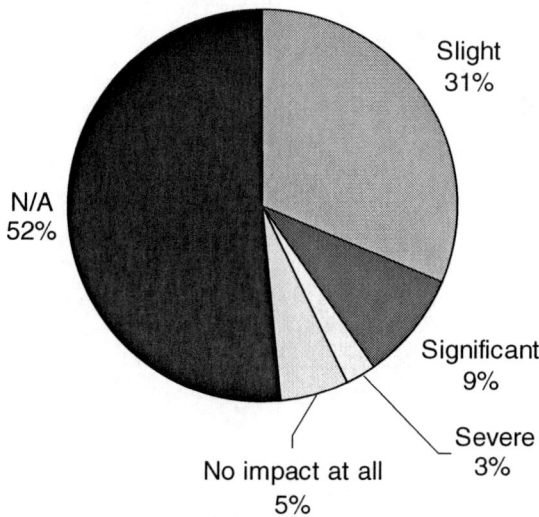

Figure 4.8 Significance to (business managers) of incidents affecting reputation

have had it 'top of mind'. Paradoxically, in one country, brand sales went up while the issue was at its hottest! (BCS24 – Senior sustainability officer)

A primary indicator of economic significance is also the impact of an event on share price. A study by Klein *et al.* (2004) measured the impact of an NGO campaign for consumer boycotts against Bremmer, a European-based food firm, after two factory closings that had received substantial media coverage. They found that market share went down for a few months because of the boycotts but returned to almost their pre-boycott levels five months after the boycott.

Managers gave us specific examples during our research of the nature of the 'fast rebound' of share price after intense NGO pressure. For example, in late 2002, Nestlé was brought to heel by the NGO Oxfam for demanding US$6 million compensation for shares in a Nestlé subsidiary (Elidco) from the government of poverty-stricken Ethiopia, at a time when the country was struggling with a threatening famine There was a proliferation of press reports on the topic. But a business manager commented later:

Oxfam created barely a 'blip' on the share price for Nestlé in the UK during its Ethiopian crisis. (BCS34b – Business manager, Communications)

Indeed, share prices of global F&B companies have shown themselves to be incredibly robust in the face of NGO pressure. In spite of the seriousness of the infant formula issue for Nestlé, the continued vigorous growth of this company indicates that the scandal did not ultimately influence either share price, or sales. (*The Economist*, 2004d).

Nevertheless, NGO attention contributed to Nestlé adopting a somewhat different stance on the Ethiopia issues, to accept less compensation and to invest the compensation back into the country.[4] A manager we interviewed pointed out:

NGOs are particularly effective at creating a sense of urgency about an issue, by forcing it on the company agenda and thus prompting companies to act earlier or differently than they otherwise would. (BCS47 – Business manager, Supply chain)

Also, no company wants share price to be threatened, even for a brief period, and marketers prefer to avoid high profile incidents due to the potential impact on brand and reputation and their own career exposure, given their 'short time stay' in their positions. Branded companies, such as Starbucks, MacDonald's, Nestlé, Coca-Cola and Chiquita will generally take rapid action when activists and the media expose strong brands upon which their corporate image relies. Industry leaders have resigned themselves to the fact that dealing with activists has become part and parcel of the act of doing business (see also *The Economist*, 2003j), and that the best approach is to 'get along with the lobbyists':

> *NGOS have always been important. Their influence is increasing. There is a two-fold influence, one positive in terms of partnerships and one negative; some will complain no matter what. We learnt from our confrontations with NGOs that confrontation cannot always be avoided, but preparation is beneficial.* (BCS39 – Top management, CEO)

Although some progressive companies have evolved from a defensive stance to a proactive stance of dialogue with stakeholders, not all managers were convinced of the sincerity of their own company's efforts:

> *To some extent, a game of bluff goes on with NGOs.* (BCS26 – Senior regional business unit manager, Purchasing)

Executives at the more well-known NGOs are no longer the sandal-wearing, flower-power stereotypes that they were characterized as being in the past. They have become slick and professional in their approach, act strategically and can present a formidable challenge to business. Some of the company managers we interviewed have welcomed the more professional approach of some NGOs, as opposed to what they describe as the chaotic and incoherent approach of others:

> *It is important to make a distinction between 'cowboys' and genuine stakeholders pushing the sustainability agenda.* (BCS48 – Senior manager, Strategy and business development)

Managers not only recognized the potential for company learning by working in partnerships but had observed that NGOs could also benefit:

> *As we worked in partnership with Greenpeace, we noticed that there was a gradual maturing of their approach; they started off with little technical knowledge and today, they are extremely well-informed and understand*

much better the dynamics of industrial change. (BCS08 – Senior business manager, Communications)

In dealing with NGOs, managers had come up against significant obstacles, mainly related to NGO's capacity to focus on single issues and act rapidly while the often fragmented, multi-dimensional and decentralized nature of the industry does not allow such a focus:

> *NGOs are better equipped to deal with sustainability issues because of their ability to 'speak with one voice' and focus on single issues, whereas food and beverage multinationals find sustainability issues a challenge to manage because of the fragmented and decentralized nature of the industry and the sheer number of issues that can be raised and linked to its operations.* (BCS01 – Senior regional business unit manager, Sales)

While NGOs may partner with companies on some issues, NGO managers declared that this would not stop them from activating the public against those same companies on other issues if deemed necessary.[5] Managers find this kind of behaviour disconcerting, being, as they are, accustomed to working generally with eager and loyal business partners.

> *We have a partnership going with an important NGO and it is taking some time for staff to realize that an NGO may work in synergy with them on some agendas and can go against them on others.* (BCS47a – Business manager, Supply chain)

In spite of the difficulties of facing NGO criticism, managers felt that their organizations had become much more adept at dealing with activists than in the 1980s and 1990s when companies found it much more difficult to predict how NGOs would approach issues (Steger, 1998b). The tables have turned somewhat since the era of corporate scandals in the 1980s and 1990s. Interestingly, IMD empirical research on stakeholders ending in 2006 indicated that NGO managers were now frustrated at 'being managed' by industry and were seeking new strategies to leverage companies to more accelerated action on some issues. Overall NGOs ranked themselves low on their effectiveness at influencing companies. Our own research indicates that despite the substantial hype around the subject of pressure groups and their influence on companies, companies are still not under sufficient pressure to regard NGOs as a serious competitor in 'the stakeholder stakes' to their customers, end-consumers and shareholders. However, NGOs can also influence other stakeholders, and

Chapter 3 shows several examples where this has proven to be a powerful dynamic. One of these is the regulator (ActionAid International, 2005), and we address the importance of this stakeholder in our next section.

2.2.2 Regulators

Legislation has been a key tool in setting the boundaries of minimum standards in corporate social and environmental behaviour across industries. This is often referred to as the 'level playing field' by managers. Also, regulation can have positive internal paybacks within companies in terms of awareness and behaviour. Although our concept and definition of a BCS is mainly related to efforts that companies make in environmental and social domains *beyond compliance*, it is important that we look at the dynamic between legislative and voluntary efforts as, by managers' own admission, much of what companies do voluntarily in terms of their individual BCS is intended to stave off impending legislation and reduce uncertainties in this area. One manager pointed out the importance of proactive CSR as a licence to operate from regulators:

> Government relations are very important to the licence to operate in certain countries. In the European market, Brussels exercises a huge influence. If we can use corporate responsibility to demonstrate positive contribution to rule of law and improvement in developing countries, this can be a powerful instrument in dialogue with political bodies. By being bad actors, companies lose political backing. (BCS05 – Senior business manager, Communications)

Since, as managers were quick to point out, the F&B industry is already highly regulated in Europe, we noted during our research that it was clearly important to the industry that its voice be heard in the corridors of the European Commission.

Sustainability officers we interviewed stated that pressure from governments and regulators was initially the principal driver for sustainability action in the industry, mainly for environmental impacts. A sustainability officer we interviewed commented:

> While regulatory pressure was most useful in the earlier stages of promoting a business case for sustainability, it is less of a driver for more progressive companies. (BCS47 – Business manager, Supply chain)

Food law was in a rather accelerated and dynamic process of evolution within the European Union up to and including the period of research.

In the past ten years, food manufacturers at all levels have had to respond to increasing regulation of the industry, and have had to provide transparent evidence of quality and regulatory compliance. The Green Paper on Food Law (European Commission, 1996, 1997), represented the birth of discussion on the development of European Food Law into a coherent and comprehensive system. The European Food Safety Authority was established in 2002 and is currently taking shape.[6] There are many examples where company lack of compliance with food or worker safety regulations would have served shareholder interests by saving companies from legal sanctions and reputation impacts: Examples are the 1999 withdrawal by Coca-Cola Company of trademarked products from the Belgian market due to a health scare, illegal mercury dumping in 2001 from a Unilever factory in India and in 2004, withdrawal from the market of Coca Cola's newly launched mineral water when the bromide content was found to be above legal limits. Regulation ensures that a strong level playing field for food safety exists.

However, companies generally take the view that as long as all players conform to legal requirements, regulation itself does not put them at a competitive disadvantage:

Legislation is a minimum hurdle being raised all the time. As long as everyone conforms, this does not affect competitive advantage. (BCS45 – Senior business manager, Corporate economist)

But managers were concerned about the threat that impending European legislation might have on their future global competitiveness. The balance between control to safeguard the consumer, environment and farm animals, and freedom in order to assure competitive advantage was of critical importance to them. We identified a strong view within the industry that costs of regulation and taxation or overly standardized norms can constrain ability to compete and innovate:

Companies do not react positively to increased levels of regulation. Regulatory bodies represent the negative aspect of stakeholder intervention. If you over-regulate, you create a backlash, with lawyers finding loopholes. For this reason, companies should see CSM as a necessity rather than optional. (BCS14 – Senior business manager, Finance)

Business managers evidently considered that in a global business environment there is probably an optimum level of regulation beyond which it does not make sense to regulate. However, a level *global* playing field is as yet far from reality, as is reflected in the IMD stakeholder study on European corporate customers and suppliers in 2006 (Ionescu-Somers, 2006b; Steger *et al.*, 2006). Several managers felt that the level of existing regulation placed Europe at a global competitive disadvantage and that a wave of deregulation should be forthcoming:

> *Some environmental regulations coming out of the EU are absolutely ridiculous. Regulation does not motivate the industry to be more resourceful. Some regulations are commendable – but we are currently over legislating suppliers and producers to the point of paralysis. There has to be deregulation – Europe has to start to live in the real world. The EU can remain competitive if business has less regulation – some countries need a 'tsunami' type change, but instead, it is happening at snail's pace.* (BCS30 – Senior regional business unit manager, Purchasing)

Nevertheless, we deduced from our interview and desk research that in future, legal requirements related to food safety, particularly in the European Community, will probably intensify and remain an important driver of sustainability action particularly for the laggards in the industry. Undoubtedly, there will be increased requirements regarding disclosure (social and environmental reporting) and advertising (labelling), collective bargaining and governance.

However, it is unlikely that legislative pressure will increase on procurement procedures, including social and environmental considerations in contracts. In Europe, national governments regard global companies as acting beyond the scope of national states, and that they are no longer directly accountable to them. They therefore do not jeopardize their national competitiveness through imposing national regulation regimes, and tend to favour standards on a European or international level for this reason. The EU commission does not perceive corporate responsibility as a purely legislative issue as is laid out in the EU green (European Commission, 2001) and subsequent white (European Commission, 2002b) papers on corporate sustainability. Overall there is an expectation by the European Commission that companies will engage voluntarily in the process of being socially responsible. During our interview research, we observed that, for the leading companies, the key business case opportunity that impending regulation presents is the possibility of 'being ahead of the posse'. It is in the corporate interest to deter regulators from imposing so many costs and administrative burdens on companies that they lose shareholder value:

> *Enough warning signs have been given to the industry – what is necessary is to be proactive and shape the agenda rather than having it shaped for the industry.* (BCS17 – Senior business manager, Communications)

Also, by becoming an industry 'first mover', a company achieves greater visibility through association with ground-breaking new approaches while avoiding 'wrong' legislation at the same time:

> *We need to be first movers because otherwise something will be introduced that suits us less.* (BCS08 – Senior business manager, Communications)

Leading companies in the industry are often strategically applying a conscious 'beyond compliance' approach for this very reason. Whilst one could argue that taking sustainability action may put 'first mover' companies at a competitive disadvantage compared with their rivals, managers at such companies stated that this apparent disadvantage can be offset in several ways over time since it improves corporate reputation among consumers and other companies may imitate the first mover until a practice eventually becomes enshrined in a non-regulatory norm.

The latter argument suggests that the line between choice and compliance is porous and emphasizes the importance of collaborative efforts to raise the bar. However, there are related risks should competitors not follow the 'first mover' example:

> *The worst-case scenario is that after considerable work done, others do not follow, and retailers do not require it. If effort is not rewarded in the market place, managers will wonder why they are doing it. We can make a difference by demonstrating what can be done and by setting a standard and raising the bar for the industry. But it is important to work with other influential stakeholders to ensure that others take up the issues.* (BCS05 – Senior business manager, Communications)

NGOs disenchanted with what they perceive as the ineffectiveness of CSM indicated that they will push harder for regulation to counter some of the critical situations they see evolving into the future. Business managers, although vehemently opposing the prospect of more regulation, seemed resigned to the possibility of increased momentum on regulation in Europe. To counter this, there have been some moves by the industry itself to reach consensus on some sustainability issues where regulatory solutions threaten. Competitors have adopted a united front on certain sustainability issues facing the F&B industry today. As an example, bilateral initiatives exist through industry associations; sustainable agriculture, water, obesity and GMOs:

> *Food industry members are closer to their peers than, say, companies in the automobile industry. Many of the discussions about eating meat, health scandals like BSE, and also GMOs showed companies the need to participate in industry discussions on such issues.* (BCS36 – Senior business manager, Finance)

> *To be effective, it is sometimes necessary to align with industry partners; we did so with recycling. Sometimes, as with the Sustainable Agriculture Initiative, there are issues that, if one company does this on its own, it will not make a huge difference.* (BCS50 – Senior regional business unit manager, Marketing and Sales)

2.2.3   Unions and employees

Employees have been successful, often using unions as a conduit, in putting pressure on their organizations to provide them with acceptable workplace conditions, taking account of employee rights and health and safety provisions; non-discriminatory practices in hiring, firing and promotion; and salary structures relating pay to performance and employee stock ownership. According to one of the managers we interviewed, the level of power and influence of employees in both developed and developing countries can depend on how much support the government of the country gives to unions. Unions are becoming increasingly important in emerging economies, precisely where F&B companies see the future growth of their markets. Some companies, such as Chiquita, have thus identified a business case for keeping a workforce motivated and engaged. In Mexico, with just such a business case in mind, Danone changed a corporate culture to stimulate staff towards innovation, sharing of ideas and employee satisfaction thus changing the traditional model of a unionized and defensive workforce.

Employees can have considerable impact on how society perceives a company, since job losses and the way employees are treated are often highly newsworthy subjects that expose the company to image damage and reputation loss. With the global trend towards mergers and acquisitions in the sector, headcounts have often been a target. How redundancy schemes are dealt with is often a reflection of corporate culture and values and, increasingly, is a sustainability issue. Companies cannot be complacent about industrial unrest. A more strategic approach to such issues may be necessary as union activity can still have a detrimental economic effect on business.

However, research at IMD in 2006 indicated that union agendas in Europe are primarily driven by globalization and pressure for regional competitiveness (Steger *et al.*, 2006), and they are thus focused on wage bargaining and sustaining employment levels and tend to prefer regulation as a solution to corporate sustainability dilemmas affecting the workforce. The IMD research demonstrated that the power of unions has waned considerably in the last two decades in Europe and industrial action is much less of a direct threat to European economies than some 25 years ago. They do not push for better CSM of issues that do not directly affect their membership on a personal level. Nevertheless, current trends to outsource manufacturing to developing countries such as India, China. Eastern Europe or Brazil, add a layer of additional complexity to the outsourcing decision that is not always considered by companies in the search for short-term efficiency gains, and there may be increased risks for F&B companies in the future. Some managers were aware of these risks:

> *Employees are much more aware of their rights and the meaning of a higher standard of conduct, particularly in developing countries. There will be a rising tide of expectations.* (BCS05 – Senior business manager, Communications)

We discovered that the power of the European employee to put pressure for more CSM in companies is largely contingent on the individual values of individual employees. Here, there are a number of rather complex considerations for the BCS that we consider very extensively in the second section of this book.

3 Synthesis

Our research on stakeholders in the F&B industry endorses Steger's (1998a) observation that stakeholders from the business sphere are of most importance to business managers, given their influence on the all-important economic sustainability of the company, and that, paradoxically, the most proactive stakeholders are those that are least relevant to managers.

We conclude from our research that key stakeholders of economic importance to the F&B industry – consumers, retailers and shareholders – are simply not yet putting F&B companies under enough pressure to internalize their externalities more rapidly and thus accelerate a sustainability agenda beyond (albeit important) incremental steps. This is in spite of the fact that F&B managers are highly aware of the relatively volatile stakeholder environment in which they are moving. The most critical factor is the mainstream consumer's unwillingness to pay for sustainability 'benefits', since these are 'wider good' benefits for the community and not personal benefits. Also, while the consumer punishes laggard behaviour in companies, she does not necessarily reward leaders. Identifying, describing and conveying consumer personal benefit through sustainability certainly requires some attention from companies before any marked change can come about.

Figure 4.9 represents the state of stakeholder pressure and response dynamics in the industry. In this figure, we observe the food processing industry stakeholder dynamics, with very strong retailer 'squeeze', augmented by strong consumer pressure, for ever lower prices and better quality, shareholders that pressure the industry for short-term returns, and an array of other stakeholders that are not exercising enough countervailing influence on the beyond compliance sustainability agenda to reverse the trend of strong industry response to the

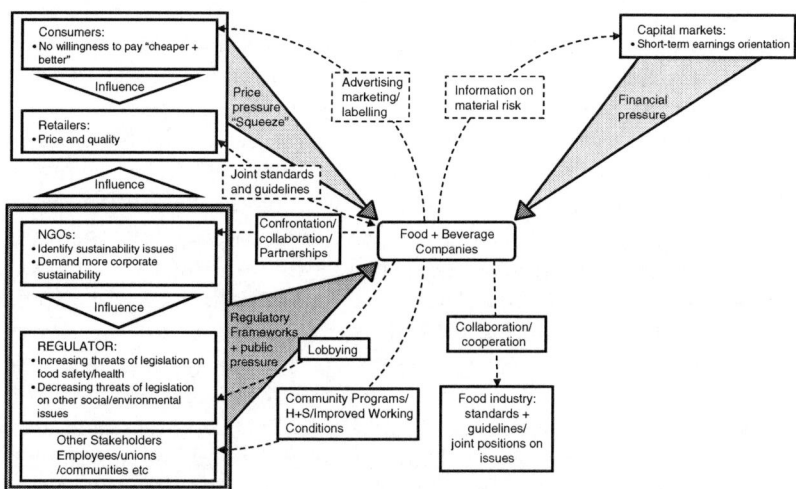

Figure 4.9 The food and beverage industry: stakeholder pressure and industry response

price/quality demands of retailers and consumers. Regulators of course, have a strong role in promoting CSM through compliance, but the industry spends a lot of time trying to stave off future potential impact so that it retains global competitiveness. Note that in Figure 4.9, we have included not only the type of pressure on the industry, but also the typical industry CSM response; the broken lined boxes correspond to the weakest areas of response. The weakest responses are in the areas of labelling/advertising and marketing efforts, cooperation with retailers on standards and guidelines, and information on material risk provided to capital markets. The strongest are the responses to public and regulatory pressure and collaboration within the industry itself.

We have referred in this chapter to individual studies carried out at IMD business school in Switzerland in the context of an extensive study of stakeholders during 2005 (Steger, 2006). The IMD research team looked at the perceptions of nine stakeholder groups of CSM and analysed the level of pressure exercised by each group on industry to improve CSM. The overall findings are pessimistic in terms of short to mid-term stakeholder pressure effects on European industry in general. Many of the stakeholders, including NGOs, ranked themselves low on their effectiveness at influencing the sustainability performance of companies. The resounding conclusion was that there is probably considerable hype behind the issue of stakeholder pressure in both the academic and business community today, and that as companies become more adept at managing their stakeholder environment, NGOs are actually regarded as much less of a threat than before. Put simply, managers in most industries do not seem to be feeling the heat.

At a forum to present the results of the IMD stakeholder research, managers were asked 'If you are not under pressure, then why are you increasingly working with stakeholders?'[7] Managers replied that while the pressure of a single secondary stakeholder may not be the issue, the cumulative pressure from several groups is nevertheless significant enough to make a difference, making the identification of strategically relevant stakeholders – and improving the quality of these relationships – a key mitigating aspect of doing business today. Companies are slow to change their behaviour on the basis of sporadic threats and it often takes several years and a combination of stakeholder pressures, both internal and external, for change to come about.

F&B managers we interviewed told us that to base company strategy on a stakeholder model allows much more scope for implementation of sustainability objectives within companies, and often gives a new dimension and economic rationale to a business strategy that would otherwise be overthrown:

> *If our company had not built up its network of stakeholders in the comprehensive way that it has, it would be insular, inflexible and unable to make decisions as well as today.* (BCS16 – Senior business manager, Strategy)

Progressive companies recognize the importance of involving stakeholders in resolving issues that the industry cannot tackle alone. They recognize the Smart Zone business benefits of attending more to secondary stakeholder demands other than those of customers, consumers and shareholders. This is because it promotes organizational learning and mitigates pressure, but also protects reputation and brand value. Probably for this reason, when the sustainability officers were asked in our survey which factors amongst several most promote sustainable business practices, 'dialogue with stakeholders' figured in the first three factors they chose.

But even for these companies, the benefits generated by collaboration with stakeholders do not surpass the business benefits of placing shareholder value and customer demands first. Furthermore, if the extensive research carried out by IMD is anything to go by, the situation is not likely to change in the near future.

Notes

1 See *The Economist*, 2004f.
2 A stock market index including all developed markets stocks in the world.
3 For a succinct description of the birth and development of stock market indexes to aid the growth of sustainable investments, read Sandor *et al.*, 2001.
4 See www.oxfamamerica.org and www.nestle.com
5 An illustrative example of WWF's actions during a partnership with Lafarge in the cement industry is described in Steger *et al.* (2003).
6 See www.efsa.eu.int
7 Forum for CSM, IMD, 21 and 22 November 2005: 'Great expectations? Corporate value chains – How far up, how far down?

5
The Value of Value Drivers

1 Introduction

At a panel discussion organized in 2002 by Arthur D. Little, food industry executives were crystal clear about the food industry mandate to primarily improve performance to benefit shareholders and the challenge that integrating social and environmental issues into business strategy brings in this context:

Food companies cannot afford to lose sight of the fact that their primary duty is to shareholders. Whatever the demands of consumers and other stakeholders, companies must ensure that corporate responsibility policies do not undermine shareholder value. Markets focus on short-term profit, while sustainability policies tend to involve a longer-term return on investment. While private companies may have more freedom to focus on the future, shareholder owned businesses must be aware of the impact of their policies on profits. (Arthur D. Little, 2002)

In Chapter 4, managers bore testimony to the virtual corporate obsession with short-term focus that dominates today's business environment. But while investors are demanding increasingly superior returns on their risk premium from companies within ever shorter time frames, it is also true that product excellence or profit focus is no longer sufficient for long-term success. Managers move in a complex business environment; share prices are often dependent on increasingly intangible concepts such as brand value or intrinsic corporate competence and knowledge. Indeed, primarily for this reason, the UK government's White Paper on Company Law published in 2002 recognized the need for more qualitative and 'forward-looking' reporting.

Assessing the relevance of a decision to a strategy today is not only a question of managers coming up with figures; highly individual assessment of problems and application of managerial knowledge of the global as well as local context of business decisions are key contributing factors. Short term measures may be ultimately damaging from a sustainable development point of view, but may also impact a company's long-term competitiveness and financial sustainability. This suggests that corporate focus should rather be on growth opportunities or building competitive advantages. In fact, it should be critical for shareholders that large global companies implement value-based management systems and focus on the sustainability of their returns more than on short-term performance.

Trends indicate that sustainability issues are, in general, more likely to crop up with greater rather than less frequency. In an increasingly sophisticated global and competitive business environment, it behoves company decision-makers to have a thorough understanding of the contribution that managing these issues may have to the process of value creation leading to the corporate bottom line. A senior manager commented:

> There *is* an 'open and shut' case for sustainability action – but companies do not see it. We did a lot of benchmarking with our peers and very few companies are really taking it on board as they should. The food and drink sector is slower than other sectors to come to the table on these issues. (BCS02 – Senior business manager, Communications)

In this chapter, we aim to analyse the extent to which social and environmental issues can be more than simply tangential to business especially when seen from a shareholder value perspective. The following sections examine how the drivers of economic success are increasingly based on sophisticated criteria that can also be linked to a sustainability agenda.

2   The concept of shareholder value

The shareholder value concept, an approach that measures the value of companies from the shareholder point of view, is described in Rappaport's (1986) groundbreaking book, *Creating Shareholder Value*.[1] Rappaport set out to demonstrate the drawbacks of the most common, accounting-based measures of a company's performance such as price-to-earnings ratio, return on investment and equity measures. He found that existing approaches were overly focused on non value-adding activities, a short-term earnings orientation and tended to look backwards instead of forwards. To illustrate a certain dichotomy in the traditional approach, we cite the example of the performance of companies defined as 'excellent' by Peters and Waterman in their best-selling book *In Search of Excellence* (1982). Johnson *et al.* (1985) demonstrate that these companies did not, in fact, demonstrate consistently superior economic performance in spite of their excellent 'earnings' performance over a given period based on the more commonly used 'short-term' measures of financial performance.

Valuing a company based on the shareholder value approach implies measuring 'value drivers' (the basic valuation parameters for a company), such as value growth duration, sales growth rate, operating profit margins and income tax rate, working capital investments, fixed capital investments, and cost of capital or equity.

So for Rappaport, value drivers are based on cash flow (rather than on profit and loss), with cost of capital acting as a benchmark for added economic value. Cost of capital determines the discount rate, which in turn depends on the level of risk; it is therefore a reflection of the relative risk of cash flows produced by other drivers. The shareholder value approach estimates the economic value of a strategy as the expected cash flow discounted by the market discount rate; thus this 'discounted cash flow' can be closely linked to strategic analysis. The cash flows in turn serve as the basis for expected shareholder returns from dividends and stock-price appreciation.

Rappaport demonstrates interconnectivity between value drivers embedded in individual company strategies – operating, investment and financial. He also shows how decisions made within these strategies, and the projected forecasts that these decisions are based upon, can have a direct effect on shareholder value. Rappaport also lends significance to the value growth duration period or the length of time over which the value adding activity is maintained. Interestingly, McKinsey & Company draws attention to the fact that even from strictly a shareholder value perspective, most stock market value – as much as over 80 per cent in US and western European public markets – actually depends on cash flow expectations going beyond the following three years (Davis, 2005).

The longer-term perspective of the shareholder value approach can be adopted usefully to determine a BCS. This is because tangible returns on sustainability activities in companies are usually based on a longer-term framework than other business activities and projects. The shareholder value concept facilitates much-needed identification of factors linked to sustainability concepts that contribute to operational value drivers. It can act as a useful tool to show managers where opportunities for value creation exist. It helps to identify actions that a company can take to improve business, justify a focus on an identified problem and thus relate managerial actions to direct economic outcomes. Example of such actions include the relation between operating profit margin and costs, productivity, resource efficiency and so on, thus encompassing all factors related to the value driver that ultimately impact economic value-added.

The concept allows managers to reflect more deeply on the underlying economic arguments that promote a voluntary internalization by corporations of corporate externalities in an effort to resolve sustainability issues, and thus identify the Smart Zone. Seen from a shareholder value perspective, the impact of sustainability value generators on corporate strategy might be substantial and tangible. We have systemized this concept in Figure 5.1.

The glaring examples are eco-efficiency measures leading to lower operating costs thus contributing to increased cash flow from operations and hence increased shareholder value. In other cases, the link is less obvious and less tangible, as is the case with reputation and brand-value benefits. These are not always quantified or quantifiable and the link to sustainability measures is not reflected in balance sheet

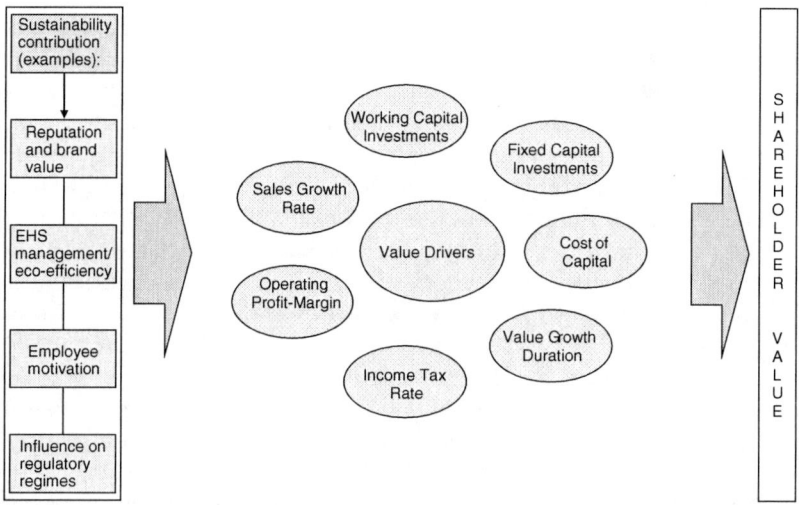

Figure 5.1 CSM's contributions to value drivers

calculations. An example would be the licence to operate benefits of gaining community trust, which in turn leads to more rapid processing of authorization permits.

Managers often fear CSM's potentially negative contribution to sales growth, for example, capital intensive investment incurring high operating costs with little to no revenue-generating capacity – such as 'end-of-pipe' technologies – can reduce shareholder value. In such cases, companies might opt to await regulation such that there is a 'level playing field' with competitors. Also, differentiation in products and operations based on sustainability concepts does not contribute to shareholder value if, as is the case according to our empirical evidence, consumers are unwilling to pay for perceived added value. In allowing us to define how sustainability issues can either positively or negatively affect the drivers of value within companies, Rappaport's framework establishes essential links between sustainability issues and economic performance. This helps to reconcile improvements of corporate environmental and social performance with either net cost savings and/or net increases in revenues. Ignoring these possibilities means that companies can miss out on what may turn out to be important elements of competitive advantage. In low margin, cut-throat business environments such as that of the F&B industry, all possibilities that may lead to additional competitive advantage need to be analyzed, understood and exploited.

To systemize value drivers in our research concept, we differentiate between two types of sustainability issues leading to different approaches to value-creating management:

- Sustainability issues that lead to **operational management** of risks and opportunities, through incremental win–win solutions. Examples of these are changes in behaviour or processes that improve efficiencies and result in immediate short-term cost saving. By their nature, these activities are cost-driven. Since they have immediate visible and tangible benefits, they are often referred to by managers as 'low hanging fruits'. Picking the low hanging fruits does not call for radical redesign of processes and products, and can be carried out while doing 'business as usual', therefore accommodating a conservative, risk-averse approach. The advantage is that they allow for an initial BCS to be founded on very tangible criteria with near-term pay backs:

Although there is also a noble desire to 'do good', like all companies, our major motivator is to make profit, and profit motivates people to use fewer resources. It is a cost issue – for example, the less packaging we use, the more money we save... (Senior regional business unit manager, Purchasing)

- And then there are those sustainability issues that lead to **strategic management** of opportunities through more radical innovation. Such an approach can result in entirely new business models, products and/or markets. Particularly in cases where companies adopt a new economic activity, a successful strategic approach based on **radical innovation** can ultimately lead to increases in revenue and duration of value growth. This is altogether a much more challenging prospect for managers as it is not 'business as usual' and involves a higher degree of risk.

In the following sections, we use our framework to focus on the principle CSM contributions to value drivers that managers perceive and use to stimulate business interest in sustainability within their companies.

3   Food and beverage industry value drivers

We asked managers to name the value drivers for the business case for sustainability in their company and rank them according to their importance. In response, business and sustainability managers in the F&B industry consistently came up with soft constructs such as 'reputation enhancement', 'licence to operate', 'brand value' and 'attracting and retaining staff:

> *The business case is primarily based on reputation and licence to operate value drivers, and to a much more minor degree on technology and innovation. By being first to deal with these issues, our brand can benefit.* (BCS08 – Senior business manager, Communications)

In our survey, we asked sustainability officers the following: What is your best possible argument when promoting the concept of sustainable development in your company? As can be seen in Figure 5.2, the three most important values contributing constructs for sustainability officers were 'improves brand value and reputation' (27 per cent of responses), 'is essential to maintaining our licence to operate' (21 per cent) and 'attracts talent and increases employee satisfaction' (18 per cent).

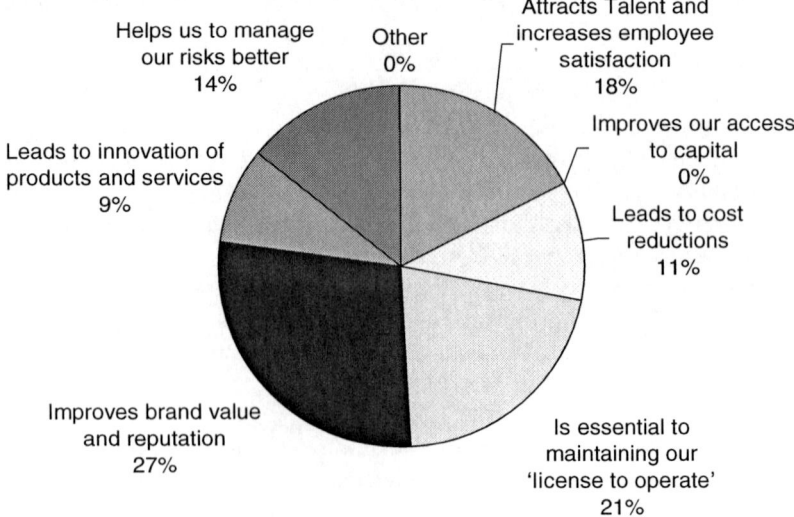

Figure 5.2 Arguments for promoting the concept of sustainable development in F&B companies (sustainability officers)

Sustainability managers only attributed 11 per cent of their responses to 'leads to cost reductions', which is interesting given the intense focus on eco-efficiency measures prevalent in the industry as a whole:

> *A lot of the industry is caught up in the tangible aspects of sustainability (measuring energy outputs and reducing impacts). Companies often ignore the intangible aspect; the social and values side. Here there is a marked difference in how companies are responding. The real muddied area is intangible.* (BCSBM6 – Food industry expert and author)

Steger (2004) classified the constructs chosen by managers as constituting CSM's main contribution to shareholder value in terms of the operational or strategic approaches to sustainability. We adapted Steger's figure to the food industry for our purposes (see Figure 5.3). It clearly illustrates how 'soft' constructs can impact both operational and strategic dimensions of management.

By emphasizing the importance of the contribution of CSM to value creation, managers at the progressive companies involved in our research confirmed the fact that conceptually they have moved beyond a cost perspective. Managers at these companies felt that cost reduction was a

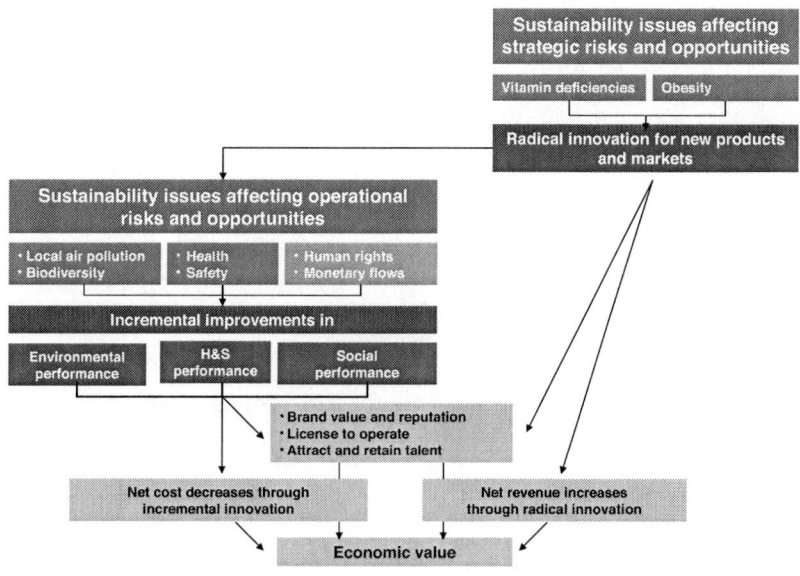

Steger et al., 2004

Figure 5.3   System of value drivers

prime motivator only for the corporate laggard. They also felt that eco-efficiency should anyway be an expected feature of good management in global companies. However, they warned that much of the industry approach still remains anchored in its sustainability actions to tangible, quantifiable, cost-driven sustainability action – such as lowering energy or water consumption. This is not surprising as managers tend to appreciate what is tangible and thus measurable best. The old dictum holds; 'what gets measured, gets managed'. While it is important and essential to exploit the low hanging fruits, the question for more progressive managers is often 'What next?':

> *For the environment, we have been concentrating on major impacts – we have 'picked off the big ones' – and set up a system establishing target setting in big areas. Now we need to go beyond that.* (BCS18 – Sustainability officer)

Managers further pointed out that the focus on intangibles such as brand value and reputation is more characteristic of large branded companies in developed economies, is scarcely part of a developing country focus and does not impact SMEs to any great extent. The business case for the F&B industry is considerably weakened by the fact that the reputation and brand value constructs that provide a strong case for global companies are much less effective in formulating the case for the myriad of smaller and less exposed food companies throughout the industry:

> *The real difference with SMEs is that they are family owned and run – there is not the same brand exposure or responsibility to shareholders. Family companies are more invisible. The driver in smaller companies is likely to be recruitment – family values drive family companies.* (BCS34 – Business manager, Communications)

Furthermore, a comparison of developed and emerging market economies carried out by SustainAbility (Cowe, 2002) shows that if emerging market companies focus on a BCS at all, it tends to be at the level of short-term savings and revenue gains – thus a cost perspective rather than a strategic value-generating perspective. Indeed, some managers felt that the cost focus of emerging economies versus a value focus of developed economies may jeopardize the BCS in the future:

> *Sustainable development is given space in Europe because of a European system of value. It's an affordable luxury. Europe is rich and has met most basic requirements already. In India and China, people struggle to survive and have a different value construct. If there is conflict between sustainability and economic development, it's a difficult choice.* (BCS45 – Senior business manager, Corporate economist)

We further explore competitive issues related to this point in Chapter 6. However, it is clear that these aspects weaken the BCS considerably for the industry as a whole.

The sustainability managers we interviewed did not perceive value drivers as difficult to identify, but they also admitted that it was sometimes difficult for managers to understand what can tangibly be done with sustainability drivers on a day-to-day basis. However, they expected the concept of sustainability to be better defined in future, and were optimistic that this would lead to better understanding by both society and companies. One manager predicted:

> *The whole sector will move gradually away from the current environmental impact focus to a sustainability context based on research and development, resource and competence management. Recognition of the*

potential of reputation and licence-to-operate impacts to affect value drivers will be enhanced as a result. (BCS38 – Sustainability officer)

3.1   Reputation enhancement and brand value

In the global 'goldfish bowl' economy in which we live today, F&B companies face substantial risks to their reputation, which can have a direct and immediate impact on their economic value, even if temporary. In a survey carried out at the 2004 World Economic Forum in Davos, Switzerland, only one in five of the 1,500 delegates there thought that profitability was the most important measure of corporate success. While only five per cent said that CSR was the single most important criterion, 24 per cent felt that reputation and integrity of the brand were the most important factors.

The more extreme side of the devastating impact on shareholder value of a loss of reputation, as well as loss of jobs and pensions, has been amply demonstrated in the public limelight of late. This can be glaringly witnessed in the fall-out from scandals such as the demise of Enron, and with it Anderson, and the crises that faced Ahold, Parmalat and Adecco and as we go to press France's Société Générale had joined the ranks. A more positive result of such events has been that progressive corporate boards are beginning to scrutinize their profiles and focus more fully on reputation risk. Interestingly however, a study in 2005 by insurance broker Aon on the F&B industry showed that F&B companies may be falling out of this trend since most had not yet begun to integrate risk to discussions at board level (Aon, 2005).

But reputation is an increasingly important barometer of company health, as is highlighted in MORI's (2004) 'Captains of Industry' study of Chairmen, CEOS, MDs and board level directors in FTSE500 firms. In today's Internet world of universal access to information, corporate reputation can be lost within a very short time frame (Murray, 2004b). Rebuilding a lost reputation is a much more arduous task. As several managers pointed out; sometimes it is only possible to know what reputation is really worth when it effectively lies in tatters.

In another study carried out by the insurance broker Aon, of more than 100 European companies, loss of reputation was seen as the greatest threat to business next to business interruption. Yet the same study reported that only 22 per cent of these same companies had a formal strategy for reputation risk.[2] Several managers we spoke to in the F&B industry agreed that risk to reputation, both from enhancement and preservation points of view was the one factor that had the potential to move sustainability into the mainstream.

The front-line characteristic of the F&B industry and the personal nature of its products also enhance reputation as a value driver. While the main focus of companies is on generating returns for shareholders, companies operate within a societal context and, thus, the criteria by which they are assessed cannot be exclusively related to economic performance. While there is a 'formal' licence to operate (LTO) given to companies by regulators on the one hand, on the other hand non-regulatory stakeholders bestow an 'informal' LTO:

> *The politics surrounding food supply and the focus companies give to the role of business in society play important roles in determining a company's ability to continue operations.* (BCS05 – Senior business manager, Communications)

Determinants of the informal LTO include vulnerability of reputation, brands and profit. Informal LTO is the result of a matching process used by stakeholders to compare their expectations of corporate behaviour to companies' actual behaviour:

> *Consumers perceive that a multinational company has a role in society and that it must maintain standards that are suited to the social fabric in which it operates.* (BCS50 – Senior regional business unit manager, Marketing and sales)

Another manager pointed to an evolution of the relationship between the consumer and the brand to more than a simple functional transaction:

> *Even if you look at it from a consumer angle, it is not good business for us to do business in an unsustainable way. In the US and EU, people want to know that they are buying from people with values. People want to know what is behind a brand and the extent to which its values align with their own.* (BCS30 – Senior regional business unit manager, Supply chain)

Managers confirmed that if F&B companies do not 'do the right thing', then consumers react and LTO and the success of business operations are jeopardized and, as LTO is directly linked to share price, this is not good news for companies. It is the perception of people that affects informal LTO and this ultimately affects sales. As a food company business manager commented at one of our interviews:

> *Winning 'hearts and minds' is what our business is all about – this is often more important than 'being right'.* (BCS47 – Business manager, Supply chain)

Interestingly, our BSC project survey demonstrated that of all nine sectors researched, LTO was considered most important by officers in

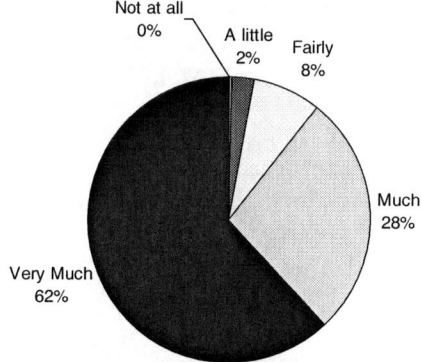

Figure 5.4 Importance of brand or reputation to the company (business managers – all sectors)

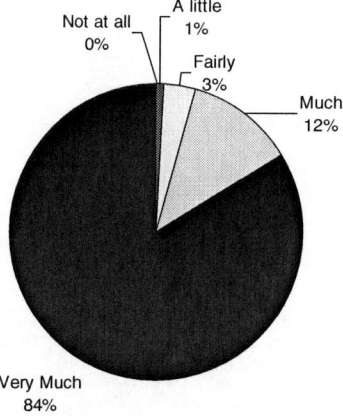

Figure 5.5 Importance of brand or reputation for the company (business managers – food and beverage sector)

the F&B, oil and gas, pharmaceutical and aviation sectors. Also, when asked how important brand or reputation was for their company, 84 per cent of managers in the F&B industry indicated 'very much' as compared to an average of 62 per cent for all sectors (see Figures 5.4 and 5.5). This revealed the distinct 'front line' highly exposed nature of the sectors business as opposed to other sectors.

This result is particularly relevant given that, according to F&B managers we spoke to, brands will in future be a more integrated part of reputation management than today. With better tracking and tracing systems, managers believe that there will be increased branding on the food producers side – indeed, some companies are moving in this direction already – or sometimes even dual branding involving both retailer and manufacturer. A beverage company manager pointed to the relationship between brand exposure and social visibility:

> *Look at Coca-Cola – as soon as the brand connectivity is there, there is pressure. Our company does not have the same exposure. There is consumer confusion about the specific brands we produce. This suits us for now. But we are going through a rapid stage of consolidation. As companies grow, they become more exposed. Over time, we will become more visible and then decide if we want more brand visibility.* (BCS41 – Senior sustainability officer)

One expert we interviewed commented that when the current wave of consolidation in the retail sector has reached saturation, it is not out of the question that retailers would move to acquiring food companies, or *vice-versa*. If this happens, the producing company will be reaching out to consumers even more directly. In such a scenario, he saw reputation and image building increasing exponentially.

Reputation is almost interchangeably referred to as brand in the industry. The gap between a product and a corporate brand identity is indeed very easily breached. Hence, a plethora of research and media articles has started to pour into the literature that explore the relationship between brand and CSR, all concluding that social and environmental performance are increasingly important strategic assets for guaranteeing brand value. Journalists surmise that leading 'brand' companies will have to accept sustainability and their obligations to be accountable for 'links in their value chains that they don't control' as a 'brand tax' (Allen and Root, 2004). The challenge for us is to understand to what extent this has entered the corporate conscience of the F&B industry.

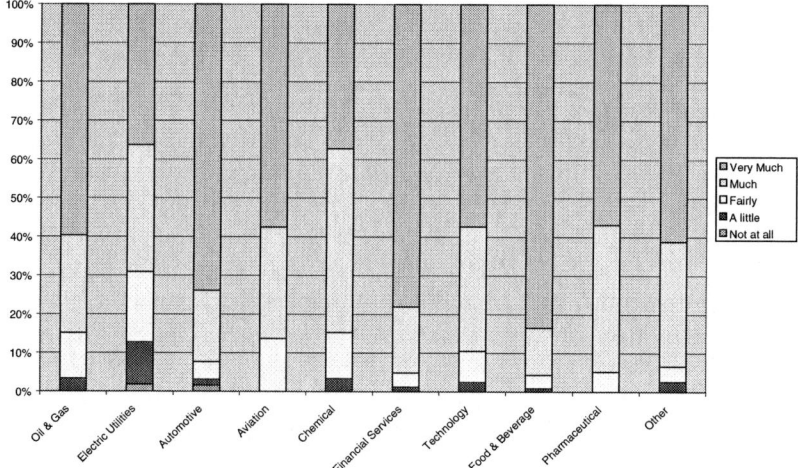

Figure 5.6   Cross industry analysis – importance of brand and reputation

Recent research indicates that corporate social and environment performance affects consumer perceptions of company brands and products. Perhaps for this very reason, of all industries analyzed in the BCS study, managers in the F&B industry lent most importance to brand and reputation (see Figure 5.6).

Brands today are given a distinct monetary value. Every year Interbrand, an international branding consultancy, establishes rankings that are worked out using complex techniques not unlike those used by stock market analysts, leading to the world brand league table. F&B companies are very much present in the first 100 most valuable global brands. In 2006, Coca-Cola had a value of US$67 billion, while McDonalds retained a value of US$27 billion. The weight of value is such that, when faced with brand threats, major F&B companies tend to switch to 'sustainability-speak' more willingly than companies in other industries whose image and brand are less intrinsic to the business. Some sustainability issues have become part of their overall risk management:

The brand is a food and beverage company's' most important asset; whatever tarnishes its image has a negative effect on whatever premium the brand brings. (9BCS04 – Senior regional business unit manager, Marketing and sales)

The association of value with a brand is fundamental to brand differenti-
ation and thus competitive advantage, especially when a company name
is tied tightly to a brand, as with Chiquita, or Nestlé. (BCS27 – Senior
business manager, Supply chain)

Also, the greater value a firm places on its brand, the more susceptible
its managers will be to activist pressure. We observed that many of the
companies participating in our research have been prime targets (see
Chapter 3).

Given the push–pull relationships between manufacturers and
retailers, producers such as Nestlé and Unilever have decided to become
more visible and to ensure that all products carry some degree of corporate branding. In this way, they can compete more effectively with the
private brands of retailers and even make inroads on the direct interface
that the retailer has with the consumer. Unilever, for example, was until
relatively recently mostly not recognized by the general public as a
brand – rather, consumers recognized its individual products, such as
Lipton tea, Dove soap and so on. The Unilever brand was 'one step
removed' from the consumer. But in recent years, the company has
taken expensive steps to make its logo more friendly and visible in order
to advertise its corporate name more prominently on its products.
While this is likely to increase the company's exposure to consumers
and campaigners, it will also allow Unilever to capitalize on the opportunities this gives to differentiate its brands in today's competitive
environment, and thus gain more of the coveted retail shelf space that
all food companies seek. If sustainability can enhance the brand and its
ability to deliver value; it therefore presents an additional opportunity
for competitive advantage:

The aim is to expand product concepts beyond technical or physical perfor-
mance, thus leading to product differentiation. Sustainability concepts con-
tribute to that. (BCS05 – Senior business manager, Communications)

F&B companies devote enormous budgets to marketing and advertising.
Coming into this millennium, the world food industry was estimated
to be spending a total of US$40 billion on advertising annually (IACFO,
2003). At the time of writing, Nestlé alone was spending more than
US$2 billion annually on advertising, making Nestle the industry's num-
ber 1 advertiser,[3] with Coca-Cola, McDonald's and Mars not far behind.
At a time when the F&B industry is much criticized for irresponsible
marketing, sustainability and the brand trust it can inherently promote

can contribute to alleviating this type of heavy investment with more positive offshoots. As a small but, for once, quantified example, Marks & Spencer, a retailer in the UK, calculated that it gained the equivalent of £1.7 million in advertising through widespread coverage of its 1997 decision to be the first retailer to stock only free-range eggs. As companies move to expand across the world, the asset and cost base of F&B companies are increasingly focusing on intangibles and capital efficiency. Studies by the Forum for the Future (2003a and b) concluded that intangible assets can present, in an increasingly competitive and weightless economy, invaluable 'unique and hard to replicate, capabilities, competencies and quasi assets', allowing companies to innovate and extract themselves from the 'competition rat race'. Goldman Sachs estimate that the level of intangibles as a proportion of gross cash invested in the F&B industry (as much as 40 per cent[4]) is a reflection of investment in advertising and brand promotion (Goldman Sachs, 2007a). Small wonder then that accounting firms such as PriceWaterhouseCoopers are getting into the foray and offering services such as 'Reputation assurance' (2003a).

The bottom line is that any BCS will have a major acceptance and take-up rate within organizations if it can be demonstrated that sustainability increases brand equity. Although the fact remains that companies largely do not quantify these benefits or have so far botched the job, there is a case for taking a serious approach to evaluating sustainability's contribution to retaining brand value. Very few serious attempts to look at the hard numbers of sustainability's contribution to reputation and brand benefits exist; certainly not within the F&B industry.

Goldman Sachs (2007a) has found the F&B industry relatively closed in terms of providing access to information about their CSM efforts. Reticence to be transparent is not specific to the F&B industry; given the extensive legal risks in the USA, for example, companies hesitate to publicize their actions. Nevertheless, some US high profile FMCG companies, such as Nike, have recently decided that, from the standpoint of building a reputation, it is well worth the risk – and this company has gone so far as publishing a list of suppliers on its website.[5]

It is difficult for the industry to ignore the fact that literally billions of dollars of shareholder value is indirectly jeopardized as the result of sustainability issues affecting the drivers of corporate performance. Seen with a shareholder value perspective, the BCS in the F&B industry becomes more convincing. While it is very difficult for a company to assess in advance when an attack on its reputation will cost sales and whether this will be permanent or temporary, there is still considerable brand risk. Coca-Cola's reputation suffered during its dioxin dilemmas in Belgium in 1999, apart from the substantial financial costs. To compound matters, its competitor Virgin Cola doubled its market share in Belgium in June 1999. During the Perrier benzene scandal in the US in February 1990, there were also a few dramatic financial impacts (market share in the USA fell from 44.8 per cent to 20.7 per cent and product recall cost US$ 30 million), but Evian replaced Perrier as the top-selling bottled water in the USA by the end of 1990 (Tsang, 2000). The incident also led directly to the takeover of Perrier by Nestlé. As yet the brand has not retained the glory that it had previous to these scandals (Tomlinson, 2004).

But messages can be mixed; a Cefic cross industry public opinion survey carried out in 2004 revealed that the overall image of the food industry was intact in spite of considerable food scandals previous to the survey, with 76 per cent of the public indicating a positive rating for the industry, as opposed to 72 per cent in 2002. Industry resilience may be contributing to a certain amount of complacency about reputation risk in the sector. Although leading companies include loss of reputation and the resulting licence to operate as an important business risk, overall our interview research confirmed that managers believe that not enough attention is paid to analyzing this risk, particularly aspects pertaining to sustainability. In a 2006 study, Aon singled out potential loss of reputation in the F&B sector as one of a host of emerging risks and pointed to the rapid change of the industry's risk profile while stating that management of this risk is not changing quickly enough. Another Aon report (2005) identified a growing gap between the risks that are most likely to damage a food company's viability and the risk management measures that companies actually take to protect themselves. Aon calls for F&B companies to review critically the way in which they monitor and analyze risk, and to ensure that risks are fully understood at the highest management level. We will come back to this point when we look at CSM in the F&B industry (Chapter 6) so as to understand the practical constraints that explain apparent gaps.

3.2 Attracting and retaining talent

In the 1950s and 1960s, employees felt secure in their jobs and a 'job for life' perspective prevailed in many sectors, encouraging a sense of loyalty and commitment to employing organizations. A 'social contract' determined the nature of the relationship between the employer and the employee. Then, in the 1970s and 1980s came an unprecedented era of redundancy programmes, mergers and acquisitions and restructurings. This produced a situation whereby, since job security was no longer assured and hard work and loyalty not necessarily rewarded by a secure job and promotion opportunities, the 'new' employer/ employee relationship became more fickle and short-term. With this new philosophy came the resulting risks for companies of employees not investing time and effort in organization-specific knowledge acquisition.

Given the prospect of the baby boomers in the developed world now reaching retirement, companies have begun to find it more difficult to retain employees, specifically those that are trained and highly skilled. Long-term trends indicate increased competitiveness for companies in the war for talent. Demographics in Europe, for example, indicate that the population segment that will supply companies with future leaders will further decline. Companies will have to compete intensely for a limited number of qualified managers over the coming decades, and it will take a substantial and long-lasting slump in the economy for this pressure to ease (Michaels *et al.*, 2001).

European employers thus face new and significant challenges; those of maintaining loyalty and commitment amongst their most highly qualified employees, attracting and retaining ever more talent, and creating a working environment within which employees will self-actualize. As the leading consultancy firm, McKinsey points out, companies have still not prepared themselves for the challenge of attracting and retaining capable people despite their indication that this was a critical need even a decade ago (McKinsey, 2008).

But how important is the view of the employee about her employer? While Nike's sales may not have overly suffered after its reputation was targeted by anti-sweatshop activities, employee morale certainly did, and the company regarded this as one of its primary risks. Moreover, Chapter 4 discussed the fact that consumers do not necessarily act on their stated values. But managers told us that employees often do – not only by how they behave but also in what they say to outsiders. And companies should not take this lightly; according to a MORI poll, three quarters of the British public say they would believe an employee's word about a company's social and environmental record over that of a corporate brochure or advertisement (Lewis, 2003a).

The Future Foundation and the Work Foundation carried out a study in 2004 to test whether CSR had an impact on the employer brand as an employer. The main findings, after over 1,000 interviews, were that approximately 20 per cent of employees found employers with a good CSR image more attractive. Also, employers that matched the organization's values with those of its employees increased retention. A strong positive correlation was found between companies seen to take their responsibility toward society seriously and those seen as a good employer.

The desire of employees to match business practices with their personal values is seen by managers as a strong potential driver for sustainability action. As managers we interviewed pointed out:

Employees have an underlying desire to be good citizens, to work with an internal sense of satisfaction and pride and will accept and protect core values that relate to this desire. (BCS04 – Senior regional business unit manager, Marketing and sales)

Employees do not leave their principles at the reception area of their workplace on the way to their offices; they are motivated by corporate values if they correspond with their own. (BCS16 – Senior business manager, Strategy)

Starbucks employee turnover is less than a third of the average for the retail food industry; 60 per cent as opposed to 220 per cent (Argenti, 2004, p. 98). The company attributes this performance to its socially responsible practices, which include a full benefits package for even part-time employees. According to Starbucks, this provides economic efficiencies that balance higher costs with the lower costs of staff recruitment and training.

Reichheld (1996) postulated that a far-reaching loyalty effect that forges a link between employee motivation, customer retention and more rapid growth than competitors can be created with employees. Goldman Sachs, in 2007, found this to be truly the case for F&B companies, where maximizing the productivity of their global workforce is a key to industry success (2007) and that motivated workforces clearly generated higher cash flow in the F&B sector.

Managers we spoke to recognized that one of the most important tasks for a successful global company is the development and deployment of people. The F&B companies we researched are leading companies that have begun to realize that, in a world that is increasingly knowledge-based and skill and service oriented, it is crucial for employees to be motivated and committed to the organization's objectives. If not, companies can be subject to competitive disadvantage. From our interviews, it was evident that senior managers in leading companies realized that sustainability objectives can gain considerable buy-in from employees:

> *Having your house in order is important. Employees have to have the feeling that they have joined the best company. Motivating employees is high up on our agenda.* (BCS35 – Top management, Supply Chain)

Several F&B managers pointed out during interviews that, although in the past staff turnover had been relatively low, the F&B industry in OECD companies is currently not perceived as one of the lucrative or attractive options for new graduates. As an alternative to offering higher salaries in a tight margin situation, such as that of the F&B industry, one way of competing in a tough competitive environment is to provide a work environment that enables greater levels of personal fulfilment in employees' lives.

Also, the move of companies in the F&B sector to functional foods,[6] and the resulting higher complexity in food ingredients, implies that key positions in the industry will have different demands in the future. Awareness of this is high in the industry, and several managers pointed to this shortage of talent:

> *In the future, food ingredients will be more scientific knowledge based than before. There is a need for more scientific-oriented people of which there is a shortage. Fewer graduates are qualifying as scientists than before.* (BCS10 – Senior business manager, Business development)

> *To get innovation, you need empowered, motivated people working under good conditions. People have strong views of how they want to work within the world.* (BCS30 – Senior regional business unit manager, Purchasing)

Diageo has even gone so far as to quantify the value of the relationship between employee engagement and performance and found a positive correlation (Diageo, 2003).

We conclude that there is a weight of empirical evidence – including that emerging from this study indicating that attracting and retaining talent in a competitive business environment will increasingly be very much stronger in the economic interest of any F&B company and that sustainability can be part of this. However, we take note of comments from our interviewees also indicating that economic circumstance can, albeit temporarily, overthrow this as a driver:

> *I am not sure whether this is a 'real' driver. When jobs are abundant in the market place, sustainability is a motivating factor When there is a downturn, I'm not so sure.* (BCS47a – Business manager, Supply chain)

3.3   Innovation and revenue increase

When asked which factors most promote sustainable business practices, only 9 per cent of sustainability officers surveyed saw process and product innovation as one that was most relevant. It did not even feature in interviews as a factor that would promote the business case. Some felt that the inherently conservative nature of the F&B industry was a factor influencing how managers perceived the relationship between process and product innovation and sustainable development:

> *The food industry is one of the most conservative industries in the world.* (BCS39 – Top management)

> *There is a 'herd' instinct in the food industry – trade associations dictate. The food and drink sector has been slower to come to the table on the issues. This is due to conservatism in the industry.* (BCS02 – Senior business manager, Communications)

Several senior managers were concerned about the sustainability impacts of this perceived industry inertia:

> *There is too little innovation within the food industry. While we cannot have exceptional growth rates, a business model of sustainability has to be about the capacity to innovate in order to balance demand with supply so as to continuously improve profit and growth.* (BCS27 – Senior business manager, Supply chain)

But as Placet *et al.* point out, mature industries tend to have an overall characteristic of inertia, resistance to change and scepticism when it comes to adjusting business models, making it difficult to instigate change (Placet, *et al.*, 2005, p. 35, Ettenberg, 2003). External stakeholders were also highly critical of what they perceived as a lack of creativity inherent to the F&B industry:

> *An 'industrial' type mindset is dominant in the industry; that is, the belief that you can find a quick fix, a technological solution, approach issues like you would a machine ... readjust the engine, and restart. This is a backward looking approach...* (Food industry expert and author)

> *Most managers do not think creatively about perception at the consumer end. Managers in many companies still have an old-fashioned view of the world.* (Senior business manager, Agribusiness company)

The press has also been critical of the industry from this point of view (*The Economist*, 2005c).

We address the question of overcoming internal mindset difficulties more holistically in the second part of this book. However, we observed that, excepting the (albeit belated) rebound effects of the obesity issue, few innovative products and practices built around sustainability concepts can be observed in the sector, even in the most progressive companies. Senior business managers commented that sustainability was simply not yet far enough up in the corporate agenda to warrant inclusion in important processes affecting innovation:

> *Sustainability now has an enhanced profile within our company. It's conceptually clear. But its translation into activity is not clear. For instance, it may not feature at a high enough level in the innovation process. A greater level of trade-off will be necessary in future but building mechanisms for this is not systematic.* (BCS52 – Top management, Finance)

> *We don't include sustainability criteria in our innovation award system; it's not fundamental enough to the business to make a difference.* (BCS45 – Senior business manager, Corporate economist)

Whether the innovation agenda should be a matter of orienting consumer preferences, or simply responding to them seemed to be subject to differing opinions amongst managers:

> *Pleasing the consumer is a main value driver for our company. We are driving value in our food strategy around consumer 'hot spots'. Consumers*

buy brands because they deliver 'what I want'. (BCS48 – Senior business manager, Strategy and business development)

Many great ideas had nothing to do with cost-benefit analysis. Giving consumers only what they want all the time does not create long-term business. For example, did people ever ask for walkmans or mobile phones? (BCS46 – Senior business manager, Sales and marketing)

Managers confirmed that it is even a considerable struggle for more mainstream products to make it through the tough competitive environment that exists in the industry, with every product line, potential new product or marketing initiative under intense scrutiny and pressure to prove how they can be profitable. However, could it be that by focusing too much on the 'responsibility' aspects of sustainability, managers ignore the 'opportunity' aspects of social and environmental performance that drive, for example, entrepreneurialism, innovation and even access to new markets in the developing world?:

More research is needed in process innovation and sustainable agriculture – currently, things are way behind what is needed. Breakthrough technologies are necessary. (BCS47a – Business manager, Supply chain)

Sustainability should be a parameter in innovative management processes, and added to the checklist of our innovation process: This would make it more explicit. (BCS48 – Senior business manager, Strategy and business development)

Western European companies cannot compete on price. New ideas are needed – blockbuster ideas and creative innovation. Sustainability is an implicit part of this. (BCS30 – Senior regional business unit manager, Purchasing)

More food for thought. Our Chapter 3 is testimony to the fact that many industrial-style, process-oriented innovations in the F&B industry in the last several decades also backfired to some extent in terms of crises of consumer confidence, both in the areas of food safety and nutrition. Some first movers are showing themselves to be more progressive:

We are changing the innovation culture at our company and making it much longer-term. We have moved our planning cycle from one year to two years, for example. We are charging R&D/innovation teams to own an innovation pipeline. The business unit presidents are in charge of making sure this works. Other progressive companies are, I think, doing similar things. (BCS20 – Senior business manager, Innovation)

In the following sections, we will attempt to demonstrate that product and process innovations, when seen through the sustainability lens and filtered through a more strategic internalization of key sustainability issues, can bring competitive advantage benefits through increased sales, but that this fact has been mostly either unrecognized or undervalued in the industry.

3.3.1   Obesity and innovation

Bringing the obesity issue into a business perspective, there are unparalleled opportunities for innovation that have belatedly been recognized by only a handful of manufacturing and food service companies. Some managers viewed the obesity issue as one that could 'make or break' the industry, and that the industry needed to innovate to fill demand for products and services, channel that demand toward healthier choices, set principles for marketing and advertising to encourage healthy lifestyle choices and even partner with other sectors to create an environment that supports those choices:

The industry has been in denial; it has been hoping to grow volumes, but this is not the way to go. People need and want new products, less fat, less sugar, not health options. Our managers need to realize that consumers want different products. (BCS08 – Senior business manager, Communications)

Some leading companies have finally started to think about obesity strategically and are starting to capitalize on the fact that the industry is set up to 'listen to consumers'. While 'listening' in the past has meant focusing on consumer buying trends and adjusting to them while contemporaneously stimulating the demand side of the market. However, the explosion of the obesity issue showed that market orientation could go much further in the areas of customer satisfaction and confidence.

How the food industry is reacting to the global obesity crisis is being carefully monitored by the press, which witnessed a rush of frantic efforts in the F&B industry around 2002 to capitalize on the huge popularity of low-carbohydrate diets (Atkins, 1992), for example. It must be said that F&B companies were remarkably slow to act on the obesity issue, given its capacity to affect companies' economic *raison d'être*. The drop in share price experienced by Kraft before and after the 'low-carb craze'[7] in the United States could at least partly be attributed to short-term thinking about obesity and health issues, as the company began to feel the economic effects of a massive public swing away from its products. (Morgan Stanley Equity Research, 2003a). The company belatedly tried to turn the issue into a business opportunity by launching an obesity initiative to give advice on food-marketing practices, labelling and portion sizes (*The Economist*, 2003a). However, this move was possibly 'closing the stable door after the horse had bolted', since despite all efforts, the company later encountered severely reduced profits leading to substantial reduction of its workforce. Another example: in 2005, PepsiCo overtook Coca-Cola in market capitalization for the first time ever. PepsiCo had diversified away from reliance on sweetened colas towards health drinks while the Coca-Cola Company still relied on sweet soft drinks for 80 per cent of its revenues; the company has since diversified more (*The Economist*, 2005d). However, Goldman Sachs carried out a study in 2007 that showed that in spite of increased focus on health and nutrition owing to rising obesity rates, there was no discernible trend in the proportion of health innovations across the industry from 2002 to 2005, with a particularly poor record in the beverage industry.

Surely the real opportunity for food makers, rather than a quick fix, is to respond with quality products using a high level of research and development technology while giving the consumer accurate information at the same time. Consumer needs in developed markets are in any case fragmenting, introducing new complexity into the business environment. Investment analysts are starting to encourage companies to adjust their portfolios and develop new product strategies (Morgan Stanley, 2003b; Goldman Sachs, 2007a). The type of innovation required implies a much longer-term investment, but it would have the potential to change the way people eat and drink into the future, and make a real societal difference at the same time.

One manager pointed out that obesity was 'not a sustainability issue, but a business issue'. We found the dichotomy he made interesting since it is difficult to see how economically relevant sustainability issues are not also business issues. It seemed that what he meant was that from being a dormant issue on many companies' agendas, obesity had attained visible and tangible business relevance. However, this does not mean that as a sustainability issue 'waiting in the wings' at it were, it did not have that inherent relevance to begin with. It seems that some companies will only regard an issue as economically relevant if they have 'hit the wall' with it:

> *If risk is high for the business, the business will wake up and deal with it. There is no pressure to do anything yet for many sustainability issues. If an issue hits the business, managers do not look at it as a 'sustainability' issue, but as a business risk. My view is; sustainability can work as 'anything to anybody'.* (BCS23 – Senior business manager, Communications)

The fact that the obesity issue rebounded on companies (in terms of increased calls for legislation and labelling, as well as litigation challenges) was entirely predictable, given the increased governmental and multilateral spending on obesity as a health issue, increased public exposure of the problem by the media, and the early litigation incidents. We identified much regret about this 'missing the boat' in the industry and one of our interviewees attributed this to the daunting nature of the task of tackling this issue:

> *We tend to think of sustainability as long-term, but now obesity is short-term. We were late in reacting and we should have reacted earlier. We should have realized that there are social trends and we are all part of the problem. We got stuck in a defensive mode of 'It's unfair – why attack us?' One of the reasons it was not tackled earlier is that the issue is 'bigger than' the industry.* (BCS08 – Senior business manager, Communications)

Views from managers and experts were that if companies had a closer ear to the ground, the obesity issue could have been turned into opportunities for competitive advantage considerably earlier. Instead, companies were caught off guard and were forced to adopt a defensive position:

> *Companies approach it from the point of view 'it is better to defend what we have than to change'. Official stances from the Food and Drink Federation are: 'We are doing everything we can!' The tension does not go*

away with these statements. The industry is still in denial and defence. The attitude is 'Those silly consumers!' (BCSBM1 – Food industry expert)

Some research in 1999 showed that in the UK, management systems at F&B companies in general were, on average, less well-developed than other industries and that, while the industry in that country was strong in the areas of resource and process management, it had weaknesses in areas related to policy and strategy, customer satisfaction, people satisfaction and impact on society (Mann *et al.*, 1999). This could have been be viewed as surprising even then since everyday operations of F&B companies should theoretically provide them with deep insights on consumer trends. Managers we interviewed seemed proud of their acquired knowledge of the consumer. They commented:

The industry is driven by consumer trends. It is all about health and/or well being and people wanting to live well and longer. These are industry trends. Scanning intelligence around the globe ensures that we stay close to understanding consumers. (BCS52 – Top management, Finance)

We work on understanding consumer trends; this means also understanding social trends – and we think about how to position ourselves in relation to these trends. (BCS14 – Senior business manager, Finance)

However, a consumer organization representative that we interviewed felt that F&B companies do not really listen to the true voice of the consumer:

Companies base themselves too much on 'buying' criteria, and then the trends escape them. (BCSBM19 – European consumer organization)

Comments from managers indicated that there may be some fundamental problems with the research approach within their organizations not allowing information flows about social trends to interfere with statistical market research based on consumption trends:

Marketers observed that consumers said they wanted healthier food (no salt, no sugar and so on), but noted that they were not following these values up with purchasing behaviour. Until intention translates into consumer behaviour, the marketers will not move. With the obesity issue, the press ensured that consumers got increasingly aware to a great extent, and they then started to act. (BCS20 – Senior business manager, Innovation)

Managers described another problem; the comparatively small budget and attention allocated to R&D in the F&B industry, as compared to other industries:

R&D in the food industry is probably only 1 per cent of sales. In contrast, R&D can involve huge investment in other industries. (BCS20 – Senior business manager, Innovation)

R&D is not so important in the food-processing industry. Agriculture is a less important sector of the organization. For the food products sold, there are no special approaches per se. Risk assessment is measured in terms of public acceptance of the product. (BCS49 – Senior business manager, Manufacturing and supply chain)

It is thought-provoking that the latter comment was made by a senior manager just prior to the obesity issue hitting the radar screens of the industry.

However, it is not easy to remedy the problem. F&B companies are challenged to judge when social trends have reached critical mass such that it makes sense to reposition their brands. Repositioning is highly cost intensive and to do so around short-term trends may end up alienating more profitable consumer bases in the meantime. After all, the 'low carb' trend came to an end and some of the products introduced to meet public demand started to be left on the shelves..... Consumers can be fickle.

The wake-up call on obesity has at least caused leaders in the industry to think differently about sustainability's contribution to innovation from a strategic point of view. Nestlé for example, has reformulated its corporate strategy around wellness concepts and Unilever is pursuing a 'naturalness' route in its own strategy. Sustainability and CSM is more at the centre of the core business strategy in both companies as a result.

3.3.2 Poverty and innovation

In Chapter 2, we identified that future markets for F&B companies will be from an emerging consumer base in the developing world. These are consumers with aspirations to a better quality of life, but with currently much less purchasing power than consumers in developed countries. Key current markets; EU, USA and Japan have stagnant or falling populations and low economic growth, while future high economic and population growth is expected in currently low-income groups in emerging economies. Some managers we spoke to felt that it was a 'no-brainer' that this mass of people was likely to become economically more important in the future:

> *Africa and Asia are main markets and it is there that there will be massive increases in population. The business potential is outside of OECD countries.* (BCS27 – Senior manager, Supply chain)

Others felt that global companies had a responsibility to communities in developing countries:

> *Value drivers in the future will react to pressure from third world countries to give back to the community. People are becoming increasingly aware of disparities and are exercising public pressure on companies to toe the line.* (BCS12 – Senior sustainability officer)

Indeed, some 4 billion people are living at what Prahalad and Hart (2002) referred to as the 'bottom of the pyramid' (BOP); a huge sector of world population that earns less than $1,500 per year. This substantial chunk of the world's population is trapped in a vicious cycle of poverty, lack of education and avoidable deaths that developing world governments have failed to address adequately. Furthermore, international aid has failed woefully to provide models of sustained development and growth in the affected countries (Prahalad, 2005). On the other hand, business and economic development has been found to be an effective weapon in fighting world poverty by bringing to bear positive externalities; job creation and development of skills, creation of new sources of supply, stimulation of SME growth, creation of new consumers, and, simply, access to a huge resource base of business DNA. And as WBCSD rightly points out, 'Business cannot succeed in societies that fail' (Timberlake, 2006).

According to Prahalad, the BOP can present a business opportunity for companies (Prahalad, 2004; Engardio, 2006). Business gurus may at first appear to suggest that they may be right:

> *The consumer landscape will change and expand significantly. (....) By 2016, annual consumer spending power in emerging economies will*

increase from $4,000bn to more than $9,000bn – nearly the current level in Western Europe. (Davis, 2006, p. 12)

However, if the BOP is such an opportunity, we might well ask why all companies are not on the bandwagon, to win the consumers of tomorrow? Prahalad's answer is that to exploit these opportunities right now requires new and creative ways of thinking and acting in companies (Prahalad and Hammond, 2002). However, arguments in this chapter have so far demonstrated that the F&B industry is not set up for optimum creativity, risk-taking and innovation. Traditional business models do not provide guidance on how to operate in poor markets where the margins are slim even if unit sales are high.

The growth strategies of even the leading F&B companies are only just beginning to focus on rethinking ways of creating, manufacturing, distributing and marketing new products in emerging economies – their markets of the future. Only a sub-group of companies amongst those that we included in the study was seriously looking at revising business models for developing country environments, creating new ones based on volume (greater levels of growth) and smaller margins. Table 5.1 illustrates the different areas of focus of these companies.

P&G refer to this process as 'linking opportunity with responsibility'. Its managers point out that the real business case is not in seeking

Table 5.1 Areas of focus for companies seeking new business models

Business area	Activities
Manufacturing	• Scrutinize costs by extracting any non-value-adding activity • Outsource production (thus enhancing local economies, entrepreneurship and creating jobs) • Develop partnerships with local manufacturers, investing time resources and training to help raise quality standards
Pricing and packaging	• Draw on experience in similar environments elsewhere in the world • Resize packets to sachet size to place within the price reach of poorest families
Marketing	• Find local solutions for distribution outreach • Where rural reach is difficult, organize different promotional methods (such as road shows, demonstrations, alignment with partners).[8]

competitive advantage in green marketing or in the diminishing returns of eco-efficiency where, in any case, the focus was on eliminating what never actually had value for consumers to begin with (Carpenter and White, 2004). Companies should rather think about the opportunities within the concept of sustainable development, and how to make sustainable development part of the goods and services they deliver. In this way, companies can contribute to sustainable development goals while at the same time harvesting either first-mover access to extensive market opportunities, or accessing the hearts and minds of local people to establish permanent long-term competitive advantage:

> *For our company, 'the first to get there' is a major driver for the business case for sustainability also.* (BCS47a – Business manager, Supply chain)

> *If a company comes up with first mover advantage, it distinguishes itself from the rest and there is an economic benefit to this.* (Senior regional business unit manager, Marketing and sales)

Both Unilever and P&G have discovered through their experiences with the BOP that working with partners can bring the missing links required in corporate learning to make their products successful in such markets.[9] They discovered several advantages of working with business and non-business local partners:

- Establishing of a leadership position in the industry, thus improving reputation and brand value while acting as a catalyst for rural wealth creation
- Anchoring a brand at a lower cost, entering the 'hearts and minds' of local people
- Building trust between the company and key stakeholders
- Creating new competencies within the company for
  (a) more effective stakeholder management; and
  (b) marketing products differently by using a collaborative strategy, or adopting a poor-centric' approach
- Increasing corporate knowledge of markets
- Facilitating early identification of attitudinal shifts in consumers
- Improving access to markets or rural reach

Notwithstanding these advantages, there are still considerable challenges in establishing an economically efficient product development and distribution model at the BOP. But to be innovative is always a challenge. There are only a handful of companies in the industry capable of discerning features that matter to consumers in order to produce leaps in value. A manager commented:

> *(Company X) is good at innovation. Their whole principle of R&D is around 'If I accidentally find something, can I link it to my superior knowledge of consumer demand?' They are good at what to do with perception.* (BCSBM3 – Senior Business manager, Strategy, Agribusiness company)

The focus of such companies is not on the competition, but on the consumer. They work outside of dominant business logic of retaining and increasing already existing customer bases, or working with assets and capabilities that already exist. They build primarily on the products that people need and value. They think 'out of the box':

> *If I had a key open question, it would be; how do we translate an in-depth understanding of both consumers and downstream consumer demand (existing or latent) into value-adding business opportunities for our company? This is the central question for the company. And sustainability is part of that paradigm.* (BCSBM3 – Senior Business manager, Strategy)

Working on translating knowledge into opportunities can be a 'win-win' situation; consumers get access to better prices or quality and increased choice, while the company creates new markets for products and services. However, companies need to find the new business models that will work for their specific circumstances, review their entire value chain to limit cost and develop strategies to increase volumes. It is not an easy ride. In a highly competitive business context, only a handful of companies are moving slowly and with great caution into the BOP.

4 Synthesis

Our analysis of value drivers for the F&B industry revealed several constructs that impact value drivers economically relevant to the sector. The message from experienced managers is that by interpreting shareholder value too narrowly, companies risk undervaluing or ignoring the value driving potential of sustainability. The obesity issue has demonstrated the danger of focusing exclusively on short-term business performance and neglecting the longer-term opportunities that attention to sustainability issues might generate. Excessive focus on the short-term could mean that companies are missing growth prospects, and it could also be argued that this goes way beyond the sustainability agenda. However, given perceived shareholder pressure for short-term earnings, companies hesitate to make investments focused on sustainability that are not clearly linked to near-term cash flow. To illustrate, we add the value driver dimension to the figure already provided in Chapter 4 to show the dynamics between stakeholder pressure and corporate response. We remind the reader that the broken lined boxes represent the weaker responses; see Figure 5.7. Note that in the diagram the radical innovation for new business products and processes is weak, while more incremental innovation based on eco-efficiencies and step-by-step improvements on existing business models are the stronger industry response. Although there is still a clear emphasis on incremental innovation in the F&B industry, we suggest that CSM's contributions to value drivers are important for the F&B industry and constitute the essence of its BCS, while also encompassing potential for more radical innovation. Because of the food industry's front line profile, CSM's contribution (in terms of reputation enhancement and brand value) to business value drivers is probably stronger than for the other industries examined in the BCS project.

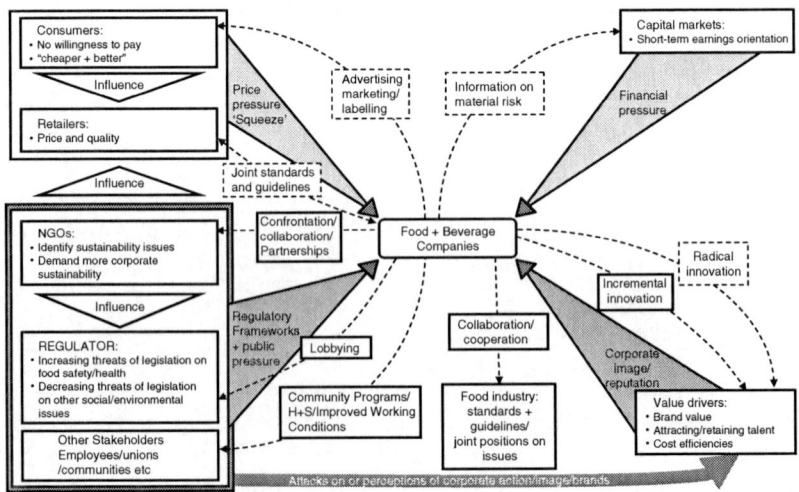

Figure 5.7   Industry value driver response

Given its exposure, it is important that the industry moves from a defensive, and thus more vulnerable, position to a proactive and involved position as a legitimate member of the society in which it operates. The industry makes substantial positive contributions to society but, given where its future markets are likely to be, even in the mid-term, it can be in its business interest to do better. Pioneering companies are already experimenting with radical innovation, but, risk averse, even they adopt a 'softly-softly' approach, mainly due to the cut-throat business environment in which they find themselves. To remain competitive, these companies have to manage an already existing, strong strategic position while moving very slowly into a new one.

Leading global players believe that the positive impacts of taking into account these contributions will be increasingly recognized and rewarded through consumer trust in their brands, benefits to reputation and loyalty of top quality employees. However, smaller scale F&B companies evidently do not gain as much from those dynamics in the same way, leaving a much weaker BCS for a large part of the sector.

By defining CSM's contribution to corporate value drivers, we can better capture and describe the importance of sustainability issues for the formulation of corporate strategy. This, in turn drives the importance of being aware in advance of potential issues, tracking these issues, mapping long-term options and responses to the issues while identifying those that can affect core business drivers such as regulation, consumption trends and so on. In general, anchoring this process to strategic development within companies will ensure that companies do not treat sustainability tangentially and remain vulnerable to major shifts in what is, ultimately, a socially driven business environment. Some companies are making these links:

Links have not been made on the triple bottom line by the food industry. Issues of supply chain, sourcing, GMOs, pesticides and new food issues including ethics and advertising are now coming together in our company. There is an internal framework in place to enable change with the objective of long-term sustainable growth in shareholder value. (BCS02 – Senior business manager, Communications)

While it may be true that society punishes sustainability laggards rather than rewards sustainability leaders, global companies are nevertheless increasingly simply expected to take on these leadership roles. Even for these companies, the business case for sustainability is not just there for the taking: it has to be built. This implies rethinking old business models and being a pioneer ready to innovate more radically than incrementally. While innovation must reap bottom line benefits, it should in the future be more value-oriented:

> *The most essential factor for driving the business case for sustainability through the food industry will be if bottom line benefits of an innovation can be found; that is, if you are saving natural resources and money at the same time. It is important to find win–win situations where the aim is to make money, or at least not lose money, and at the same time contribute to sustainable development.* (BCS45 – Senior business manager, Corporate economist)

However, no matter what the strategy or how innovative the business model, another key factor for success with a sustainability strategy is undoubtedly organizational alignment. And we have dedicated the second part of our book to this formidable challenge.

Notes

1 Rappaport's book was revised and updated in 1998.
2 See www.aon.com
3 See www.mind-advertising.com/ch/nestle_ch.htm
4 This compares with 20 per cent intangibles for consumer cyclicals, 17 per cent for industrials, and less than 10 per cent for fixed asset intensive sectors such as energy and utilities.
5 Nike set new standards in transparency in April 2005 by publishing a list of their suppliers on its website, a move considered daring by other companies.
6 Functional foods, or nutraceuticals as they are often termed, are foods or food components (whole, fortified or enriched with functional food components) that are scientifically recognized as having physiological benefits beyond those of basic nutrition.
7 The Atkins diet, and other low carbohydrate diets took America by storm during 2002 with consumers switching massively to new ways of eating.
8 A review of Unilever's approach, 'Global Challenges Local Actions', can be read online or downloaded at www.unilever.com/environmentsociety.
9 For examples, see Steger & Ionescu-Somers, 2001; Steger *et al.*, 2002.

Part II
Rolling Out the Business Logic

6
Corporate Sustainability Management

1 Introduction

Conceptually, managers must build the most robust business case possible for sustainability, but the use to which the business logic is put in devising strategy around sustainability and integrating that strategy into overall business strategy brings its own challenges. Successful roll out of sustainability concepts within organizations means integration of sustainability into the mainstream of strategic planning and decision-making processes within the company:

> *Aligning an organization behind the business case for sustainability means aligning with the business purpose of the company.* (BCS40 – Senior sustainability officer)

Our aim in this section is to ascertain the extent to which the perceived presence, or lack, of a BCS in the F&B industry influences the dynamics of organizational change required for effective sustainability performance. Mainly because of the complexity that globalization brings, every company we looked at in the research admitted to having problems with alignment of even the best constructed sustainability strategies. In fact, we did not find managers to be generally enthusiastic about the ability of food companies to fully align their organizations to sustainability strategies:

> *There is a long way to go before we take sustainability fully into account in our operations.* (BCS12 – Senior sustainability officer).

In the following sections, we comprehensively cover all the stages of strategy conceptual design and implementation in order to illustrate and analyze the *status quo* of internal barriers and limits to the exploitation of the BCS in the sector. We provide some direction on the agenda for change that F&B companies could adopt in order to better implement their sustainability strategies and hence develop, communicate and fully exploit the BCS.

Galbraith (1995) argues that, increasingly, forces outside organizations shape their design; such as demanding customers, changing environments, proliferating product lines and increasing emphasis on speed. The parameters of the company have thus become much less clearly defined, bringing a certain increased complexity to the business environment. Research we have presented so far suggests that managers may find it somewhat challenging to match that complexity internally. This chapter will throw light on how organizations and their managers are coping with this challenge.

Galbraith (1977) also proposes that organizational design is based on achieving harmony between strategy, structure, people, rewards and processes. He uses a 'structure follows strategy' framework and emphasizes that all of these aspects must have inherent capacity for change and be aligned to assure success with corporate strategy roll out and for an organization to be effective. He suggests that strategic ideas must be converted into programmes for corporate success through organizational alignment. And so it is with sustainability strategies; their success or otherwise will depend on the extent to which they are integrated into organizations from strategy, through structure, values, incentives and finally through human resource management.

In this chapter, we first examine corporate cultures and then look at company goals and objectives determining the direction companies want to take. Next, we assess how the location of decision-making power (structure) within F&B companies influences the company's ability to deal with the complexities presented by sustainable development, moving to an overview of the information and decision processes cutting across structure. We assess the importance of key functions and internal structures influencing or affecting the success of sustainability initiatives. Then, we move to the processes and systems that F&B companies put in place to roll out the BCS within organizations, specifically looking at some of their most difficult challenges. We also assess the extent to which reward systems are aligning the goals of the employee with the goals of the organizations we included in the research, thus providing motivation for the completion of sustainability strategy applications. We finally examine some relevant additional factors such as the internal and external communications strategies.

2 Corporate culture, vision and the mindsets of managers

Corporate culture is the sum total of beliefs and values that affect behaviours of employees within an organization. According to managers, culture is probably the single organizational attribute that is most resistant to change. But once anchored, culture can outlive products, services, founders and leadership and all other physical attributes of organizations. To apply a strategy, the corporate culture acts as an important backdrop onto which the strategy is projected. Sustainability managers were convinced that obtaining the right corporate culture – one that is open and receptive to the complex concepts of sustainability – is also one of the greatest challenges for the alignment of an organization behind sustainability objectives. For a handful of companies within the F&B industry, their historical past gives them a helping hand. The idea that business has societal obligations was evident to leaders of some companies even as early as the late nineteenth century. A few such visionary companies were in the food manufacturing arena, presumably because of visibility and profound early social impact. Unilever and Cadbury Schweppes for example, are companies that have a long history of innovative leadership inspired with goals and a vision expressing concern and respect, not only for consumers but also for employees and communities. The early actions of these companies were motivated by both an intrinsic desire to 'do good' and 'enlightened self-interest', the latter being an alternative phrase for a 'business case'. Simple business logic applied; if workers had improved living and working conditions, they would be more productive and if society moved in the direction of better and more affordable nutrition, then this would be good for both F&B business and society; a win–win in every sense of the word.

Managerial discretion implies that management is free to impose objectives upon the firm that reflect their own values. In more modern times, there are examples within the F&B industry, of CEOs with a vision of sustainability that carried itself into the culture of organizations, such as Antoine Riboud of Danone who had a profound effect on corporate employment policies in France in the 1970s. Managers at Unilever, Cadbury Schweppes and Danone felt that their companies were in some ways predisposed towards sustainability concepts because the moral beliefs of their founders became established in the company culture at a very early stage:

> *We have a strong corporate culture of sustainability action. In 1906, our founders were already taking action on social issues. There are greater expectations of us than of other companies.* (BCS02 – Senior business manager, Communications)

External stakeholders were less convinced that these legacies had permeated the cultures of even prominent companies in the industry:

> *Many food companies have been around for many years – longer than the average Fortune 500 company, which is only 30 to 40 years! But surprisingly, instead of being attuned to their social realities, they are stuck in mass market attitudes and fixed perspectives.* (Food industry expert and author)

Schein describes a three-level organizational model (Schein, 1992). The first level includes the organizational attributes that can be seen felt and heard by the uninitiated observer; the facilities, furnishings, visible awards and recognition factors, dress code and human interactions within the company. The second level includes the declared culture, company slogans, mission statements and even the local and personal values widely expressed within the organization. The third, and deepest, level relates to the elements of culture that are unseen, and are not cognitively identifiable. These are not discussed openly within organizations and interviews and survey data do not necessarily draw out these attributes. Using the model, organizations may appear paradoxical; that is, they can profess very high standards on one level, but may have deeply entrenched opposing behaviour at the third and deepest level of culture. We need to bear this in mind during the remainder of this chapter as it throws light on some of the paradoxes we found in F&B companies.

Schein's theory gives us some insight as to why it may be difficult for staff, especially newcomers, to assimilate organizational culture or be protagonists in changing it. We have already mentioned (Chapter 5) the increasingly rapid turnaround in staff at companies in the modern era and the disappearance of a certain loyalty factor that existed in past times. To continue to exist in competitive environments, companies have to be flexible and open to change, and that includes their employees.

Our interviews indicated that the establishment and maintenance of a culture that is amenable to sustainability concepts is probably the biggest challenge for alignment of a sustainability strategy within F&B companies today:

> *Companies can be dysfunctional and this can be due to different cultures. It is better to try to understand how to optimize relationships.* (BCS30 – Senior regional business unit manager, Purchasing)

Global companies are increasingly more far reaching geographically; the business units of a European based F&B company can be found in places as far a field as Shanghai and New Delhi. Global corporate cultures encounter local cultures and, unless potential clashes are foreseen, the ambitious hope of global alignment is dashed or certainly weakened. To minimize risk, global F&B companies devote resources to ensuring that their diverse business units adapt to the company culture. In 2006, when we spoke to food supply chain managers, companies were expanding rapidly into China and India. In these countries, they had encountered differences in the way in which even human life was valued (thus affecting attitudes to safety), not to mention the environment.

Collins and Porras (2000) carried out research on what they called 'visionary' companies and revealed that 'maximizing shareholder wealth' or 'profit maximization' was not the only dominant driving force or primary objective for the companies they looked at. In fact, they identified that economic gain was only one of a number of objectives – and at that not even the most important one. There were other objectives, such as responsibility to customers and to the community at large that were given more importance internally. In fact, the companies they looked at all tended to have a core ideology that included core values and a sense of purpose beyond simply making money.

Davidson (2003) carried out interviews at 70 companies – including Diageo, Unilever and Tesco – to identify best practice in managing vision and values. He concludes the 'trick' of managing the complex brands of today that have multiple stakeholder constituencies is to 'develop a vision and a set of values to unite stakeholders, by aligning these with the brand proposition and then tailoring the message to each stakeholder'. When Arthur D. Little carried out a survey in 1998 of 481 environmental, health and safety and other business executives in North America and Europe to ascertain the business value of the sustainable development pathway to business growth and prosperity, an overwhelming 75 per cent of respondents pointed to their companies' vision and strategy as the area where most change was needed in order to implement a sustainable development approach. Second to this was innovation in technologies and processes and, third, alignment and motivation of staff (Arthur D. Little, 1998).

We found during our interviews that for the respondents that had worked on a company sustainability strategy, the common starting point was indeed the normative development of the company's vision and values. When sustainability officers were asked what approaches or initiatives are used in their companies to overcome barriers to sustainability, 22 per cent of answers pertained to corporate values, policies and standards, and a further 14 per cent related to management development, which we can also link to the concept of instilling values in the corporate culture (Figure 6.1).

However, it is also worth bearing in mind that there are often substantial gaps between values as stated in companies and actual applications in

Figure 6.1 Approaches used by food and beverage companies to overcome barriers to sustainability internally (sustainability officers)

the business. Enron, a company that had a coherently tuned and values laden mission statement, was a company that evidently did not 'live' its values. Therefore, a number of strategies or clear descriptions of how to achieve the vision have clearly to be put in place such that operations are aligned to corporate strategy. A supply chain officer told us that his experience had shown him that sustainability was an iterative, 'learning by doing' process. He complained that, too often, sustainable development initiatives come top down from corporate decision-makers rather than bottom up from operating companies. This greatly compromised ownership of the activity by business units which we noted is often not firmly in place. An open, consensus-building organizational culture lends itself to a much more robust roll out process.

There is a fairly uniform desire across countries in Europe to meet certain social and environmental standards but, when it comes to implementation, managers in the industry that we interviewed mostly acknowledged that northern European and Scandinavian countries are the strongest players. When we asked Scandinavian based companies why this might be, the answers related to the consensus building non-'top-down' management approaches common in Scandinavia that suit very well the complex needs of sustainability implementation and buy-in within companies. Interviewees felt that Northern European cultures lend themselves well to such consensus driven sustainability approaches, and that managers bring their values and their ability to make concessions 'into work' with them. Nordic managers saw their countries as leading the field in corporate sustainability:

> *Sustainability in Scandinavia is part of national mindsets – and plays a bigger role than in other parts of Europe. Social awareness has been fine-tuned in our cultures over a long time. We are way beyond compliance.* (BCS10 – Senior business manager, Business development)

> *In our company, there can be discussion and consensus-building. The CEO cannot shout top down, as happens in the US.* (BCS49 – Senior manager, Manufacturing and supply chain technology)

While senior managers felt that a global organization has to address all cultures and accept differences at the same time, they also realized that this constituted a substantial challenge in terms of roll out:

> *The business case for sustainability is very much related to countries, the corporate culture and where the office is based. That is what makes roll*

out a particularly challenging task. (BCS36 – Top management, Finance)

Managers perceived the way corporations apply sustainability as being a matter of stages of cultural and economic development. They strongly felt for example that issues are interpreted differently in developing countries than in the developed world:

With 170 countries involved, we got further in some areas than others. Some areas did not see that this was crucial to the business. (BCS17 – Senior business manager, Communications)

Notwithstanding this fact, managers insisted that if multinationals establish a principle in one country, it must be equally applicable in another and that global companies were an excellent conduit for 'raising the bar':

We never compromise on our corporate standards across the world. This is the best conduit for sustainability; global companies have had a massive impact on how countries have evolved and are evolving. (BCS26 – Senior regional business unit manager, Purchasing)

Managers had experienced the sharp end of the challenges of getting 'buy in', with sometimes sharply contrasting points of view within the same organization:

Getting everybody on board is a real challenge. I have been in tricky situations where two managers think entirely differently about the same issue. (BCS14 – Business manager, Finance)

There was a real culture clash. Managers were genuinely surprised that others in the organization thought so differently. (BCS47 – Business manager, Supply chain)

Managers expressed the acute need for the building of management awareness about sustainability issues and concepts in manager's minds before the business case can be exploited to the full:

Sustainability issues and their implications for the business need to be more clearly defined in the mindsets of the people working in companies. (BCS27 – Senior business manager, Supply chain)

The lack of prior understanding upsets the 'continuous feedback mechanisms' necessary for early identification of issues. (BCS36 – Senior business manager, Finance)

Assuring this prior understanding is, in itself, a significant challenge. Managers running businesses have a focus on the brands under their responsibility and are busy dealing with pressing initiatives related to product and market development:

Time and resources are 'pull' factors that create, if not active opposition to sustainability, then at least passivity and inertia in managers faced with what is often simply perceived as an extra management burden. (Senior regional business unit manager, Marketing and sales)

Even if sustainability is integrated in the strategy, the pull of short-term gains can be so strong that it is still difficult to overcome:

We have to keep reminding ourselves and taking out the red flag and saying: 'Be careful – this doesn't fully fit with long-term.' (BCS14 – Senior business manager, Finance)

There is often scepticism in managerial ranks about the added value of sustainability action, with fear of high costs and little or no return. A manager referred to this perspective as the 'What's in it for me?' mindset. Interestingly, middle managers are sceptical of what they referred to as 'trends' or 'fashions' picked up by their senior managers and unless sustainability is an integral part of the DNA of companies, there is resistance and behaviour does not change:

Changing behaviours is a challenge. It is easy to persuade top managers and workers. Middle management is the main problem. It is necessary to change values – create consistent values – and introduce a simple basis for how people do business. Then you can constantly remind your managers of those basic values. (Food industry expert)

We asked managers: 'If corporate environmental and social initiatives had little or no success in your organization, what are the main barriers?' Manager's mindset, organizational culture or simply lack of knowledge – all related paradigms, accounted for a total of 28 per cent of responses to this question from business managers. Interestingly, the proportions of responses for mindset and lack of knowledge were very

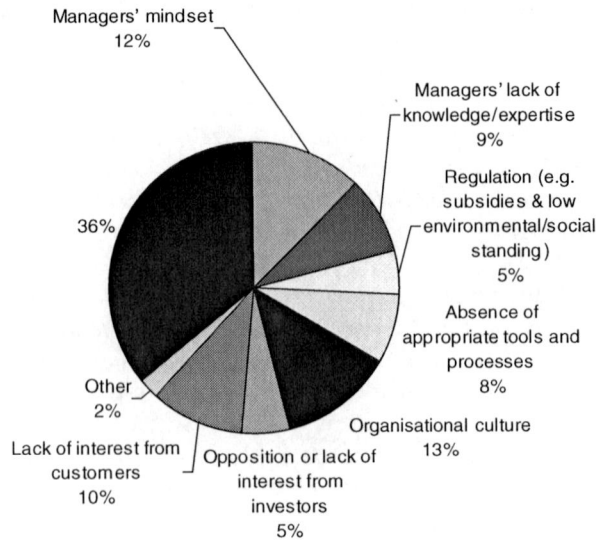

Figure 6.2 Barriers to success of sustainability initiatives – all sectors (business managers)

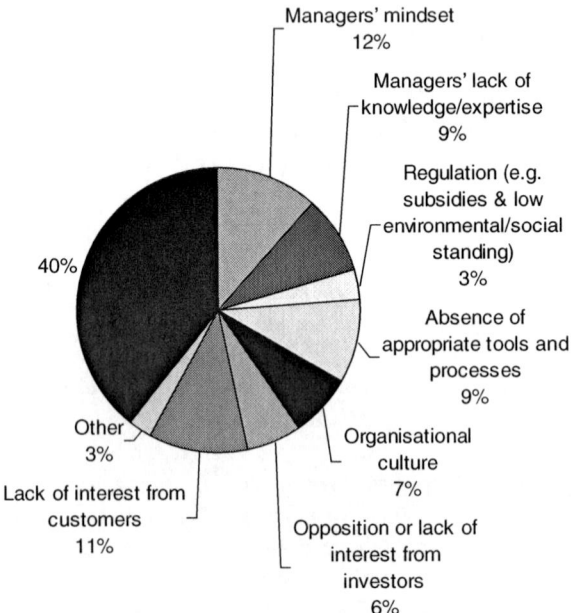

Figure 6.3 Barriers to success of sustainability initiatives – F&B sector (business managers)

similar when we averaged total responses for all sectors examined in our BCS study (see Figures 6.2 and 6.3). Thus, the F&B industry is not alone in this respect.

Again, the large number of non-responses indicated lack of knowledge and degree of uncertainty on the part of managers as to the reasons why sustainability initiatives are not always successful. It was clear in interviews that not many had given thought to this question.

The small sample of sustainability officers was asked a similar question and their view attributed a 60 per cent of responses to these same categories; mindset, organizational culture and lack of knowledge. This demonstrated their conviction as to where the problems lie. As our

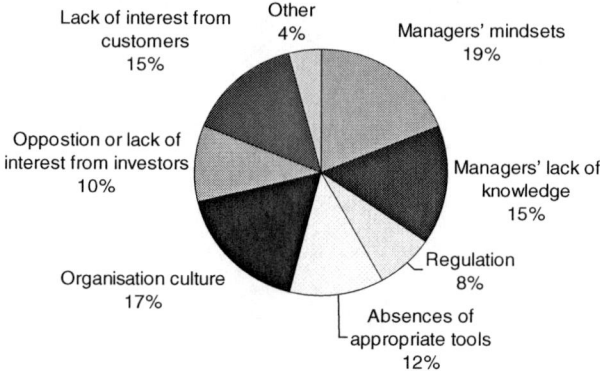

Figure 6.4   Main barriers to sustainability – all sectors (sustainability officers)

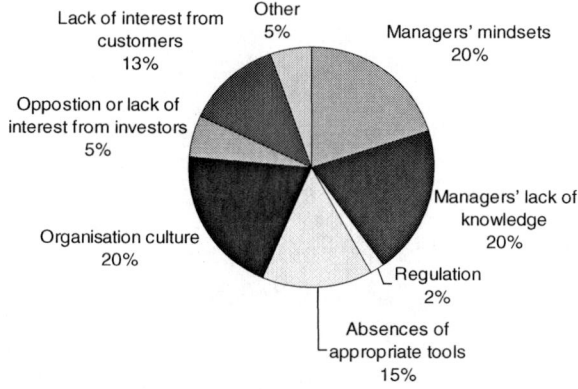

Figure 6.5   Main barriers to sustainability – food and beverage sector (sustainability officers)

F&B sample was small, here we benchmarked against the results for all industries and found a similar result (compare Figures 6.4 and 6.5.

Lack of knowledge and fixed mindsets are internal barriers. Thus the good news is that breaking down these barriers should be entirely within the reach of each and every company. However, we remind the reader of Schein's (1992) view that mindset is an aspect of organizational behaviour that is exceedingly difficult to change since it is working on that critical non-cognitive third level.

How can fixed mindsets be reached? According to sustainability officers, it is a question of 'speaking the language' of these managers and taking a company, if not unit- or project-specific approach. If the push for sustainability action should come from business units, as many managers believed, a key prerequisite is that these units understand the link between sustainability activities and their business results:

> *The significance of sustainability is not always clearly understood. It is not always clear to all staff how they can make a meaningful contribution.* (BCS52 – Top management, Finance)

> *We have a selling job to do – convincing people, consensus building in a bottom up way. If you choose the wrong level of abstraction to sell the concept, progress will be immeasurably slow. You need to speak in a language that others understand.* (BCS47a – Business manager, Supply chain)

Interestingly, several sustainability leaders professed that they actively seek staff that come into the business with this understanding, or mindset, already firmly in place:

> *The marketplace needs people that can handle complexity; sustainability will appeal to these minds.* (BCS47a – Business manager, Supply chain)

We examine case examples of how different organizations have set about changing mindsets later in this chapter.

3 Sustainability strategy design

3.1 What good is a sustainability strategy?

Corporate strategy-making has to take account of developments related to several dimensions of the business environment such as governmental, socio-cultural, economic and competitive aspects, with the end objective of formulating a product/market portfolio that gives comparative advantage to a company. This is also the framework for corporate sustainability focused as it is on the relationship between the company and society. A sound sustainability strategy firmly linked to the corporate strategy forms a basis for broad corporate policies and detailed plans and programmes. Managers commented on the importance of setting objectives in the formulation of a sustainability strategy, since it creates unity of purpose and lends coherence to supporting activities:

The only way to get the top guys on board is if these issues get to the top of the agenda of the corporate entity. The key is to have a clear and coherent strategy for sustainable development with defined objectives and goals that are communicated and implemented with passion. Integrating sustainability as part of the way of doing business is the challenge. (BCS46 – Senior regional business unit manager, Marketing and sales)

The risk of not integrating sustainability into the business through objective setting is clear; the sustainability strategy will be sidelined by busy managers:

Given that sustainability issues are complex and long-term, food and beverage managers, with more short-term demands on their time, tend to put sustainability action 'on the long finger' unless a strategy is clear and integrated. (BCS16 – Senior business manager, Strategy)

Sustainability officers felt that a clear and fully integrated sustainability strategy helps to shape the company's relationship with all its stakeholders whether suppliers, customers, other companies or policy makers, as well as making sustainability issues more visible at management level. A coherent sustainability strategy can guide competency development within corporations but, even more importantly for the food industry, it may even ultimately give companies the power to influence the way customers and consumers think.

But at the outset of our research, few F&B companies had formulated a comprehensive and fully aligned sustainability strategy. In our survey, we asked managers: 'How much does your company aim to integrate environmental and social criteria into its business strategies and operations?' Given that we had managers from a number of highly visible sustainability leaders responding, surprisingly few business managers in the sector answered 'very much'; only 22 per cent – although, again, we stress that this was more than the 16 per cent average for all sectors at that time. Unsurprisingly, our small sample of sustainability officers – thus, those working directly on such strategies – were more confident, with 32 per cent believing that this was the case (see comparative Figures 6.6 and 6.7). These results allowed us to observe a contradiction with what we already observed in Chapter 4; that 84 per cent of managers expected that sustainable development will 'very

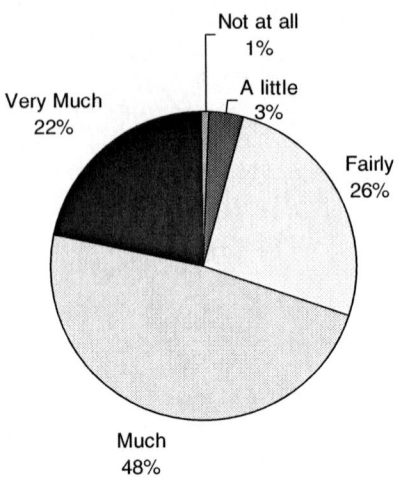

Figure 6.6 Perception of company's integration of environmental and social criteria into business strategy and operations (business managers)

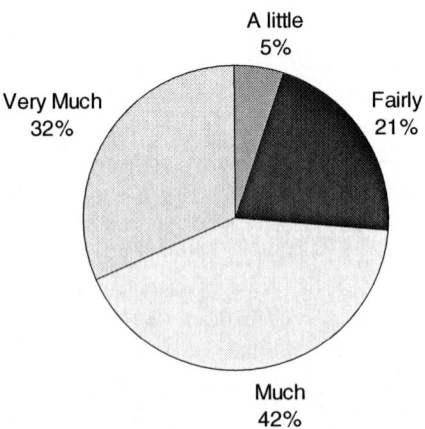

Figure 6.7 Perception of company's integration of environmental and social criteria into business strategies and operations (sustainability officers)

much' increase in importance for corporations in the future. We sur-mised that unless more companies 'very much' intend to integrate environmental and social criteria to business strategies and operations, the corporate momentum on sustainability was not actually likely to increase significantly at all.

We also pointed out in Chapter 5 that a little more than half (52 per cent) of business managers felt that capital markets would only slightly change their tendency to largely ignore sustainability issues over the forthcoming five years, and a further 15 per cent expected no change. Given the importance attributed to shareholders by managers, our view was that significant pressure for a move to integrate social and environmental criteria into business strategy was unlikely to occur under such circumstances.

In an attempt to better understand the attitudes of managers to integrating sustainable development or social responsibility into corporate strategy, in our survey we asked managers to agree or disagree with certain statements, ranging from the more radical cut and dried market-based view of Milton Friedman (1962) – 'the business of business is business' – to progressively more moderate views. The majority of respondents tended to opt for a 'middle of the road' option, and chose the following statement:

Companies should consider social and environmental issues/expectations and try to actively integrate them into their strategies, because, by doing so, they gain long-term-competitive advantage.

This indicates goodwill on the part of most F&B managers to try actively to integrate sustainability issues into strategy, which is a hopeful sign.

Smith has described what constitutes a sustainability strategy:

Developing the right CSR strategy requires an understanding of what differentiates the organization – its mission, values and core business activities. (Smith, 2003)

Effectively, leading companies have focused their attention on sustainability issues in areas that are most relevant to their business and where they can have most influence and impact; this provides management with the strongest business case:

The focus for design of our sustainability strategy was to ascertain how the businesses could best contribute to sustainable development.

Strategically, this led the company to create a focus in its sustainability actions on a number of areas of global importance upon which it could have most influence and around which the company could build some long-term initiatives. (BCS47a – Business manager, Supply chain)

The search for differentiation in the formulation of sustainability strategy not only allows companies to tailor-make strategies but to distinguish themselves from strategies of customers or competitors:

If what your competitor is doing is considered 'the' guiding star, then you have to find another guiding star – you have to gain another perspective. To surpass your competitor, you have to look at an even more outstanding company, look abroad, globally, to find your guiding star. You can do this by looking at industries that have a tough job with sustainability – and not necessarily just the food sector. (BCS11 – Senior business manager, Investor relations)

Effectively, we sometimes found companies looking towards other fast moving consumer goods companies to emulate or build upon their better practice example – Nike as regards child labour, for instance – yet adapting the model to their own purposes.

The sustainability strategies we looked at often reflected what the company stood for or built on areas where there is a genuine business case for involvement through the companies' stakeholders. We noted that often strategies were not necessarily comprehensively spread over the three 'pillars' of sustainability (environmental, social and economic) and were often more heavily weighted in either an environmental or a social direction. Unilever and Nestlé have taken the lead on sustainable agriculture in the supply chain and Chiquita and Starbucks have made excellent headway with employee satisfaction, but, at the same time, in very company-specific ways. This also allowed companies to use established skill sets:

The heart of the business case is to adopt environmental and social policies that use skills that the company has anyway. Then, you use those skills against achieving an objective which is consistent with the aims of the business. (BCS44 – Top management)

Once companies have strategies around certain key sustainability issues, these are dealt with as true business strategies, and not only as a mirror of corporate responsibility. One company showed us its com-

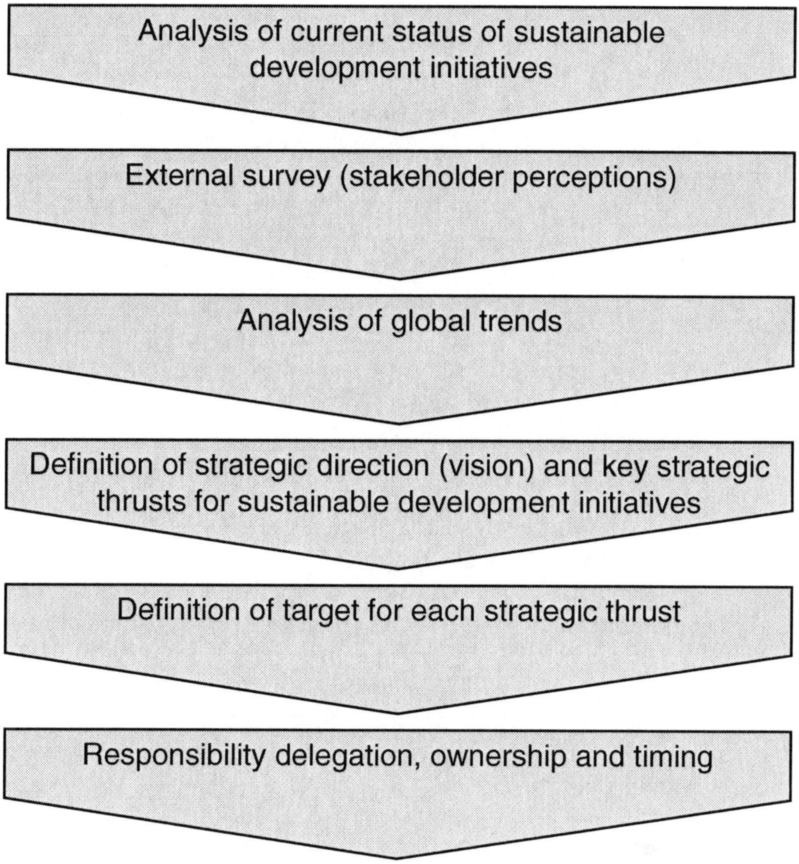

Analysis of current status of sustainable development initiatives

External survey (stakeholder perceptions)

Analysis of global trends

Definition of strategic direction (vision) and key strategic thrusts for sustainable development initiatives

Definition of target for each strategic thrust

Responsibility delegation, ownership and timing

Figure 6.8   Steps in building an environmental strategy

prehensive environmental strategy review, which had all the ingredients of a highly methodological business approach. (see Figure 6.8 for the steps involved)

Unilever had one of the rare, consistent strategies we found in that it had issued a commitment to meet sustainability criteria with respect to three areas within a specific timeline. However, we noted that no F&B company involved in our research had yet developed a fully comprehensive and binding commitment across the entire range of raw materials it used. Given that we included sustainability leaders in the research, one can assume that such a comprehensive strategic approach is either nonexistent or at an early stage throughout much of the industry.

Business managers insisted that if the sustainability strategy is properly integrated in the business strategy, it becomes an essential prerequisite to doing business. However, interviewees at consumer organizations were suspicious of many companies using sustainability to enhance their public relations efforts. For those that do, the risk is that if sustainability is merely a 'PR add-on', it will be 'first to be axed' during such hard times:

If the global economy turns down and companies look for savings, this could be an area which, if not implemented fully, could be hit by cost cutting. (BCS11 – Senior business manager, Investor relations)

As long as the economy and company are on a 'good run', the sustainability element will be expanding. If the going gets tough, only a core of activity would still be kept. (BCS34 – Business manager, Communications)

On the other hand, sustainability leaders warned against the company being perceived as fickle by starting with a strategy and not following through when times get tough:

Under financial hardship, it is unlikely that we would phase out our sustainability programme. From a reputation standpoint, a company cannot just pick up the issues to let them down when it likes. The public would quickly suspect that this was only done because it was 'fashionable'. This would damage our overall strategy. (BCS50 – Senior regional business unit manager, Marketing and sales)

The days of insular logic are over. This makes large companies re-evaluate. The danger is to dilute sustainability because things are on a downturn. Companies should no longer do this. The financial shape will have to be maintained. (BCS46 – Senior business manager, Sales and marketing)

4   Organizational structure

There is not a lot written about the organizational structures and change processes needed to implement sustainability strategies. In this section, we let F&B managers speak and lay some groundwork for such studies.

4.1   Structure and interaction between key business units

Organizational structure varies considerably from one organization to another in the F&B industry. Given the very specific nature of the products and context of each company, this is hardly surprising. However, it was possible for us to identify the common denominators that contribute to providing an optimum backdrop for building and promoting a BCS in the F&B industry.

As with many multinationals, the F&B company corporate headquarters takes on a role of central policy-setting and strategic overview. In the companies we included in our research, operational responsibilities (business units) were most often decentralized. Business units for global companies in the sector are often split into geographic markets in order to maintain a local focus and relevance, with the 'glue' being provided through global business overview; strategy, innovation and business development, at the corporate headquarters. While business managers suggested that overview of progress with corporate sustainability and the push for sustainability action must initially come from the corporate headquarters, it was also clear that the 'bird's eye view' required to do this was difficult to achieve:

Our business is highly decentralized. Cascading through the organization is a challenge. (BCS37 – Senior business manager, Communications)

Geographical dispersal is a real problem that hinders alignment. There are centrifugal forces separating units from each other over time. (BCS05 – Senior business manager, Communications)

Some managers proposed that in highly decentralized structures sustainability was a potentially strong 'glue' factor that helped to bring organizations together under one set of strongly integrated values.

While both business and sustainability managers unanimously felt that sustainability actions are most successful when implemented by operational units, there were several barriers involved in achieving this:

There is sometimes a mindset of 'not invented here' – even though we are the same company; this is sometimes difficult to overcome. (BCS17 – Senior business manager, Communications)

As already mentioned (see Chapter 4), due to the fragmented and decentralized structure of F&B organizations, they are also at a disadvantage in dealing with single-issue focused activists.

Companies have chosen diverse ways of locating responsibilities for sustainability issues in their organizations; in places as diverse as the public relations department, supply chain or innovation department. It often depended on how organizations started out with their sustainability strategies. Placing the sustainability function within corporate communications or public affairs departments may indicate a defensive rather than proactive starting point – a direct reflection of the corporate concern with dented image and reputation. However, some managers believed that no matter where the sustainability function is 'born', the important issue is that sustainability somehow gets on the management agenda:

> *Afterwards, it will start permeating the company in one way or another.*
> (BCS31 – Business manager, Supply chain, Purchasing)

Sustainable development activities in companies often had their origins in their environment, health and safety (EHS) departments, but sustainability leaders had moved to managing sustainability issues outside this department, keeping EHS separately as a discrete, highly technical entity. Food safety in the industry is also generally handled separately from the sustainability function.

Some companies have dedicated 'sustainability officers'. Managers felt that having this function directly to the CEO gives the entire organization a message that sustainability is being taken seriously within the company:

> *Our sustainability officer should have his own unit, and report to the CEO. This would enhance his profile. It is inevitable that this will happen eventually. Increasing the profile is of utmost importance.*
> (BCS06 – Senior regional business unit manager, Marketing and sales)

At one company researched, there had been a change of reporting line (direct to the CEO) and the officer reported major impact on credibility of his role across the company, with new exposure being given to sustainability at the highest level, at shareholder and board meetings for example. Furthermore, the previous incumbent in the position had been posted at a subsidiary, whereas the new officer was based at the corporate headquarters. Business managers at that company conceded that they had started to look at sustainability with new eyes as a result of the change.

But the existence of a sustainability function was often not perceived as the best solution, mostly owing to a fear of establishing an ineffective corporate silo:

> *There is no distinction between this and any other part of the business; there is no question of having a separate 'sustainability' department staffed with 'ivory tower' consultant-type staff.* (BCS27 – Senior business manager, Supply chain)

Interestingly, research by Aon on F&B companies in Europe (Aon, 2005) found that most F&B companies were not taking CSR seriously at an operational level. One of the main problems, the researchers concluded, was the fact that CSR teams were mainly operating in silos and were struggling to get functions, other than public relations, to integrate CSR into their operational thinking.

Managers in the industry nevertheless felt that while it was important to integrate sustainability to the business and support ownership in business units, there was a strong need for a strongly supported coordinating function so that this will effectively happen, at least initially, until a strategy 'takes hold':

> *Public Affairs, HR and the environment department have all been variously involved in sustainability in an ad hoc initiative driven fashion. It would be good to reinforce the coordination. The optimum would be to have one coordinating entity.* (BCS32 – Sustainability officer)

We noted that a large percentage of the sustainability officers we surveyed report to either a cross-cutting functional group or a strategy/innovation function, an indication of the need to network and coordinate across a number of functions across the organization.

Our research indicated that while a sustainability officer is an important enabler, this position cannot substitute for commitment from the business units.

> *If sustainable development is to be accepted by the business, then it has got to be owned by the business. The sustainable development unit is the coordinating part. In our company, the initiatives for sustainable*

development are coming through the business: this empowers them.
(BCS40 – Senior sustainability officer)

Sustainability is a moving target. The job of the sustainability officer can be to articulate whether the company is on target with the strategy and whether activities are becoming irrelevant. But according to our survey, there was considerable scope in the industry for sustainability officers to work more closely with business functions. Interaction was

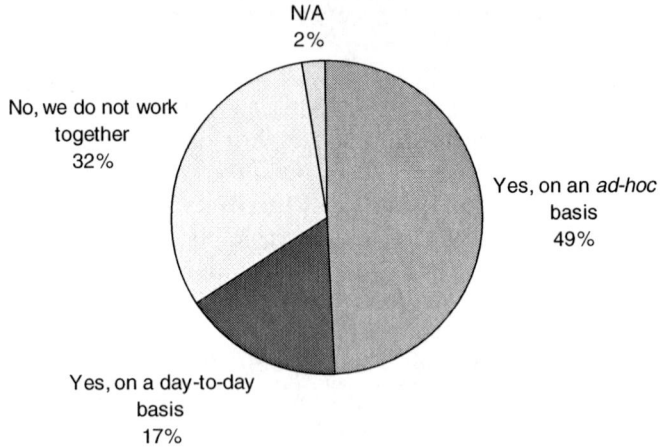

Figure 6.9   Collaboration with sustainability officers – business managers in all sectors

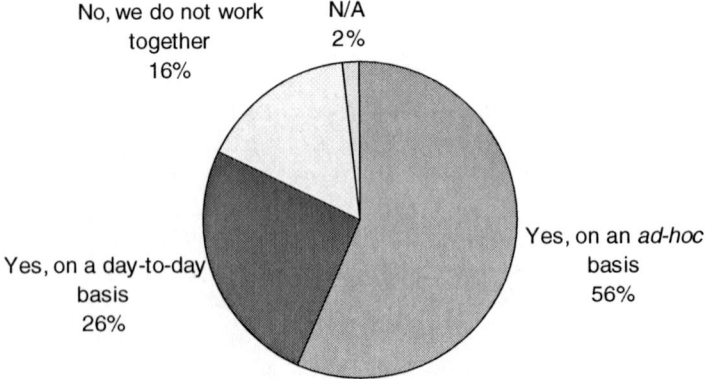

Figure 6.10   Collaboration with sustainability officers – business managers in the food and beverage industry

mostly *ad hoc*, with only a little over a quarter of F&B managers indicating that they worked with the sustainability officers or department on a day-to-day basis (see Figure 6.10).

This compared relatively favourably with the average result for all sectors researched, where only 17 per cent felt this was the case; the F&B sector was clearly above average in this regard (see Figure 6.9).

However, business managers were lukewarm on whether further collaboration would pay dividends; only 8 per cent felt that more collaboration with the company's environmental or sustainability officers would 'very much' contribute to sustainable business practices in the company, with another 24 per cent saying that there was 'much' to be gained (see Figure 6.12). This was low by any standards but, again, it was still higher than the average across all sectors ('very much' – 3 per cent and 'much' – 19 per cent) – see Figure 6.11.

Clearly, there was some work to be done by sustainability officers in convincing business managers that there was relevance in working more closely with them, and scope for further exploiting these relationships. Better practice organizations firmly believe in such collaborations:

We try to build a complete strategic framework based on 'trust'. We encourage continued and sustained interaction between sustainability and

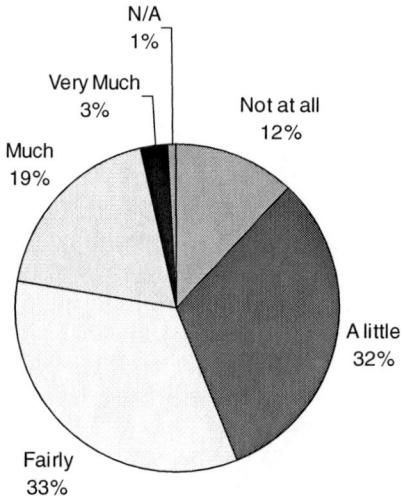

Figure 6.11 Contribution of increased collaboration to more sustainable practices in the company – business managers in all sectors

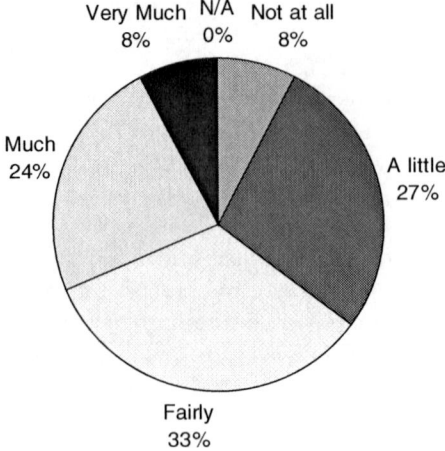

Figure 6.12   Contribution of increased collaboration to more sustainable practices in the company – business managers in food and beverage sector

business staff. (BCS48 – Senior business manager, strategy and business development)

Sustainability officers should be exposed more to line operations. (BCS50 – Senior regional business unit manager, Marketing and sales)

However, if the sustainability officer wants to be listened to, there are prerequisites; a business-friendly approach is necessary:

The sustainability officer should not forget the holistic part of his work – respect for other areas within the organization is a prerequisite. (BCS10 – Senior business manager, Business development)

In leading food companies, we identified sustainability 'champions' in the supply chain departments responsible for pushing the key sustainability agenda in the company. 'Champions' are individuals working within organizations that orient their vision, skills, experience, persuasive capacities and leadership towards issues important to them. On the operational level, larger companies have concentrated on building networks of sustainability champions positioned in the business units at senior level and scattered throughout the organization.[1] This has the effect of anchoring ownership of sustainability initiatives by the business units and ensures that questions such as budget and resources for sustainability initiatives are addressed in the context of business strategy.

It is important to identify specific individuals spread throughout the organization who take responsibility for sustainability within the network. They should not be full-time sustainability people. (BCS50 Senior regional business unit manager, Marketing and sales)

Some managers suggested that the key to successful issue identification was communication between business and strategy groups. In more than one company for example, strategy groups inform the sustainability or corporate responsibility committee on issues and *vice versa*. A few leading companies have appointed a strategic coordinating committee to lead from the corporate centre, with overall responsibility for the identification of issues. Examples of such companies are Diageo and Nestlé; and, at the time of our interviews, Kraft was also in the process of developing such a structure. Such groups are cross functional, with involvement from different business units and unions, and with an appropriate geographical representation. These groups decide whether issues should be addressed by their members or at business unit level. In more than one company, the strategic coordinating committee had nominated issue groups or 'owners' of key issues, such as human rights or ethical trading. As with the coordinating committee, issue groups had diverse membership:

Our company creates 'nets' and 'goalkeepers' for these nets to enable companies to work in a matrix structure that allows, for example, staff in the markets to communicate with global functions. This ensures cross-pollination. Information gathered in one market is transferred to another more easily, facilitating maximum use of knowledge in the organization. We refer to this process as 'search and spin'. (BCS16 – Senior business manager, Strategy)

We identified other 'search and spin' approaches; one food company was holding two-day internal sustainability seminars twice yearly, where managers define priorities on a country basis and exchange examples of best practice. The same company was also holding a company-wide sustainability conference once a year in order to compare production priorities with market expectations and exchange best practice, the objective being to feed the output from such activities into the process of establishing sustainability goals for the organization. According to managers, the participatory nature of the process ensured buy-in and endorsement of the policies.

By operating with teams in a matrix structure, it makes it more possible to put in place an 'early awareness system' to learn directly from stakeholders and consumers as early as possible, and to commercialize good ideas and innovations quickly. The process provides an opportunity for individuals to pick up issues at market level and elevate them to the appropriate decision-making processes, but has the advantage of changing company culture at the same time. A strategy manager commented:

> In order to avoid some issues being kept at a national level too long, *'radar mechanisms'* can be put in place to ensure that issue identification at market level is channelled up and out quickly enough. (BCS49 – Senior business manager, Manufacturing and supply chain technology)

At Diageo, such a process had been positively correlated by its company analysts with a year-on-year reduction in weighted average risk to the company. Managers interviewed at that company commented that the process had involved better assessment of risks overall, and had improved both engagement with relevant stakeholders and contingency planning.

Overall, we found that leading companies were still in a process of experimentation to find the 'right' set-up to build and implement a sustainability strategy within their overall corporate structure. Often this was because a sustainability function was either new or evolving. Mainstreaming sustainability, as opposed to having specific corporate functions under a sustainability banner, is the preferred orientation for the leading companies. However, as we shall see in the following sections, although structures and frameworks are important, it is people that are the key to making a sustainability strategy work at an operational level.

5 Importance of functions: 'Opposers' and 'Promoters'

Support for sustainability initiatives varied widely among different internal business groups, commercial activities and individuals within the industry. The business functions that were primarily focused on the business margin (thus, sales and profits targets) generally saw sustainability as a high-risk strategy. Often, this was because awareness about potential opportunities and pay-offs from increased sustainability performance was not at an optimal level:

> *Accommodating additional responsibility is difficult for production-oriented functions that are focusing on tight shipping schedules and so on. Personal disposition and attitude makes the difference.* (BCS05 – Senior business manager, Communications)

Business managers regarded finance and control functions as the primary opposition (22 per cent) followed by marketing and sales (17 per cent) and manufacturing (13 per cent, see Figure 6.14). Although sustainability managers agreed with them about the main 'opposers' (see Figure 6.13), they tended to see marketing and sales as substantially more of an opponent than did business managers (32 per cent versus 17 per cent). Sustainability officers also saw manufacturing units as putting up more opposition than did business managers – 21 per cent versus 13 per cent (compare Figures 6.13 and 6.14).

The findings about finance departments is perhaps not surprising, considering the proximity of financial professions to bottom-line impacts, the difficulty of proving tangible and measurable bottom-line

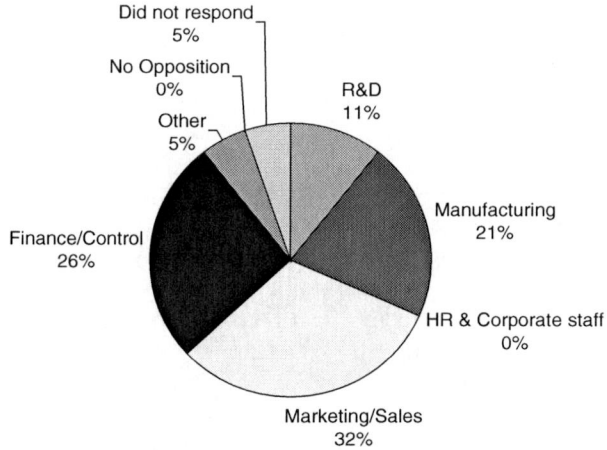

Figure 6.13 Strongest opposition to implementing sustainability initiatives (responses from sustainability officers)

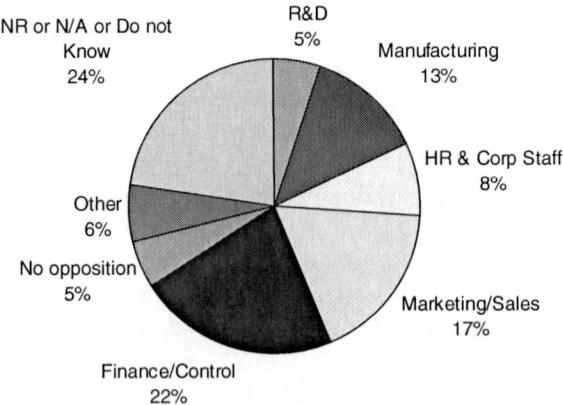

Figure 6.14 Strongest opposition to implementing sustainability initiatives (responses from business managers)

benefits of sustainability strategies and the financial function's risk-averse strategic orientation in general:

> *The typical response of financial staff to sustainability is to scrutinize costs. But that is their nature; they tend to be overly focused.* (BCS36 – Top management, Finance)

But sometimes they are simply not integrated with sustainability activities:

> *We have no strategy on investments and building the BCS and the financial controller is not involved in sustainability issues.* (BCS15 – Senior business manager, Finance)

In companies there was a mismatch between where the process for risk management resides (finance department) and where competency for sustainability risk management exists (sustainability function). Exposure can be avoided if processes and competencies are well linked within companies. Could it be possible that the negative publicity that Nestlé got over its Ethiopian crisis in 2002[2] for example, could have been avoided through more collaboration between financial and sustainability risk management staff?

According to business managers, the perceived importance of functions for promoting sustainability was in the following order: human resources/corporate staff, manufacturing, R&D and finally marketing

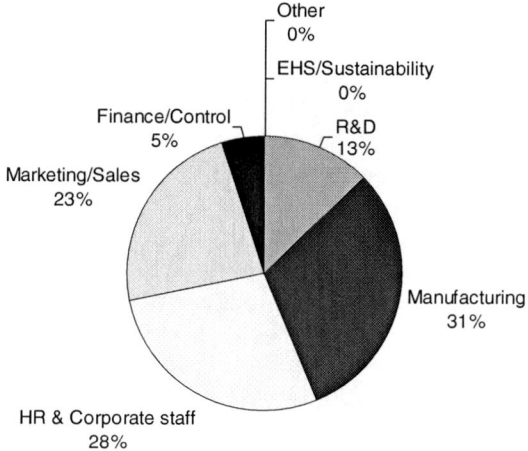

Figure 6.15 Functions that can most promote sustainability (responses from sustainability officers)

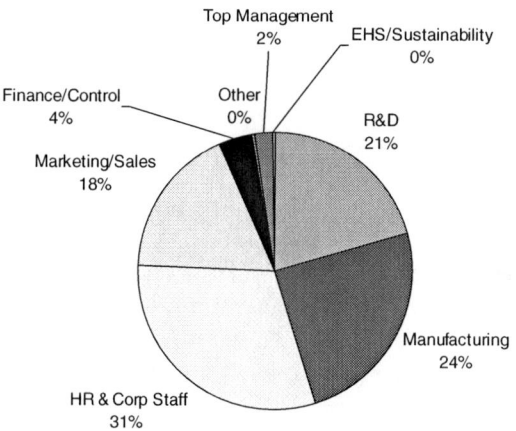

Figure 6.16 Functions that can most promote sustainability (responses from business managers)

(see Figure 6.15). The fact that both business managers and sustainability officers in the F&B industry consider manufacturing and marketing/sales groups as functions that can most effectively promote sustainability performance is interesting (compare Figures 6.15 and 6.16), since we thus deduce that at least one perceived principal opponents is also a perceived principal potential promoter. This is a factor for sustainability officers in the F&B industry to be aware of when they seek engagement on sustainability issues.

Although seen as an important deterring agent, finance and control was not perceived as a function that can most successfully promote sustainability (see Figures 6.15 and 6.16). In the perception of F&B managers, corporate staff and human resources had the pivotal role in rolling sustainability out within the organization and R&D had potential to engage in process and product innovations. We found it interesting that our small sample of sustainability officers were less ambitious about the potential for R&D to promote sustainability than business managers. This may be because the sustainability officers themselves were overly focused on continuous improvement in the manufacturing area and needed to focus more fully on promoting more transformational change through the R&D as well as the marketing departments.

5.1   Top management

Sustainability officers felt that, for a BCS to be successful, the CEO and members of the executive board of a company needed to take distinctly proactive roles on sustainability issues:[3]

> *One of our greatest strengths is our top leadership commitment to corporate sustainability management.* (BCS50 – Senior regional business unit manager – Marketing and sales)

As the driving force behind the sustainability strategy, CEOs of the leading companies have become publicly vocal on sustainability issues. One of the two CEOs of Unilever at the time of our early interview research had elected to personally support the Unilever water initiative – one prong of the company's three-pronged sustainability strategy. Several of the F&B companies we researched were members of the global compact (for example, Danisco, Danone, Scottish & Newcastle, Diageo, and Nestlé),[4] which sets out to align business leaders behind ten principles of social and environmental responsibility and implies a formal engagement from CEOs. While the Global Compact conditions of membership have been criticized by NGOs (owing to a perceived lack of rigour in assessing related corporate actions), managers we interviewed were aware of their companies' membership and viewed it as an important step in the evolution of their companies' thinking when it came to sustainability actions. Such memberships have an impact internally in raising awareness within companies, something that should perhaps not be overlooked by the critics.

In 2007, a survey of the CEOs of global compact companies carried out by McKinsey indicated that CEOs increasingly believe that they have business reasons for being more proactive on the sustainability agenda, and more than 90 per cent felt that they were doing more than five years previously. However, newly appointed CEOs may keep sustainability further down the agenda than other more pressing (for them) concerns until they have 'made their mark' on turnover and profits:

> *When our CEO took over, his main question was, what have I taken over? Then there was restructuring. It took five years before we started address- ing sustainability as a strategic priority.* (BCS10 – Senior business manager, Business development)

CEOs are increasingly subject to peer pressure outside the organization also, and sharing of information and learning has positive impacts internally; however, within limits:

> *CEOs of different companies influence each other, and this is a conduit to sharing some practices as there is some cross fertilization going on here. However there are competitive issues if one starts to share practices, so this does not tend to happen.* (Senior manager – Manufacturing and supply chain technology)

In 2001, nearly half of CEOs were in office for less than three years (Drake Beam Morin, 2001). CEOs are required to implement strategies and plans within increasingly limited time frames, reinforcing the focus on short-term business results. The increasingly short tenure of senior posts can jeopardize the sustainability agenda since constant changes bring threats to continuity:

> *It is difficult to be consistent with strategies; when there is a high level of fluctuation in top management with changes each time; managers become a little impervious.* (Food industry expert)

On the other hand, in the same year replacements for departing CEOs in 85 per cent of cases at the time of the Beam Morin research were from within the company ranks, so if a company is strategically aligned behind sustainability, there is a high likelihood of continued endorsement of the existing sustainability strategy when a new CEO is sourced internally.

Once a company has strategically integrated sustainability, having a vision for this can also become part of the selection criteria for future CEOs:

> *It was unlikely that a CEO without a vision for sustainability would be selected by the board, since corporate responsibility had already become an essential part of the company's culture, and it was a defining characteristic of the brand.* (BCS16 – Senior business manager, Strategy)

5.2 The 'second layer'

Sustainability managers often referred to the opposition of the 'second layer' of senior business managers (directly under the CEO), those oriented towards profitable growth first and foremost:

> *You need champions of the corporate citizenship cause at the senior business level. To bring disbelievers on board, having the leaders on board is critical.* (BCS17 – Senior business manager, Communications)

Even senior managers seek their comfort zone; they focus more easily on aspects that are directly linked to managing the business – for example, food safety issues are more accessible than 'fuzzy' other issues. But managers believed that although they could be 'won over' in different ways, theirs would remain a cautious approach unless pressure was intense:

> *If you can show the risks associated with say, animal welfare or the opportunity for innovation presented by, for example, aquaculture, they can be persuaded. However, pace and amount of effort would still be up for discussion. They will look at margins and costs and say: 'We are not a Unilever – the NGOs are talking but they are not influencing consumers...why should we act?'* (BCS37 – Senior business manager, Communications)

Benefits for stakeholders, including employees, and environmental protection measures may be viewed by the 'second layer' as costly or unnecessary, unless a robust and convincing business case is prepared and presented as part of the business decision-making process.

5.3 The 'old guard'

Scattered throughout the organization, sustainability managers complained of what they referred to as 'the old guard', a group of hard-line sceptics that are difficult to persuade of the value of sustainability programmes, but who, because of their sometimes senior positions and/or longevity with their organizations, can present significant barriers to implementation:

It is good is that icon 'opposers' in our company have finally moved away or have retired. (BCS27c – Senior business manager, Supply chain)

Changing the 'old guard' from strategically important places through reshuffling is important. (BCS34 – Business manager, Communications)

The 'old guard' is often supervising other staff and, as direct supervisors, constitute a barrier to change of mindset and behaviour for others:

Our company is grappling with the challenge of ensuring the embedding of sustainability action in line management responsibility. There is a 'disconnect'. (BCS50 – Senior regional business unit manager, Marketing and sales)

Unless vision, culture and reward systems align under a strategy, line managers in the industry do not necessarily exercise the behaviours that the company prefers. According to a study by Ramus (2001), leading by example is one of the most important forms of managerial support for managers in any company. The 'old guard' deter progress on promoting behaviour that can allow organizations to capitalize on their sustainability investment and hinder progress of key departments responsible for roll out of a sustainability strategy:

Our current CEO is very supportive of changing the traditional conservative approach. Our senior communications staff has been stopping us reaping the benefits of changing in key areas where we could win favour with rating agencies. (BCS24, Sustainability officer)

5.4 'New age' managers

Senior managers we interviewed felt that younger executives are more prepared to take on the integrative aspects implied by sustainability in their work:

New young marketing managers are more attuned to sustainability, particularly if they have families – as some of the realities of unsustainable behaviour will hit the next generation. But they also need a corporate mandate...... (BCS43 – Senior business manager, Marketing)

There will be change when a 30-year-old of today comes into a senior management job later. It will take new breeds of manager and conumers to get the business changed. (BCS44 – Top management, Board member)

Some managers interviewed felt that women managers were more open to sustainability concepts. Whilst we did not find evidence to back these points up in our survey data, there is evidence of this in other research (Tomkiewicz and Hughes, 1993; Peterson, 2004). Goldman Sachs (2007a) found that the failure to attract, retain and promote enough women was a systemic problem in the F&B industry that might ultimately affect competitiveness, and that lack of female leadership particularly in Europe may impede access to as broad a knowledge of consumer behaviour as possible (vital for the industry). Gender diversity was a 'hot topic' at the time we carried out our research. Human resources management in several companies we researched had recently focused on increasing diversity in the workplace, including having more women in management positions. Women may in future bring different and more positive perspectives on corporate sustainability into the F&B workplace.

5.5 Supply chain and purchasing officers

Sustainability officers in the F&B industry saw buyers of raw and semi-processed materials as key functions to be convinced of the BCS. We interviewed a number of senior supply chain officers in the industry and noted a high awareness amongst these officers of environmental and social issues. This was directly associated with a high awareness of food safety and traceability requirements. Companies can be demanding of their suppliers, depending on the pressure they receive from their stakeholders, and suppliers react positively to requests from customers:

In relationships with supplier, actions are different depending on what is being sourced. For vegetable oils and fats, coffee or cocoa, sustainability is very much an issue, but when it comes to solid board, rigid plastic or flexible packaging, the issue is rarely addressed. It relates to levels of risk. (BCS25b – Senior regional business unit manager, Purchasing)

The food companies send us many questionnaires; we have responded by putting systems into place to cope with these demands. (BCS01 – Senior regional business unit manager, Sales and marketing, Food industry supplier)

Global branded companies have considerable influence over their suppliers, and there is a significant business case for supplying companies to comply with their requests since multinational companies provide their suppliers with multi-million Euro contracts:

The business case is simply ... more business with our company. We give preference to companies that meet our social and environmental performance criteria. We are a customer of choice and suppliers can link to the reputation of our brand. In return, the supplier gets long-term assurance of contracts within the parameters of quality and food safety. (BCS26 – Senior regional business unit manager, Purchasing)

At the time of our research, large companies were moving out of primary processing; those that still had some business concerns in this area were planning to phase out gradually. Dependence on suppliers was increasing, exposing F&B companies to added degrees of risk:

We are talking of a shared responsibility; we will be more dependent on suppliers than before. We will have to have new guidelines for suppliers as we are losing transparency. (BCS26 – Senior regional business unit manager, Purchasing)

In recent times, with increasing sourcing in developing countries, and with a trend towards relocation of manufacturing bases from Europe to Asia in the search for ever more economically advantageous alternatives, buyers and purchasing managers of goods traditionally sourced through European companies are finding it much more difficult to fathom their risks. While managers could somewhat take social and environmental frameworks and regulatory enforcement for granted in Western Europe, the same could not be said of Asia and Africa:

We need to have a sufficient warning system for China. Recently we had our fingers burned there; a supplier used a production process outlawed in

Europe. It was clear that we would not touch it. But it raises competitive issues. For the first time we were really worried. We need processes in place to evaluate the supplier. (BCS25 – Senior regional business manager, Purchasing)

Managers felt that they should be looking towards other companies in other FMCG industries such as Nike and Gap to emulate how these companies were dealing with such issues.

Purchasing managers were very aware of potential competitive disadvantages involved in applying high standards to their activities in developing countries, when other less exposed and local competing companies are not so discerning. On the other hand, managers knew of potential risks to corporate reputation and brand by not insisting on high standards. The F&B branded companies are treading carefully as a result and are trying to ensure that Asian first tier suppliers have at least similar standards to those expected from European suppliers. Global companies strive towards continuous improvement and, as sustainability performance is usually part of the supplier qualifying process – albeit to extremely varying degrees in the industry – incremental improvements result. All in all, we found that social and environmental audits of suppliers were in a dynamic stage of development throughout much of the industry.

In other industries, it has been possible for companies to establish long-term, close relationships with suppliers and to rationalize their numbers in order to streamline operations and have more overview (Ionescu-Somers, 2006b). This is more challenging for a global food company, where the supply base, depending on the commodity or ingredient, is highly fragmented. Some global companies will have hundreds of thousands of direct and indirect suppliers. Even direct suppliers can be in the tens of thousands. Control over suppliers has thus proved more challenging than in other industries. This poses a problem when it comes to auditing suppliers from every point of view. Supplier audits in the F&B industry are in need of rationalization, since all of the food companies source from the same numerous suppliers. A senior manager at one company told us that he had recently joined a think tank of industry managers to rethink the existing situation:

More must be done to define common approaches in one industry towards our suppliers. We want to develop and implement a third party audit system acceptable to all food industries in Europe. (BCS25 – Senior regional business manager, Purchasing)

Probably owing to the fragmentation of supply, sustainability leader Unilever only took the step of asking its approximately 50,000 *direct* suppliers to provide non-negotiable positive assurance on the company's sustainability policies and codes in 2005. The company had established an objective of obtaining overview in this area by the end of 2005 and of initiating risk assessments on those suppliers that could not provide this assurance. While a supplier sign-off on business principles does not constitute a performance measure, it certainly serves to communicate a strong message that companies are taking this seriously.

Other leading companies are concentrating on improving relationships with as many major direct suppliers as possible:

We get as close to the producer as we can. We align with organizations that have a direct line back to the producer themselves. Chosen traders have a relationship with suppliers that aligns all the way back. Where possible, we deal with the producer directly but if we have to use a trader, we insist on knowing where the product comes from. (BCS26 – Senior regional business unit manager, Purchasing)

In going through such processes, senior supply chain managers are eminently more aware of social and environmental issues and their complexities and risks. They clearly saw a BCS, and were supportive of it:

There is a definite correlation between corporate responsibility and making money. I firmly believe that being a good corporate citizen helped us to be more competitive. (BCS30 – Senior regional business unit manager, Purchasing)

Purchasing managers and their operations provide an excellent starting point for developing a strong BCS, and are a solid support to the BCS when rolling it out to other more challenging areas of F&B organizations.

5.6 Brand and marketing managers

Brand managers and marketing executives have a major influence on final product (design and sourcing) and sales decisions. However, we found that sustainability is generally not a high priority for this group:

Often sustainability criteria are dominated by economic criteria. For example: the packaging debate is always won by marketing and sales and lost by the environmentalists. (BCS47a – Business manager, Supply chain)

The fall-out of the marketing function from sustainability strategy-making came up time and again in our discussions with managers, but there were few solutions proposed about how they could be better involved and we identified a certain fatalistic acceptance of the situation by managers while sustainability leaders grappled with potential solutions:

The short-term conservative perspective of marketers affects product innovation– we know this and we have looked carefully at how we innovate. Marketers focus on business plans and if they get it wrong, this can affect the brand in a big way. They are risk averse. (BCS20 – Senior business manager, Innovation)

Efforts to involve marketers have so far not been successful yet this is essential to strategic fit. We need to link existing raw material supply chain programmes with consumer communication. (BCS47 – Business manager, Supply chain)

Furthermore marketing and sales managers were far from convinced themselves that 'sustainability can sell'. They did not yet see ways of using sustainability in brand communication.

Sustainability does not bring a competitive edge on the consumer side – the consumer is not knowledgeable enough to be pushing the issue. The consumer buys the quality brand and a good feeling. It is not productive to spend money on explanations to consumers about sustainability programmes. I cannot see how our company could have the media power to bring this concept to people. (BCS07 –Senior regional business unit manager, Marketing and sales)

According to several sustainability managers, the root of the problem was, again, lack of knowledge:

Salespeople need to know more about how products are made. If they see the potential for a product to be positioned differently through sustain-

ability, they will hold on to this concept. (BCS12 – Senior sustainability officer)

Raising awareness of the potential of a BCS in the sales and marketing functions and with brand managers can go a long way towards ensuring its ultimate strategic implementation especially since, in the F&B industry, the line of succession to the CEO often runs through these dominant functions. But finding the right language and enough spare time to convey the message is an essential prerequisite:

> *To win over marketers – you need to cash into their 'culture' as it is entirely different to supply chain. Job rotation in sales and marketing is often too fast for the complexity of sustainability – it takes time to win people over.* (BCS47a – Business manager, Supply chain)

The managers we interviewed in the F&B industry did not comment negatively on marketers' attitudes to social responsibility but focused more on the fact that marketers have in general, not reinvented their approach to their work although many other aspects of business operations have changed in recent years (distribution, new product development, the supply chain). Interestingly marketing managers owned up to a conservative approach:

> *Consumers used to be conservative and slow to change their habits in the past – now they rapidly change and adjust to new realities. We have not yet learnt to deal with a world where the consumer is changing more quickly.* (BCS43 – Senior business manager, Marketing)

> *If you can put sustainability into an emotionally convincing package, then you can sell it. Why have they not done this before? Marketers have not been forced to think in this direction. The model for brand and product development is always the same.* (BCS50 – Senior regional business unit manager, Marketing and sales)

A careful and more sophisticated approach to marketing sustainability is called for, one that is not based on traditional approaches but on a new kind of relationship with the consumer.[5]

One food industry expert was sceptical about industry openness to using sustainability in its marketing of products:

> *The industry is frightened that the brand will become associated with something uncontrollable. So they say that sustainability cannot be used*

> *to market products. They're worried about opening a Pandora's Box that they cannot control.* (BCSBM01)

But external stakeholders warn that marketers will eventually be forced to change and one expert we spoke to commented that marketers will have to cater for a growing group of consumers interested in sustainability attributes, with more sophisticated ability to choose between products.

Sustainability officers saw the development of an internal understanding of the contribution of sustainability to the corporate reputation value construct as a step that may help to bridge the current reality. However, developing such an understanding is a time-consuming process, and marketing and brand managers have a swift turnaround time in their positions, 18 months to two years on average, with tightly set deadlines and objectives:

> *Marketers think in terms of four month time blocks. Not only that, but frameworks are becoming shorter and shorter.* (BCS43 – Senior business manager, Marketing)

Successful senior managers, particularly those in sales and marketing in FMCG companies are either moved around the world constantly and change jobs regularly; this curtails opportunities for more long-term *in situ* organizational learning, and compromises the continuity preferable for rollout of sustainability concepts:

> *Staff turnover especially at senior level is a problem. This is greater at senior level. We don't have a marketing or senior manager that has been in the position for more than three to four years.* (BCS14 – Senior business manager, Finance)

While mindset is a barrier to managers adopting sustainability concepts willingly, lack of time and continuity can be major barriers to a change of mindset.

Consumer organization officers felt that marketers, and the media that carry their messages, must urgently respond to public health issues such as obesity and become more accountable to customers in the marketplace about their sourcing practices. Yet we found little evidence of collaborations with these organizations to transform the framework that limits sustainable consumption to its current niches and contributes to maintaining the *status quo*.

For solutions, marketers may look towards companies that have been under pressure for some time; for example, efforts by Diageo to promote 'responsible drinking' (Mason, 2003). If a message for responsible drinking has an effect on consumption, it would demonstrate the potential of commercial brands to steer societal change. In this way, brand strategy becomes influenced by the business strategy and reflects the same strategic visions and corporate culture. Such a dynamic takes companies away from classical brand management, with its emphasis on sales and share driven criteria, and causes marketers to focus on more complex concepts. The strategy then becomes driven by brand identity and the promotion of multiple brands with a much more global perspective.

Few mainstream brands are making sustainability integral to their products and services, to their business model or to the general appeal of their brands, other than a few niche brands, such as The Body Shop or Ben & Jerry's, although a good recent example is Nespresso's partnership with the Rainforest Alliance aimed to associate sustainability with quality. In spite of a fairly recent proliferation of Fair Trade brands amongst the global food companies, most represent only a tiny portion of the companies' total product mix. As already mentioned, NGOs fear that the real intention of the companies is to stifle competition and avoid mainstreaming niche brands.

Unilever's acquisition of Ben & Jerry's in 2002, or Cadbury's purchase of a 5 per cent stake in Green and Black (a UK organic chocolate manufacturer) in 2005 provided opportunities to the companies for corporate learning about manufacturing businesses that earn higher margins than those of global manufacturers based on more sustainable products. Managers were open about their objectives:

> *Over time, we acquired a major stake in this business; it was a question of getting to know it, trying to leverage that knowledge – and then we took full control of the company. It is a small business, but experimental. We gain insights on why this company works so well.* (BCS14 – Senior business manager, Finance)

Indeed, organic companies complain of employee poaching as the global companies moved to understand the successes of these brands (Moules, 2004).

Some interviewees indicated that even in better practice companies, problems arise with including sales and marketing executives in strategic coordination groups in charge of overseeing sustainability strategies:

> *Since the industry does not associate specific brands with specific sustainability issues, marketing executives drop out of the equation because of their direct association and preoccupation with brand and not issues.* (BCS03 – Senior sustainability officer)

We suggest that an integrated sustainability strategy that leads to true sustainable development and market transformation will probably never be successful unless marketers are brought on fully on board with sustainability strategies, task forces and related processes in F&B companies. This problem affects everything, from R&D and innovation to the messages that consumers receive downstream. A study by Ionescu-Somers (2006b) revealed that while the corporate customer was somewhat pressured to influence the social and environmental behaviour of companies, the same was not true for the corporate supplier. The difference was in the customer buying power; quite simply, pressure goes up the supply chain, not down:

> *We do not scrutinise our customer's social and environmental behaviour. We are reactive to their needs, not proactive to influence how they are behaving.*(BCS01 – Senior regional business unit manager, Sales)

A consumer organization representative expressed the contradictions in the dilemma we have just been describing better than we could have:

> *There are fundamental flaws in the way companies do business. Some take action in their supply chains, but at the other end of the chain, they allow marketers to call the shots. This waters down their efforts and they forget that crucial interface with their consumers. Marketers are detached from the production process and take things over at a critical point when more continuity is needed, not less, particularly within companies that are strategically integrating corporate sustainability. The advertising world needs a seismic change for anything to move. Companies need to re-evaluate their marketing strategies to see if they integrate.*

Sustainability strategies lose considerable momentum in the industry because of these gaps. Progressive companies such as P&G, frustrated with the failure of 'green' marketing to bring top line growth in the form of new consumers or markets are realizing that sustainability may bring opportunities as well as responsibilities:

> *In focusing on 'responsibility', we have focused only on eliminating things which never had value for our consumers in the first place...pollution, waste, natural resource depletion.* (P&G Director of Sustainable Development George Carpenter, cited in *Marketing Week*, 2003)

New dynamics in the industry may also give opportunities:

> *More recently, marketers are under less pressure than before; the time horizon has changed. Because of new systems, the retail trade is able to plan ahead and is more stringent about cutting costs and their own supply chains are more efficient. Nowadays, they plan a promotion some 6 months ahead and carry stock for a minimum period. This is good news for sustainability.* (BCS43 – Senior business manager, Marketing)

Sustainability officers strongly endorsed the idea of building the business case around strong pilot projects in the supply chain before moving to the link to brand benefits:

> *If you want to build a business case for sustainability, don't start with the marketers.* (BCS – Senior business manager, Supply chain)

> *Now that the supply chain has many models up and running, our next step is to convince marketers. We will hold a workshop with marketing executives of foods with a view to sharing agriculture stories. The definition of the brand is an essential part of this. What does it stand for and what is the consumer expecting?* (BCS49 – Senior business manager, Manufacturing and supply chain technology)

Transformation of markets will involve changes in both the supply and demand side, and must include cooperative activities with other stakeholders to change frameworks limiting sustainable consumption behaviour. Currently, our empirical evidence suggests that in spite of some encouraging examples, one important side of the equation is largely missing.

6   Processes and systems

But even in the leading F&B companies we looked at, we found that the daily practices and realities of implementation often did not echo the care that has gone into developing the corporate sustainability strategy. Herein lay the greatest challenge, even for the corporate leaders and first movers. The complexity and constant evolution of sustainability issues in a global context makes roll out a significant challenge:

> *Sustainability is a constantly moving target, and I am often reminded of an old saying by Heraclites 'No man ever steps in the same river twice, for it's not the same river and he's not the same man'.* (BCS16 – Senior business manager, Strategy)

Nevertheless, by internalizing some of their most strategically relevant issues, F&B companies can ensure that their issue management[6] moves away from reactive and defensive modes evidenced in some well-documented cases,[7] and addressed by primers for managers such as 'Dancing with the Devil: Crisis Management in the Food and Drinks Industry'; (Leatherhead Food International, 2000). Non-reactive issue management integrates an early awareness system (EAS). An EAS helps companies to see issues as an integral part of what they do, to antici-

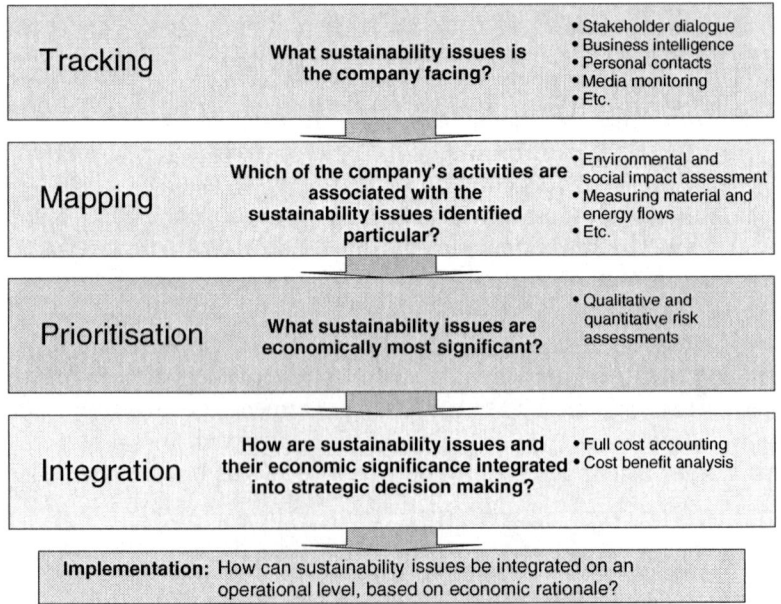

Figure 6.17   Stages in the system of issue management

pate demands and constraints, and decide more strategic options for dealing with them. But overall managers are not sufficiently abreast of the issues:

> *We carried out research on awareness of sustainability issues on mid- to senior management. There was low awareness – the message was not getting out there.* (BCS42 – Senior sustainability officer)

In the follow section, we can examine how F&B companies identify issues, map and prioritize them, and then integrate them into strategy (see Figure 6.17).

6.1   Issue tracking, mapping and prioritization

When companies in the sector have robust issue management systems in place, this has frequently been as a result of incidents involving defensive confrontations with stakeholders. The infant formula issue for example for which Nestlé was targeted by its stakeholders was not only a catalyst to create a strong public affairs department within Nestlé, but also a more effective issue management system. Chiquita also changed its entire company focus – including issue management – as a result of press and media exposure. An issue manager described his view of the *status quo* in the industry:

> *The more affected a company has been by a major issue in its past, the more it treats the potential risks of issues seriously and the higher it places responsibility for issues in the company hierarchy.* (BCS34 – Business manager, Communications)

This is clearly more reactive than it need be. As Cardinal Richelieu once said, 'Experience shows that, if one foresees from far away the designs to be undertaken, one can act with speed when the moment comes to execute them'; in other words...early awareness generally pays dividends. Across all sectors in our Forum for CSM/IMD study, we found that strategic EASs that track the development of weak signals associated with issues, thus assisting with their conversion to strategic awareness, were mostly not being implemented.[8] Not only that, but managers were aware of these shortcomings:

> *Some issues are kept too long at a national level and are not shared in other countries early enough. The coordination across business is extremely*

important. (BCS49 – Senior business manager, Manufacturing and supply chain technology)

Systems to evaluate risk already known but where details are lacking were more prevalent than EAS.

For effective issue-tracking, the more progressive companies have put in place radar mechanisms to ensure that information in the markets is transmitted around the network:

You need to look at the critical environmental social and economic issues in different parts of the value chain, and understand where your company is positioned. Some businesses are affected in the upstream and others in the downstream. (BCS49 – Senior business manager, Manufacturing and supply chain technology)

Managers favoured a decentralized approach:

Each market should have responsibility for the corporate affairs agenda and identify strategic issues that need to be addressed. Then you can set up a continuous strategic action agenda based on value creation. (BCS16 – Senior business manager, Strategy)

It was also clear that interaction with external stakeholders was a major source of information:

To keep our 'ears to the ground', we network with various future-oriented organizations. Large organizations with complex worldwide activities need an up-to-date list of probable, potential issues. This facilitates making choices. (BCS05 – Senior business manager, Communications)

The importance of the coordinating role of the corporate headquarters was also underlined:

The 'centre' (corporate headquarters) needs to take the proactive role and make structured and specific requests. (BCS16 – Senior business manager, Strategy)

One strategy manager described a process adopted to assess the company's strategic position in relation to sustainability issues:

We looked at the corporate affairs strategy, first identifying issues common to all markets and then bigger issues preventing managers from reaching financial targets. Each strategic area head was asked, 'What would ease your licence to operate?' Every market looked at public policy, stakeholder dialogue and how it was addressing corporate citizenship. We increased awareness of the positive things being done. People had addressed corporate responsibility in different ways. We used the information to build strategic alternatives to reach our goals. (BCS16 – Senior business manager, Strategy)

Issue tracking is currently carried out at different levels within F&B companies, using diverse approaches and tools that are laid out in Table 6.1.

Overall, interviewees felt that more resources need to be dedicated to defining a best-practice framework to flag the status of issues at an early stage, and to developing issue-tracking tools.

Table 6.1 Issue tracking within food and beverage companies

Process	Examples	Benefits
Stakeholder dialogue	Relationships/partnerships with NGOS Local and national government Academic bodies Neighbourhood groups	Allows for understanding of viewpoints and issues of many diverse entities in different countries Companies can better define their approach and priorities, select objectives and define key performance indicators. If network of stakeholders is constantly updated to remain relevant, companies are less insular and inflexible and more able to make decisions well.
Networking	Future oriented organiza-tions (i.e. WBCSD, Global compact) Trade associations Industry groups and federations Personal contacts	Ensures active monitoring of issues Early awareness communica-tion at the non-competitive level
External expertise	Academic bodies Independent consultancies External PR agencies Corporate reputation monitors Press groups	Flag issues and through independent advisory boards, provide input on how to address the issues

Table 6.1   Issue tracking within food and beverage companies – *continued*

Tools	Examples	Benefits
Risk management reviews	Carried out by divisional directors of business units at operating companies on supply, environmental and safety risks Bi-annual/annual reviews of food issues (contaminants, GM, allergens) Focused forums up to several times a year	'Radar net' for emerging issues The business unit can take responsibility for defining how to tackle the issue Can be carried out on a continuous basis
Internet	In-company monitoring services enter and follow key words (brands and issues) Public discussion forums Rates of public queries	If issue comes up on a regular basis, it will be highlighted to management Momentum behind an issue is constantly monitored
Print and visual media	Intelligence scans NGO and media-watch mechanisms	Company media service monitors consolidates, analyses and classifies this information
Surveys	Scans of both internal and external views and opinions	Can be carried out and repeated on a regular basis
Database	Comprehensive list of probable potential or future issues	Keeps track of issues identified Can be constantly updated with information from the markets Facilitates the prioritization process at a later stage for large organizations with complex worldwide activities Ensures coordination across businesses

Issue mapping is the assessment of relevance and strategic fit with identified value drivers. Mapping builds an internal awareness of the stakeholders and business activities that are relevant to each issue. This allows the building of a business case on a more cognitive level.

Rather than producing a detailed quantification of their sustainability efforts, companies tend to create matrices to prioritize resources and efforts. This allows analysis of issue threats and opportunities, and facilitates structured discussion:

The relative importance of issues relevant to us was debated over a three-month period. Communication strategy meetings contributed to this process. External PR agencies also helped. In a decentralized company like ours, energy is going in all directions. It is essential to focus on areas of importance and persuade the key people that this is important. Done in a consistent and structured fashion, top managers will be convinced of the relevance of the issues to the economic sustainability of the business. (BCS37 – Senior business manager, Communications)

By submitting issues to the corporate function, using the routes we already mentioned, business units assure more holistic and long-term 'big picture' assessment. Making such a process operational necessitates the use of a framework for processing and managing knowledge; a leveraging of knowledge throughout the organization, expansion of knowledge based on existing expertise, and the acquisition of knowledge from partners. Where such informed prioritization goes on, if the environmental or social risk is high for the business, it will automatically be rated high on the company's agenda and sustainability issues become business risks earlier than otherwise would be the case.

A number of data management tools are used to inform the mapping process for environmental issues, such as the continuous measurement of material, energy and waste flows and emissions, as well as more *ad hoc* environmental impact assessment tools. The development and implementation of key environmental performance indicators (KPIs) had been part of an organizational learning process leading to greater understanding of sustainable development. KPIs for monitoring and controlling environmental externalities within the context of an environmental management system, for example, ISO 14000, were more commonly used in the industry than instruments and processes to monitor social issues mainly because the latter are perceived as more difficult to assess. Companies were increasingly looking towards standards such as AA1000, SA8000 for guidance in this regard. However sustainability managers regretted that quantification tools for intangibles were missing:

For a more effective mapping and prioritization effort, we need more information and better tools on to measure intangibles – for example, for

measuring the impact of relationships with NGOs and so on. (BCS47a
– Business manager, Supply chain)

Companies also benchmark internally and with other industries or
companies in order to assess the relative significance of an issue. For
example, during debates on obesity in the USA, concerning litigation
against fast-food companies for example, the sector drew parallels with
the experiences of the tobacco industry.

Companies we researched mostly tended to assess sustainability
issues informally. Few companies were using risk assessment processes,
internal and external, to prioritize their issues. Only the most evolved
companies use risk assessment tools including qualitative and quantitative assessments and parameters such as probability forecasts and
assessment of consequences. Again, few were prioritizing risk and/or
creating risk registers to be used as tracking tools, and where they
existed, they were not often used to their best advantage:

> *Our issue catalogue should be more upfront in the company. It is not
> widely known that it exists and how it is put together. Staff should think
> about issues more. Issue management is important – we are never speedy
> enough in identifying the real issues. We should anticipate them, take
> action, and develop strategy around them.* (BCS50 – Senior regional
> business unit manager, Marketing and sales)

> *Our approach is more reactive than necessary. There is no framework for
> flagging up the status at an early stage. More resources need to be devoted
> to this – and to developing related tools.* (BCS03 – Senior sustainability
> officer)

There was little evidence in the industry of auditing systems to scrutinize identified critical sustainability risks and establish whether action
plans are in place and are being implemented. Such schemes can
inform decisions about action related to the identified risk including
integration of priority issues to strategic decision-making processes.
Diageo had the most evolved approach – its so-called 'Navigate' system
allowed a business issue to be viewed from various angles including the
CSR angle.

F&B companies are thus still vulnerable to the prospect of issues
turning into a crisis, with little opportunity to resolve conflicts at as
early a stage as possible. This has higher cost implications, both in
terms of cash and reputation. Apart from believing that the way issues

are tracked, mapped and prioritized needed to be more transparent and more thoroughly understood in their companies, managers felt that companies should observe their competitors more closely in this regard:

We do not know how issues are being mapped and prioritized by peer groups and competitors either. This could eventually disadvantage our own competitiveness. (BCS10 – Senior business manager, Business development)

Aon's survey of the 50 F&B companies in 2006 found that 20 per cent of companies do not address the issue of reputation risk at board level, and there was little scenario planning for major brand-threatening incidents that could have severe financial impacts (Aon, 2006). Aon drew sobering conclusions about F&B industry lack of preparedness to deal with impending business risks. The Aon report also showed that risk management needed to be integrated across all functions and that high risk threats were not being acknowledged by senior managers.

6.2   Integrating issues into strategic decision-making

To convince decision-makers of the BCS, sustainability officers in the F&B sector mainly rely on interactive communications based on speeches, presentations and papers outlining concepts and plans. The BCS they have evolved is primarily focused on the concept and value drivers behind sustainability initiatives rather than on a fully completed business case with figures to back up the proposals:

I avoid referring to costs, and place the emphasis instead on product differentiation, competitiveness and investment to cut costs in the medium term. (BCS05 – Senior business manager, Communications)

Sustainability managers in the leading F&B companies said that their CEOs implicitly recognized a strong BCS based on reputation and licence to operate value constructs without a need for much further quantification:

We took certain decisions because of vision and found other ways of promoting sustainability objectives than quantification. Our CEO was not interested in quantifying. We chose to focus on key strategic areas and

> *tested the market for sustainability internally.* (BCS49a – Business manager, Supply chain)

But for business managers, monetary considerations can never truly be set aside:

> *I am trying to find out internally whether we have a way of trading off financial performance against money spent to support our sustainability initiatives. The answer will be that we do not have a formal mechanism for trading off, using judgement instead.* (BCS45b – Senior business manager, Corporate economist)

Putting a value on reputation loss (the strongest value driver for CSM) is a challenge that the sector has not tried to address and managers found this to be a shortcoming:

> *If it has been possible to value a brand, why should it not be possible to value reputation?* (BCS50 – Senior regional business unit manager, Marketing and sales)

> *There should be instruments for measuring sustainability impact. If you can do it for advertising, then you can do it for sustainability.* (BCS36 – Senior business manager, Finance)

F&B companies have made various mostly half hearted attempts to quantify sustainability benefits. Some had tried hard to reach some valid conclusions based on quantified data, but to no avail. One company had made considerable attempts to quantify the effect of applying sustainable practices in farming on specific relevant sustainability parameters, and had produced a thick stack of related reports only to realize that the four to five years' of data; farm and field level data, collected on five key crops did not show any dominant trend whatsoever. The supply chain manager's comment had a note of despondency:

> *It leaves us without a story to tell.* (BCS47c – Business manager, Supply chain)

The company is now considering looking at a different balance between business relevant and farm relevant measurements in relation to sustainability, based on a number of pilot projects.

Quite a few managers re-echoed the famous remark made by Einstein; 'Not everything that can be counted counts, and not everything that counts can be counted'. They were convinced that looking for figures at all costs missed the point. Indeed, we noted that the earlier companies were in their strategy making, the more their managers asked for figures quantifying the business case:

It is not always possible to translate things into money terms. It has more to do with vision – and the fact that if you do not do it, business value is at risk. (BCS49 – Senior business manager, Manufacturing and supply chain technology)

Quantification is subject to doubts and criticisms, as managers felt it sometimes provokes more debate than it resolves. There are of course some important exceptions; measurement tools to increase transparency are regarded as powerful support tools, since they certainly allow for a quantifiable argument for and endorsement of the BCS. Few managers in the industry would dispute the efficiencies achieved and costs saved by quantifying environmental compliance, applying targets and then measuring continuous improvement. Managers consider use of such tools as a 'no-brainer' tantamount to good management. Measuring the social dimensions of sustainability was considered much more of a challenge. With some issues such as child labour, managers pointed out that the normative, moral argument for doing the right thing is primordial.

Measurement without belief is not compelling. Some issues are not measurable in money terms, and not even always quantifiable – it is often simply the 'right thing to do', based on best practice and pending legislation. Making direct links between the investment and return on investment becomes exceedingly difficult. (BCS16 – Senior business manager, Strategy)

Interestingly, we found that once senior business managers are convinced of the BCS based on reputation and licence to operate value drivers, they are less convinced of the need for quantification than even the sustainability officers:

Quantification makes decision-makers go by short-term numbers, but benefits of sustainability are greater in the longer term. Measurements in the same short-term snapshot as financial performance will never tip the balance. There is never a single quantified reason for action on sustainability issues, but a network of reasons. (BCS16 – Senior business manager, Strategy)

Some senior business managers agreed that the boundaries of quantification needed to be pushed further, but on a very project-specific level:

It is important to measure financially as well as to measure intangibles. We need more information and better tools on how to measure the intangibles of relationships with NGOs and so on. (BCS16 – Senior business manager, Strategy)

Supply chain and sustainability managers clung to the belief that in specific areas, if they could show, with numbers, that sustainability action was having an impact on profitability, there would be powerful arguments to promote a BCS: Sustainability officers felt that by accompanying figures with intangible criteria, the BCS could gain considerable weight, but they were critical of the means currently available to them:

There is a need for new sets of indicators. The quantified argument is still important. The same rigorous assessment procedures should be applied to sustainability projects as to other projects, but both tangible (economic impact), and intangible (relationships with stakeholders), sources of value have to be looked at. (BCS49a – Business manager, Supply chain)

A food industry expert endorsed this view:

A story is needed and numbers are storytellers. To get onto the radar screen of sceptics, numbers are helpful. You could call it the carrot approach. Once on their radar screen, it you can make the case more nuanced. (BCSBM1)

Sustainability officers were concerned that normative and intuitive position of sustainability, no matter now strong, did not allow answers to hard-nosed questions from business people such as how much should be invested in corporate sustainability, and how the investment could be assessed, or even benchmarked, to assure continuous improvement. They felt they had far from exhausted the potential for quantification in their companies:

Measurement is the weak part of sustainability. There are too many indicators for environmental aspects. These are in need of harmonization. There are not enough for social aspects. This makes the business case much more difficult to explain. It is difficult to set objectives with concepts. We need to set social targets indicators and quantifiers. Figures are more expressive. (BCS32 – Sustainability officer)

Sustainability officers felt that quantification could be a risky business if corporate responsibility was not part of the overall business strategy, if there was no practical guidance for identifying potential priority risks and improvement opportunities along complex product chains, if there was no systematic measurement tool in place and if the measurement tool was not linked to established strategies and value drivers.

We produced the following schema (Figure 6.18) to elaborate on ways of approaching sustainability benefit measurement that allows for a business-specific approach.

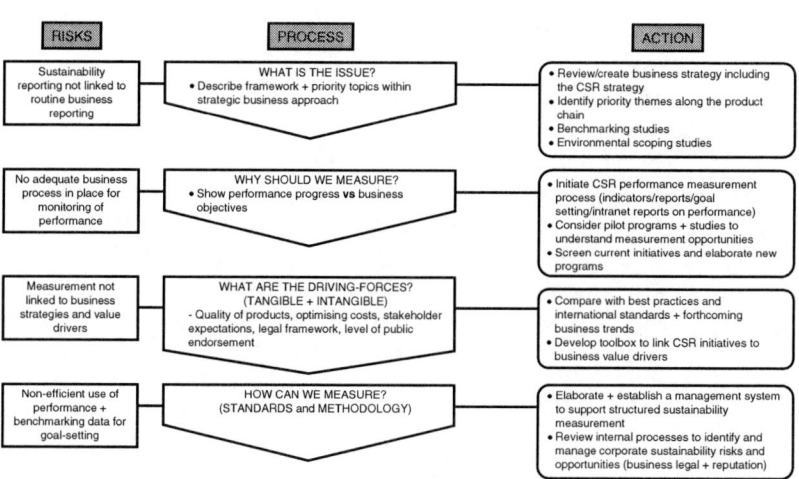

Figure 6.18 Elaborating the 'What?', 'Why?' and 'How?' of sustainability benefit measurement

However, there was little evidence of adoption of specific quantification techniques:

No particular method is being used currently to quantitatively evaluate the economic benefit from driving the business case for sustainability through our organization. (BCS45 – Senior business manager, Corporate economist)

We were once shown various quantification methods used for incorporating sustainability aspects into finance, but I am not aware of the extent of these being used in the company. (BCS50 – Senior regional business unit manager, Marketing and sales)

One company was adopting a shareholder value approach to its policies and practice, making the firm link between its sustainability activities and policies and final outcomes. The company had established a close link between its risk management and CSR programme, and could make a correlation between year-on-year reductions and weighted average risk facing the company.

A cross-sector study out at IMD in 2005 supports our findings (Salzmann *et al.*, 2005). IMD examined how important quantification is to managers, and how commonly it is carried out, as well as identifying its drivers and effects. The study concluded that companies quantify costs more frequently than benefits. This is because of the diffuse nature of benefits, the difficulty in attributing them to a specific initiative, and also to the immateriality of benefits, which have to first be leveraged into cost reductions or revenue increases, making the isolation of CSM effects extremely difficult.

Scenario-building has been used by some leading F&B companies to push issues into strategic decision-making, helping to build momentum around an issue, by facing strategic decision-makers with the consequences of inaction. For years, one food company was a target of intense NGO campaigns threatening to link the company's brands with their campaigns if the company did not take proactive measures to improve agricultural and business practice in its supply base for a certain product. The company developed a scenario to understand the potential financial impact should the company not take a pro-active stance. The company could then evaluate the effect on sales in Europe, particularly in the environmentally sensitive North-Western European and Nordic countries. Based on realistic scenarios for different campaign durations and recovery periods, a substantial sales loss on an annual basis was forecast, with a potentially severe trading contribution effect, due to non-recoverable fixed costs and extra spending on PR/advertising to counter the campaign.

Although the Aon study on the F&B industry (2005) stressed the importance of introducing more scenario management in the industry, we found mixed views about scenario-building amongst managers:

Scenario analysis is not for reporting to the outside. They sometimes depart from reality. Forecasts are very difficult to make in business today. They have to be reliable, not based on theory. In our company, it's even difficult to come up with a budget for next year. (BCS36 – Top management, Finance)

Managers discussed some novel approaches to bringing decision-making more in line with the long-term strategic objectives of sustainability:

We want to prove that a short-term campaign can bring the company to the wrong side of an issue, to state 'Here is the financial benefit from this short-term, but this will drive sales in a negative way long-term'. The management can then make the decision based on the full picture, and not only the short-term picture as it is today. (BCS08 – Senior business manager. Communications)

What is important is to work backwards to make a business model that makes a proposition viable – we can thus work out what the consumer will pay for a product in a country and then work backwards to a cost target. Sustainability is an essential cost of doing business that has to be compensated elsewhere. We can avoid consumer niches by ensuring that the more sustainable product costs the same. (BCS46 – Senior business manager, Marketing and sales)

6.3 Implementation: working with mindsets and getting managers on board

The following sections explore some applied aspects of sustainability strategy implementation that demonstrate the complexity of what companies are dealing with and how the business case is built on a very company-specific, and even department- or business unit-specific basis.

6.3.1 The framework

For successful issue integration into operations, better-practice companies work within an agreed set of policies and management systems. As we have pointed out, central to this are statements of principles

– codes of conduct, and values that provide a framework within which to operate. For the all important mindset change and culture re-orientation, managers felt that it was essential to involve business units in development of frameworks, in order to assure buy-in:

> *There should be no surprises. People at market level should be engaged in the process and an extensive review process for all documents needs to be undertaken. By the time something is introduced, the mindset has changed.* (BCS27 – Senior business manager, Supply chain)

Companies also establish position papers on the most important issues. As pointed out earlier, if a single issue is very significant; traceability, for example, then a focused strategy is articulated and a strategic action plan related to the issue is developed.

We asked business managers to identify which tools and systems in their company related to the concept of sustainable development or corporate social responsibility internally (see results in Figure 6.19). Interestingly, the response proportions relate almost exactly to the average of responses from all sectors in the cross-industry study. Managers had a high level of awareness of tools and systems devised to deal with such

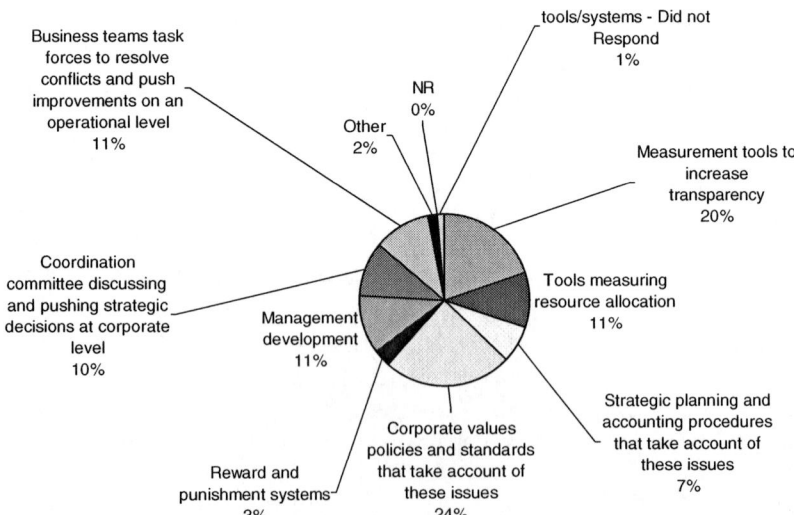

Figure 6.19 Tools and systems used by companies relating to the concept of sustainable development (responses from business managers – food and beverage industry)

issues in their companies. Managers are pragmatic people and if a practical and useful tool exists, they will generally adopt it willingly.

As can be observed, 24 per cent of responses related to corporate values, policies and standards that take account of sustainability issues. In interviews, managers gave more detail:

Tools are inherent to the company for direct costs. Softer issues are trickier. To take sustainability beyond compliance, you have to build a commitment and use mechanisms to get people to connect with a vision. (BCS46 – Senior business manager, Sales and marketing)

Tools are not necessarily the issue. The starting point is to create an awareness internally of the issues. This comes from working in several areas: the innovation phase, working on the mindset of people in the business, publicity, better articulation of policies and rationale, seeking partnerships. (BCS52 – Top management, Finance)

Clearly, tools that create more heightened internal awareness also create an operational framework within which the BCS can be promoted throughout the global organization.

The second most important contribution to a framework, with 20 per cent of responses in our survey, was the use of measurement tools to increase transparency. As mentioned earlier, these are measures, metrics and assessment systems that provide important feedback for a company's progress towards goals and targets, and are essential prerequisites to formulating a quantified business case in areas where quantification is possible. During our interview research, the phrase 'What gets measured, gets managed' was used so often by operational managers we interviewed that it left no doubt as to the importance to them of being able to measure as much as is possible, particularly environmental performance, in order to establish a robust business case for their actions. As margins come under extreme pressure in the competitive food industry environment, there is increasing interest from companies in achieving greater profitability through continuous improvement and more efficient operations; more efficient environmental management is one contributing factor. These factors contribute very positively to improving sustainability performance and often provide a solid business case for doing so. In fact, Bank Sarasin conducted research that showed that European and Japanese F&B companies had much higher levels of production efficiency than their US counterparts, mainly due to the more developed environmental management systems (EMSs) in these regions (Fawer-Wasser *et al.*, 2001).

Many such systems are company-specific, since companies tend to orient the development of measures and metrics to what is important for them. The following table sets out tools that are available to F&B companies to promote sustainability strategy roll out. We have retained the F&B empirical data results against those tools that were mentioned in the survey:

Table 6.2   Tools available to F&B companies to promote implementation of sustainability strategies

Tools to identify the BCS:	Tools to build the BCS:
• Stakeholder industry dialogue • Media screening • Surveys/public opinion polls • Benchmarking • Risk management tools	• Coordination committee discussing and pushing strategic decisions at corporate level (10% : 18%) • Business teams, task forces to resolve conflicts and push CSM (11% : 14%) • Strategic planning and accounting procedures that take account of environmental and/or social issues (7% : 8%)
Tools to implement the BCS:	**Tools to monitor and control implementation of the BCS:**
• Corporate values, policies and standards that take account of environmental issues (24% : 22%) • Reward and punishment systems (for example, salary partly based on social and/or environmental performance) (3% : 3%) • Management development (such as environmental training courses, workshops on SD with senior executives) (11% : 14%) • Sustainability/environmental innovation awards • Product stewardship • Communication tools to create awareness and understanding • Internal information systems/ services (e.g. Intranet, corporate TV, corporate magazines) • Sustainability indices and ratings • Sustainability reporting initiatives	• Measurement tools to increase transparency (such as measuring material and waste flows) (20% : 18%) • Tools measuring resource allocation (such as environmental expenditure) (11% : 4%) • Environmental (EHS) and/or social auditing • Eco-efficiency analysis • Environmental accounting • Due diligence environmental assessment

Note: Percentages indicate level of response from 116 general managers versus 19 sustainability officers.

Senior managers stressed the importance of obtaining buy-in from business units:

> *The corporate message on sustainability has to be received in a way that is relevant and modified based on region or country; otherwise it will not be effective. Operational units have an important role in developing and transmitting this message.* (Senior regional business unit manager – Marketing and sales)

> *The headquarters is far away from the operating companies – it is necessary to translate the message to people in charge of the operating company and give them the tools.* (BCS36 – Top management, Finance)

In the early stages of corporate sustainability strategy development, companies rely on the attitude and persuasive power of the senior staff member responsible for sustainability or corporate responsibility to drive the BCS. Indeed, in the course of our research we met with several sustainability officers who claimed that their job was to carry out basic networking through 'management by walking around'; taking on a subtle political role, leveraging opportunities to talk informally to key people about sustainability issues, events and potential strategies in the office corridors, and discreetly identifying allies within the organization. One officer referred to this process as 'setting the seeds'. The building of such informal internal alliances by the sustainability officer is regarded as a key success factor for roll out:

> *The sustainability officer needs to carry out internal marketing. Sustainability is a tool for knowledge building. Our sustainability officer has been travelling around to promote 'the case'. Our competitor has 19 people dedicated to travelling around testing sustainability – quality assessors – as well as others dedicated to sustainability at the centre.* (BCS11 – Senior business manager, Investor relations)

In several companies, senior officers within supply chain departments have been delegated the task of dealing with upstream sustainability concerns:

> *Building and implementing the business case for sustainability cannot be separated. It is a question of learning by doing, through a process*

of iteration and interaction. (BCS47a – Business manager, Supply chain)

The most innovative examples of learning by doing can be found deep in the supply chains of some global companies. One of the most effective ways used by the F&B industry leaders to create a network of sustainability champions is to use pilot demonstration projects and to have business managers working on sustainability issues directly during daily operations: pilot projects or focused actions effectively introduce the concepts of sustainability in a hands-on way, and allow sustainability officers to 'speak the language' of managers, while building on the motivation of managers to carry the concepts further throughout the organization:

> *We can try to find proof that we can be sustainable without jeopardising the bottom line through pilot projects. If profit can be maintained while being sustainable, this will be an unbelievably effective business case argument.* (BCS47a – Business manager, Supply chain)

The economic case for sustainability is not made in the abstract, or even with data from other companies. Companies want to apply it to their own data, and often only one operation at a time. If first experiments turn out well, they will do more. However, strategically, it is important that the first issue be chosen in such a way to 'guarantee' the result that will generate most interest.

The CEO of one of the 'younger' companies we researched greatly valued the companies' potential for learning for his company from such experimental work:

> *To close down our pilot sustainability projects would make us lose one of the main reasons why I stayed with this company for so long – the opportunities that the company has to create long-term value. This company offers incredible opportunities for innovation and sustainability concepts are part of this.* (BCS39 – Top management, CEO)

As Mark Twain once pointed out, 'Few things are harder to put up with than a good example'. Therefore, with a view to understanding how a business case for sustainable agriculture might be built effectively, we propose examining some corporate efforts to do just that in our next section.

6.3.2 *Working business case examples: sustainable agriculture*

We discussed many of the challenges of sustainable agriculture already in Chapter 3. Leaders in the industry have recognized the need for a change of mindset in the industry regarding sustainable agriculture, and for the food industry to speak out on the challenges posed by agricultural production systems. Unilever created its sustainable agriculture initiative in the mid-1990s, its primary concern being continued access in the future to its key raw materials. The company is experimenting with pilot sustainable agriculture projects within its sustainable agriculture initiative, testing ten broad indicators of sustainability on key crops such as tea, oil palm, tomatoes, spinach and peas with a view to creating sustainable standards for these crops (Unilever, 2002b). Unilever is also assessing the world market and supply chains with the intention of establishing market mechanisms to enable the sourcing of raw materials from sustainable suppliers without losing competitive advantage. The ambition is to integrate sustainability much more robustly within the business:

Our sustainability group is taking a supply chain approach. This will lead to good impacts in terms of integrating sustainability into the supply chain. There will gradually be a move from supply chain ownership to ownership by everyone. (BCS48 – Senior business manager, Strategy and business development)

By using local partners' know-how jointly to develop sustainable agriculture best-practice guidelines for farmers, and then providing information to those who shape the market; such as other producers, buyers, processors and consumers, the objective to gradually create market mechanisms that favour sustainable practice can be achieved. Unilever is working on imbedding sustainability in the corporate agenda by placing heads of leading brands and business units on a learning curve. Value chain analysis can, in Unilever's view, support the business case for sustainable sourcing:

There are many opportunities to improve, cut costs and promote food safety, limit unnecessary storage, preventing mixing or cross contaminations. Value chain analysis can greatly help with breaking down barriers with supply chain managers. (BCS47a – Business manager, Supply chain)

By defining the main value activities throughout the value chain, and analyzing the costs of each step, it becomes possible to identify areas where a surplus value for consumers can be created, thus justifying a price premium for a unique product. This allows for product differentiation. By using this concept, purchasing criteria for consumers and stakeholders can be defined in terms of value, not only in economic terms, but also as social and environmental values for stakeholders. The company is reaching a profound understanding of how non-economic value is generated and how to manage these processes.

In collaboration with the Forum for CSM at IMD, Unilever carried out a value chain analysis in the framework of its own sustainable agriculture initiative. A focus group was chosen, which included Unilever agronomists, and supply chain professionals such as buyers/ purchasing officers. Buyers in the F&B industry are at the centre of corporate accountability for suppliers' behaviour and many officers in this function are unaccustomed to taking sustainability criteria into consideration. Many are simply unfamiliar with application of sustainability concepts in their daily work. However, buyers generally have a good understanding of local issues. Thus, once they are engaged and convinced of the concepts and their application, they can ensure that these principles are communicated and applied throughout the value chain. At a special workshop held at Unilever for these managers, value chain analysis was carried out in multidisciplinary teams. In this learning-by-doing experiment, the main take-home value for managers participating in these hands on workshops was the recognition that redesigning the value chain provided more cost-saving opportunities than cost increases. Also, the managers saw that roll-out challenges were probably not insurmountable, and well within the control and sphere of influence of the company. Unilever managers shared with us the important factors for failure or success in the implementation of such strategies as described above:

- Programme leader with dedicated budget and resources
- Clear definition of the sustainable development principles relevant for the initiative
- Indicators on how to measure success
- Set priorities, by not starting too many projects – first get experience, build understanding and success, and then extend
- Senior ownership for each of the sustainable development initiatives by a business group and/or operating companies

- Vision (defined early on) of how to make it part of the way the company does business in the future
- Early involvement of external experts and stakeholders

The company has learnt not to rely only on internal expertise but to include stakeholders primarily at a local level:

> *They have relevant know-how and understanding of local issues. Involve the best locally available NGO and where possible leverage cooperation with global NGOs if they have resources on the ground.* (Business manager, Supply chain)

This BCS should not necessarily assume higher profits, sales or margins. By providing very specific examples, it is hoped that breakthroughs in sustainability initiatives can be achieved with either positive or neutral impact on the bottom line:

> *It would be very compelling if there were initiatives that just had benefits and no cost, or that showed saving of costs in the production process, or for an identical product, produced cost savings due to sustainable action.* (Senior business manager, Strategy)

Unilever is going for what one of its managers termed the 'opportunity argument':

> *If we succeed in building a business model that is profitable, adds to natural capital and enhances social improvement, then who could compete with that? Our experiments show: 'If you want to, you can'.* (Business manager, Supply chain)

Analyzing the business case for sustainable agriculture initiatives, and creating the right tools and instruments to implement them and roll them out to pilot markets, is a time-consuming initiative for those championing the cause. Efforts to create sustainable practices in the supply chain contribute to the continuous improvement capabilities of businesses and do not imply the development of new sets of skills. Often, it simply amounts to good management practices being implemented by organizations.

One of our supply chain interviewees had been engaged in a process over several years of promoting the business case for sustainable agriculture and gaining buy-in from a network of future champions identified throughout the business that could assure rollout. At the outset, his first defined objective was to create a coalition, a group of influential managers with similar values. These coalitions eventually, either formally or informally, influenced the decision-making apparatus within the organization. Over time, it became clear that this investment of substantial time had paid dividends in terms of gaining buy-in to the business relevance of sustainability in his organization.

During the period of research, a major strategic move affected the business case for sustainable agriculture at Nestlé. Nestlé repositioned itself from being a world leader in F&B to being, primarily, a world leader as a nutrition-focused, health and 'wellness' company. This implied sometimes substantial changes in the business model. Productivity, quality enhancement, and also sustainability were placed at the core of Nestlé's vision for growth, and this was increasingly reflected in internal discussion about sustainable development within the company involving Nestlé's CEO. Risk management involving supply chain sustainability was clearly increasingly in the company's business interest, for example. During our study, the company was developing a tool to help assess and manage the risks of direct procurement of agricultural raw materials to enhance supply chain sustainability.

By ensuring ownership of sustainable agriculture pilot projects by project leaders, we noted that these leaders converted into veritable ambassadors of sustainability in organizations. Also, by setting up pilot projects, it is possible to introduce and test the key performance indicators necessary to define the relevant sustainability issues and measure the success of the pilot initiatives.

Unilever, Nestlé and Danone collaborated to set up a pre-competitive platform to support the development of sustainable agriculture in 2001 – the Sustainable Agriculture Initiative (SAI).[9] This platform has clearly defined objectives. It was created to ensure that:

- best practices in sustainable agriculture are shared and overall standards improved;
- a set of international standards for sustainable agriculture could eventually be introduced;
- a common understanding of threats to the future of the industry is reached;
- synergies on supply chain management on a non-competitive level are identified;

- companies that are working on sustainability agriculture are not at a significant competitive advantage.

The creation of a horizontal alliance such as the SAI suggests that the industry requires a more level playing field in order to move more rapidly to the creation of sustainable supply chains. At the time of writing, some 20 global companies had joined the SAI and the platform had four working groups in charge of generating pilot guidelines for sustainable agricultural practices for dairy, cereals, coffee and palm oil products. The main challenge is to encourage leading international companies to share their experience and knowledge in open and transparent dialogue. At an early stage, the varying nature and level of representation at SAI meetings (communications and PR experts, as well as supply-chain professionals) was a barrier, since progress had to be made in areas demanding specific technical expertise. As time went by, the balance started to work better and working groups achieved progress:

> *We have had some very positive outcomes from steps taken at extremely influential points in the supply chain.* (BCS47 – Business manager, Supply chain)

The biggest single challenge for the SAI platform is to break down barriers in communication so that companies will effectively 'show and tell' in a transparent way that what they are doing is better than their competitors in the sustainability area. It is not surprising that it is a challenge to get companies behaviourally accustomed to fierce competitive and defensive stances regarding product and process information to open up to their competitors in this way. On the other hand, we remarked in our later discussions that the dividing line between what was competitive and non-competitive had started to become fuzzy. This, according to some managers, may be owing to an increased recognition of sustainability as a competitive advantage in some companies, something that was not a factor at the outset of the research, when we were consistently told that no company was competing on the strength of their sustainability performance.

Not all stakeholders were convinced of the industry approach to sustainable agriculture; one retailer interviewed commented sceptically:

> *For the moment EurepGAP is a more convincing approach than SAI. The manufacturing industry has been trying to put standards in*

place for years and have so far failed. They are only making small steps...

Clearly, there is still a very long way to go, but success of the SAI initiative would be a key contributing factor to breaking down the competitive barriers impeding the application of sustainability standards in supply chains across the industry.

We observed during the period of research that while there were very promising pilot projects, few if any were hitting the mainstream. Business managers were sceptical about the scaling up potential, suggesting that the pilot projects had not reached commercial viability. Some held the view that to assess sustainable agriculture, it is necessary to look towards the farming community and commodity processors, bearing in mind that food-processing companies are not in the commodities business. Changing complex frameworks is a very long-term investment of time. Ultimately, even if they can apply pressure, the multinationals are not the owners of their suppliers' operations:

> *We can't go into a country and dictate. We can only show how we believe how it should be done. We hope to create momentum. It will take 20 years to have an impact – you can't change agricultural practices quickly in emerging markets.* (BCS26 – Senior regional business manager, Purchasing)

Some managers were sceptical and saw the pilot projects as a 'PR exercise':

> *Our sustainability projects will not have much impact. They are more publicity stunts than changing fundamentally how business is done. They are restricted demonstration projects to show NGOs that we are doing something. There is a difference between demonstration and what is actually being done.* (BCS26 – Senior regional business unit manager, Purchasing)

A food industry expert we interviewed wondered whether the advantages of collective action, in the case of the SAI, would surpass the first mover advantages of being a 'front-runner'. Good question – and the answer is not yet forthcoming....

Also out of concern with the fact that it is so difficult for pilot projects to reach the mainstream, Unilever has participated in setting up the Sustainable Food Laboratory (SFL) in the context of a Global Leadership Initiative.[10] Its purpose is to accelerate the movement of food produced in a sustainable way from niche to mainstream by creating more prototypes and pilot projects that can become large, mainstream and, most importantly, economically sustainable for all actors in the chain. The SFL adopts a holistic approach born out of a need for collaboration between key players in order to resolve the key food chain dilemmas leading to the global 'race to the bottom' in the industry. It is a coalition not only of global companies, but also NGOs, policy organizations, and other stakeholders, and has it has designed six initiatives that are destined to reverse this race to the bottom in the food production cycle. Again, learning by doing is the primary focus of the Sustainable Food Lab. The fact that some major food and retail companies (Unilever, Starbucks, US Food Service, Carrefour) have joined this initiative demonstrates that these organizations understand that the current food system brings its fair share of risks and that sustainable agriculture is increasingly being regarded as a strategic issue. Participants in the SFL feel that the only way of achieving some effect is to work with others to shift mental models and design an alternative sustainable food system while engineering the social capacity to absorb change.

However, participation from the industry is scant as yet, even if some important players are on board. Nevertheless, the SFL is working both upstream and downstream, and is providing organizational learning at a contextual level. Reviewing the many questions on purpose, design, objectives and process in reports from meetings of participants indicates that the initiative is at the start of a very long journey (Sustainable Food Laboratory, 2005a and b). The ambitious targets will be extremely difficult to meet and not all major food companies were convinced:

> *For me the Sustainable Food Lab seems a fuzzy initiative. It is difficult for a business manager like me to engage in such a time-consuming 'think-tank' process. SAI is a more efficient way forward. People believe in the methodology and the US is increasingly interested.* (BCS27 – Senior business manager, Supply chain)

In 2007, a memorandum of understanding for collaboration was signed between the SAI and the SFL. At the time of concluding our study it seemed that mainstreaming pilot projects still appeared to be a long way off. As we go to press, while the interest of major retailers in, say the SFL, was encouraging, substantial increases in food prices worldwide and a threatening world recession was likely to impact the pace at which either SAI or SFL advanced the cause of sustainable agriculture. The jury was still out on the extent of impact.

6.3.3 Partnerships, stakeholder dialogue and engagement

We have mentioned that the nature of business – NGO relationships has been evolving to include opportunities for close collaboration. Increasingly partnerships and stakeholder dialogue bring together one or more businesses with one or more NGOs, sometimes also including government agencies (Webster, 2004). It is probably in the F&B industry that many leading examples of industry public/private partnerships can be found, for example:

- Unilever's partnership with Ghana's health ministry and UNICEF to increase consumption of a low-cost brand of salt (Annapurna) fortified with iodine in Ghana
- P&G's NutriStar, a drink developed with the United Nations Children's Fund that addresses micronutrient deficiency in school age children.
- Chiquita's partnership with the Rainforest Alliance to certify its banana plantations for application of social and environmental standards.[11]
- The Coca-Cola Company, McDonald's and Unilever's work in 2000 with Greenpeace, UNEP and their suppliers to develop, test and deploy hydrofluorocarbon-free[12] refrigeration technologies – the 'Refrigerants Naturally' initiative.[13]
- The Roundtable on Sustainable Palm Oil; an initiative of Aarhus United, Migros, MPOA, Golden Hope Plantations, Sainsbury's, Unilever and WWF that promotes the growth and use of sustainable palm oil through co-operation within the palm oil chain and an open dialogue with its stakeholders.[14]

In many of these cases, companies have been going through a first experience in working closely with NGOs to attain a sustainability objective; 'living with the enemy' as some managers referred to it:

NGOs are challenging. We try to find solutions but there are always sticking points. Sometimes, I wonder whether things will ever be fully agreed. The process can be very bureaucratic and we can, at times, lose sight of the main objective. Some stakeholders are inflexible and are unwilling to change. (BCS31 – Business manager, Purchasing)

But in general, managers engaged in partnership alliances reported how positive these experiences had been, primarily in terms of changing mindsets within the company and also modifying business practices. And in our survey, when managers were asked what works best to improve their relationships with stakeholders, many managers found that the choices we offered; public relations, listening more to ideas and feedback, donations, greater transparency, did not adequately cover the ground. Thus, under the 'other' option given in the questionnaire, respondents invariably added such approaches as 'partnerships/alliances', 'joint projects', and 'setting up common forums' as being some of the most effective mechanisms (see Figure 6.20).

But are such initiatives successful? Again, the answer is; it depends. In Chiquita's case, a robust business case has proved itself through the partnership with the Rainforest Alliance. The US$20 million spent to certify its farms under the Rainforest Alliance standard has been more than repaid in cost savings from reduced pesticide expenditure and recycling. Also, the lower risk profile has allowed the company to refinance some debt allowing savings in interest payments. Other efforts were less successful for example, Starbucks' partnership with Oxfam, initially proclaimed as a collaboration for sharing ideas on tackling coffee crises and regaled by the press for its potential to have real impact should it be scaled up. The partnership prematurely ended with Starbucks being accused of 'greenwash' and Oxfam of being partisan.

However, all of these start-up efforts show a willingness by F&B companies to deal better with their stakeholder environment. Managers felt

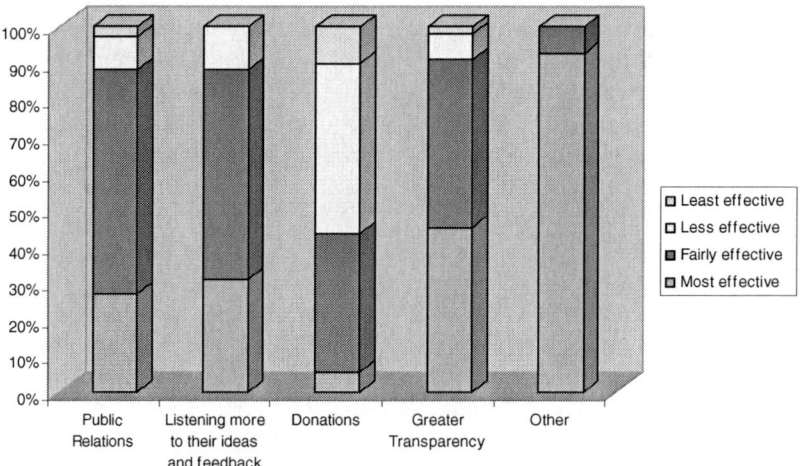

Figure 6.20 Most effective means of improving relationships with stakeholders

that such initiatives bring real opportunities for company learning that make managers think of the world usually substantially differently than if no partnership had ever been instigated. Through dialogue and partnerships, companies are exposed to multiple points of view on different issues. Companies also learn how to communicate with their stakeholders 'using their language'. Managers reported changes in mindset as a result of engagement in partnerships, but also innovation and, ultimately, modifications to the more tried and true business models:

Our multi-stakeholder process is a journey – an education process and we are learning how far upstream we can go. (BCS31 – Business manager, Purchasing)

Faced with the dizzying rate of disintegration of fish stocks in the world's global fisheries, Unilever, the world's largest buyer of seafood, entered a partnership with WWF to create the Marine Stewardship Council (MSC) in 1997.[15] The objective was to attempt to reverse the decline in world fisheries and to assure long-term sustainability of global fish stocks by putting into place an environmental standard for sustainable and well-managed fisheries. The MSC developed a fisheries certification scheme that could endorse sustainable fisheries management and operational practice. This built on work already done by WWF and other corporations on forestry conservation and certification through the Forestry Stewardship Council.[16] In 1999, the MSC began to operate independently as an independent, global, non-profit organization (Steger *et al.*, 2006; Unilever, 2002a).

This unique green-business partnership is much cited as an example of how NGOs and corporations can work together to achieve mutually beneficial objectives (Steger and Raedler, 1999a, 1999b; Steger *et al.*, 2006).[17] Shoppers can identify the distinctive MSC logo on packaging and thus choose fish products from well-managed fisheries. In this way, market forces are harnessed to encourage a more responsible approach to fishing worldwide.

Unilever undertook to buy all its fish from sustainable sources by 2005, and introduced a 'traffic-light' system, a sustainability assessment tool based on the FAO's Code of Conduct to ensure that fisheries were classed according to their level of sustainable management. However, by late 2003, reaching the target was looking more and more challenging and in 2003, the company stated publicly that it was unlikely to meet this objective. The conversion to sustainable fisheries had turned out to be a long and painful process. By the end of 2005, it looked as if only 60 per cent sustainable sourcing was feasible; given the will of the company to succeed, this was a reflection of just how difficult it is to get certified fisheries onboard with such schemes. UK consumers showed substantial consumer resistance to efforts to change their traditional cod consumption habits (Jones, 2003a). Second, the consumer was receiving confusing messages. Competition between supermarkets actually drove down the price of cod, making it even cheaper than *hoki*, the sustainable alternative. Far from sparse supply, confused consumers saw gluts of cod in the supermarkets, and given the slow growth of sustainable fisheries, there was a contrasting dearth of sustainable fish on the shelves. This contradicted the message that Unilever and the MSC were trying to give about cod as an endangered species. Proof, yet again, that price and taste take precedence over sustainability concerns, except for a minority of consumers, and that sustainability is a 'tough sell'.

This case demonstrates the extent of the challenges linked to mainstreaming the BCS within organizations, even where a business case for a sustainability agenda is strong since based on dwindling supplies of a key raw material in a mid-term framework. For Unilever, the learning curve was steep. The methodology used to assess fish stocks has heightened company awareness of the status of fish stocks and fisheries worldwide, but also provided a benchmark for the greater issue of sustainable agriculture:

> *The difficulty is to get the first model going. In Unilever, the fish issue brought everything else into focus. The fish purchasing officers at Unilever spent a lot of time on this strategic issue because it was no longer a long-term issue but had become uncomfortably short-term. In agriculture, the short-term issue is less clear.* (Senior business manager, Manufacturing and supply chain technology)

While other F&B companies told us that they saw Unilever's missed objective as a failure, managers at Unilever emphasized instead the incomparable opportunities for organizational learning:

> *We are on a journey. The most important aspect of this ambitious target setting was to be moving purposefully in an agreed direction. There is a lot of learning for the organization on the way.* (BCS47a – Business manager, Supply chain)

Although Unilever is almost out of the fish business today, the MSC has attracted new partners, including major retailers such as Walmart, to their certification schemes. The withdrawal of Unilever as a major leading figure and first mover has not overly impacted the evolution of the initiative. The inclusion of major mainstream retail chains is making a significant difference to the fish sourcing BCS in the fish-processing industry.

Managers informed us that the *hoki* experience demonstrated to Unilever that sustainability had to be used to enhance other aspects of the brand such as taste, quality or, indeed, health. Unless consumers see a personal benefit for themselves, sustainability will effectively probably 'not sell'. The company decided to experiment with combining sustainability with other concepts and to try new marketing approaches. Therefore, downstream also, setting up a demonstration example can assist learning immeasurably:

> *To convince marketers, it will be important to create a demonstration case where you can illustrate how this can be done successfully. It is important to get away from the generic BCS and demonstrate to people that it works. The only way of opening minds is to show the opportunity and advantage that it can give the company.* (Business manager, Marketing and sales)

Some managers were wholly convinced that the future lay in linking personal benefits to sustainability:

> *Consumers are sensitive to what they are eating – healthy eating is the way to go. The emotional connotation may slip over into other areas and maybe there will be a trickle down effect that will take time. There may be a second wave around not so personal issues, such as sustainability.* (BCS30 – Senior regional business unit manager, Purchasing)

Interestingly, marketing officers interviewed at Unilever already had a more evolved approach than the traditional marketing dismissal of sustainability as 'hard to sell' that we found in other companies:

> *The consumer trigger is 'What's in it for me?' If sustainability cannot be translated into a personal benefit for the consumer, then there will never be a mass market for it. If we use health as a conduit and at the same time if the consumer feels as if she is doing something for the world, then this enhances the brand. To work out the cost issue, we have to look at the total business system.* (Senior business manager, Marketing, Unilever)

We are looking at what is missing in the toolkit for marketers, to help marketers to integrate this concept into their operations. The question is how can marketers be more comfortable with extending the emotions they are used to dealing with to sustainability issues? (Senior sustainability officer, Unilever)

Unilever's efforts, as well as other companies' initiatives such as the linking of quality to sustainability through Nespresso's AAA program for sustainable coffee may bring solutions to help marketers overcome the difficulties of 'selling sustainability'. Although Nespresso is a company that is autonomous from Nestlé, there are nevertheless close relationships between the two companies. The Nespresso partnership with the Rainforest Alliance around 'AAA' sustainable coffee, as it is termed, has gone a long way to changing mindsets within Nestlé itself. According to Nestlé managers, since its inception, the partnership has helped their organization to move towards a much more open culture regarding sustainability concepts.

6.3.4 Training and competence building

Senior managers recognized the importance of providing training and development programmes to ensure that the required skills and attitudes receptive to sustainability and corporate social responsibility are cultivated within organizations (DTI and Corporate Responsibility Group, 2003). However, sustainability officers did not consider that specific management courses on sustainability issues were an effective means of rolling out BCS messages internally since, with generic training modules, it is difficult to show managers specifically how sustainability is directly relevant to their work, which as we have mentioned is in their view a key to successful roll out. Conversely, managers felt that corporate training should primarily aim to reinforce values in managers' minds above all else. A senior finance manager said:

You need people in the organization that have a prepared mindset. To shift the paradigm, it is a process of education, of filtering people in progressively, not forcing. A 'Trojan Horse' – slow but determined – approach. (BCS14 – Senior business manager, Finance)

Time and again during the interview process, managers reiterated the need for appropriate internal value orientation. A higher emphasis clearly needed to be placed on employee training to increase the value alignment and internal competencies.

Training also needed to be applied from top management down to shop-floor level:

Training needs to be holistic and should touch all layers of management. Skipping over layers is a potential problem if you really want to change mindset. The concept must be interpreted such that everyone will be on board. (BCS10 – Senior business manager, Business Development)

Sceptical managers who expressed reticence about training tended to ask 'what comes first, the chicken or the egg?':

There is no current need to improve knowledge and skills as yet; our sustainable development initiatives are at an early stage and have yet to demonstrate their commercial viability. I am not sure I believe in the triple bottom line – it is not a question of black or white. One could have a philosophical discussion of what business is truly about in this context. (BCS45 – Senior business manager, Corporate economist)

Senior managers at more progressive companies expressed a commitment to increasing personal responsibility amongst employees in a gradual way so as not to deviate from the business objective too radically:

It has to be somewhat of a softly-softly approach as you cannot impose it; reactions are too drastic if you are deviating too much from the status quo. (BCS14 – Senior business manager, Finance)

Several managers were unconvinced that the requisite time could be taken from profit orientation for awareness building, since it curtailed limited time available for focus on the short term:

Often the company is in crisis mode due to market share considerations. It is difficult to take whole half days – which is what is needed for strategy building on sustainability or indeed training – and reflect on where we are with this. (BCS13 – Senior business manager, Innovation)

To overcome this constraint to some extent, leading companies use a 'train the trainer' approach to build sustainability awareness and integrate it into business operations. A large part of one company's training in this area was given by in-company managers. The company arranged for function-specific training built on very pragmatic business cases specifically oriented towards the function in order to illustrate business relevance, but it also started hierarchically from the upper echelons of that function. This allowed for the 'train the trainers' approach to be implemented at a later stage and had other advantages. Time can be lost operationally by introducing new ways of doing things at too low a level in organizations. Generally, education starts with top management, then top directors, then is cascaded downwards. Some companies had learnt the hard way:

> *We started at too low a level in the organization – we didn't involve site managers and brought their staff from the sites to the centre for an introduction course instead of arranging this locally. Later, we had no buy in at management level and all the effort was wasted. To penetrate beyond the management layer, bring the manager on board first.* (BCS12 – Senior sustainability officer)

F&B companies generally may need to train their human resources professionals and purchasing managers first and foremost, while other industries may have other priorities.

For pilot project management or labour relations, there are specific new requirements to train managers in informal skills such as conflict resolution, dialogue and facilitation owing to the stakeholder engagement activities implied by these activities. Business managers at one company confirmed that a move to sustainability agriculture involving third-party development in tandem with a strategic business move out of direct sourcing had generated a need to fill new functions within the team – a coaching function – training suppliers how to follow newly established guidelines and improve upon weak points, and an audit function. Companies have even used innovative board games in training so as to place managers in more or less complex situations requiring new approaches to dealing with problem situations generated by sustainability issues. The companies using this method regarded it as an effective way of getting managers to 'play the game' and indirectly to experience a management situation using a sustainability filter.

F&B companies are at an early stage in their processes where training and competence building in sustainability and sustainability management are concerned, and we identified significant gaps in this area:

An awareness/introduction programme linked to training was developed but has not yet been delivered. It depends on corporate strategic buy-in. (BCS42 – Senior sustainability officer)

Figure 6.21 summarizes the many-pronged potential that food and beverage companies have to change mindsets regarding the application of CSR concepts in their organizations (see also CSR Europe, 2003a):

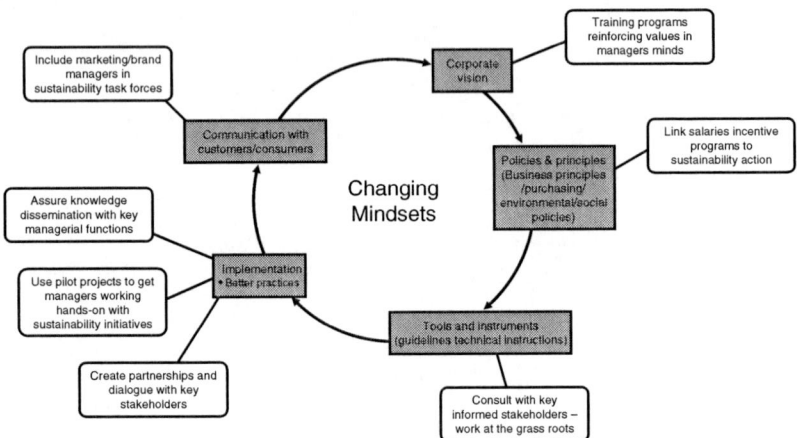

Figure 6.21 Changing manager's mindsets

Managers are starting proactively to demand training: many of our interviewees recognized the need for more systematic training on corporate responsibility issues, and certain functions – such as investor relations – were clearly aware of their own shortcomings in this respect.

Our discussion underlines the need for strong human resource departments in F&B companies:

HR is a countervailing force and balancing element to the businesses. In our company there is the Chairman and then the COO, CFO and HR secretariat underneath him all at the same level, on par with one another.

This structure makes us think twice about taking sustainability short cuts. (BCS14 – Senior business manager, Finance)

However, even in some of the largest and most prestigious companies, we learnt that managers regarded the HR function as weak:

Traditionally, the HR dimension in our organization has not been strong. HR was there to support line-management functions. Attitudes are slowly changing; a professional HR organization can add value to a company. (BCS24 – Senior sustainability officer)

When we were setting up interviews for the BCS project, sustainability managers, interestingly, did not immediately see HR as an obvious choice for talking to us about the sustainability strategies of their organizations. A possible explanation is the fact that many companies were still struggling with the challenges of formulating sustainability strategies, and had not yet moved to consider full roll out implications.

6.3.5 Evaluation and reward systems

According to sustainability officers, incorporating responsibility for environmental and social issues into employee job descriptions, job review and reward systems is a major prerequisite, rather *the* major prerequisite, for mainstreaming sustainability management into operations. However, even the most progressive companies had not moved to this level of integration. Including environmental and social criteria in assessment processes ensures that addressing sustainability issues happens from the bottom up, without direct top management intervention. The sustainability officers we interviewed argued that it is an essential aspect of internal promotion of the business case. The positive offshoot of mainstreaming in this way is that employees thus come up with creative and innovative solutions to social and environmental problems based on their practical experience in the field. In other words, solutions are not 'cooked up' at the corporate headquarters and imposed on individuals who have not bought into the process.

Clearly established targets can help business units to put sustainable practice in place. Business managers interviewed felt that agreeing targets for different businesses to implement a number of practices was paramount to the successful roll out of the BCS, thus ensuring that plans for sustainability action become an integrated part of the business model. Managers emphasized the importance of targets as a requirement for success with any business strategy:

> *We have a tool that sets specific targets for people. Target achievement is tied to corporate audits and the yearly bonus system at local level. So sustainability becomes a part of everyday operations.* (BCS27 – Senior business manager, Supply chain)

Most companies in the F&B industry are not moving towards such an integrated approach although companies recognized the need to develop the performance indicators around sustainability concepts so that the link could be made to recognition and rewards:

> *Given that sustainability has not been translated into performance indicators for the company, it is not yet part of an operational performance review system.* (BCS49 – Senior business manager, Manufacturing and supply chain technology)

There is potential, for example, to include sustainability achievement as a factor in in-company awards for innovation. This would diversify the focus adding to the existing criteria of marketplace success and roll out and would almost certainly change the way sustainability is viewed within companies.

Nevertheless, some companies prove that it can be done. In one, we observed that goals based on sustainable development were included in their company goal-setting and management-appraisal process (MAP). In another, sustainability was part of the manager's balanced scorecard.[18] However, applied research on the food industry has revealed that the traditional balanced scorecard has tended to prioritize traditional aspects such as finance, customers and employees but neglect aspects such as supply chain management, or even environmental performance.

Again, managers blamed the lack of an integrated approach on the decentralized character of management structures in the sector. Notwithstanding the current situation, several senior managers felt this problem needed to be further addressed as a matter of priority in future management reviews:

> *To break down some of the barriers, managers at operating companies and marketers need personal targets that tie their pay to doing certain things. Otherwise, you are fighting a losing battle. But we are not at this*

stage yet. Our incentive system is still linked only to sales and profits. (BCS45 – Senior business manager, Corporate economist)

But in general, managers were sceptical about the system changing:

There is still a reigning climate of 'I am judged on facts and figures and that is where I get my salary and bonus'. Let's say I don't see this changing overnight. (BCS27 – Senior business manager, Supply chain)

If a manager were meeting targets but yet had a lot of unaddressed external issues on the agenda, management would be concerned but it would not constitute a reason for firing the person, but if the problem were vice-versa, it would be different. (BCS16 – Senior business manager, Strategy)

The ability to execute strategy well is a source of competitive advantage and people are essential contributors to successful strategy implementation. A 2001 Financial Times survey of 400 US companies demonstrated that the ability to execute successfully has an impact on financial performance ten times greater than strategic choice (Becker *et al.*, 2001). The conclusion of the research was that companies are generally adept at choosing the right strategy, and that this is not really the differentiating factor. What matters is the ability to execute strategy. We suggest that given the absence, in most cases, of appropriate evaluation and reward systems related to sustainability objectives, companies are unlikely to fully succeed with their strategic focus for sustainability even if they have included sustainability in corporate strategy. This is the ultimate barrier to roll out of sustainability strategies. As one manager put it:

The main barrier for me is the inability of people to understand and implement. It is mainly a people issue and not a money issue. Unfortunately, unless there is a risk for themselves, people do not move. (BCS27 – Senior business manager, Supply chain)

The Financial Times research further shows that organizations that have performance measurement systems, such as balanced scorecards, rated the strategic focus of their employees significantly higher than organizations that based evaluation on financial data alone. When organizations' rewards, development and appraisal systems are oriented towards the execution of the company strategy, the strategic focus of employees is sharpened. Naturally, if sustainability is part of this equation, there is more of a business case for managers to come up with creative ways of addressing the related issues.

6.3.6 The internal communications strategy

Sustainability officers felt strongly that, apart from an external communications approach, a good internal communications strategy must go hand in hand with the sustainability strategy. Often, though, the emphasis is on using sustainability to promote the company in external communications.

A study carried out by Lewis (2004) reached the conclusion that, in the food industry in Germany, there was generally a high level of confusion about environmental issues amongst German food industry managers. This was primarily due to the ambiguity and complexity of both issues and impacts of diverse food scandals such as GMOs, BSE, foot and mouth disease and so on. He found that this had implications for the management and organization of companies; in particular, the organizational information structure. He recommended the inclusion of all employees in the search for information, but also more intense information exchange between employees. He also recommended the exchange of views and opinions on a regular basis with a variety of stakeholders. This very much endorses our findings so far; that the most effective contributing factor to heightened awareness amongst employees is process-related. However, a number of tools are being

Table 6.3   Tools used in the food and beverage sector to promote sustainability internally in companies

Tools used	Advantages
Awareness raising sessions such as site events, function specifics events	Engages managers and other staff in the process
Intranet/internal websites	Cross-fertilization: gives direct access to information and success stories about sustainability initiatives around the world
Quarterly business reviews/corporate news bulletins/ newsletters	Can be exploited to disseminate information about sustainability initiatives
Tailor-made training sessions Sustainability board games	Can get managers thinking of solutions to sustainability dilemmas

used to promote sustainability strategies internally in F&B companies as part of the internal communications strategy. These tools, with their advantages as described by managers, are outlined in Table 6.3.

We observed that progressive companies mainly pursue a subtle but consistent strategy of leveraging existing communication channels and 'plugging into' existing forums rather than creating new ones. However, we found evidence in even the most evolved companies of drawbacks in existing internal communications strategies, since managers in business units were often critical of the quality and clarity of communications.

Sustainability officers' feel that corporate intranets can provide information effectively but are not effective interactive communication tools, and that placing sustainability champions in the operational and business units will be far more effective in promoting the BCS internally. Again, sustainability implementers, whether they are sustainability officers or champions in the businesses, strategically identify who needs to be convinced internally in order to get a project through the organizational hierarchy. In companies where such a network is operating, these key 'change agents' are kept involved permanently and on an ongoing basis.

6.3.7 The external communications strategy

Communicating successes with sustainability actions externally is important for companies. In a world that is increasingly communications led, companies that do not exploit this potential may find themselves at a competitive disadvantage:

> Our main competitor has a higher sustainability rating than we have but I assure you that they are not more responsible than we are. They are simply better at communicating their successes. Our communications department has not capitalized on what we have been doing in sustainability. (BCS10 – Senior business manager, Business development)

At the outset of our research in 2002, KPMG had produced a briefing on better practice in reporting for the F&B sector, comparing the results to the global corporate environment. It found that only 25 per cent of F&B companies from the first 250 in the Global Fortune 500 produced non-financial reports, as compared to 50 per cent of utilities companies, for example. KPMG concluded that non-financial reporting was not yet well established in the F&B sector. In 2003, ECC Kohtes Klewes carried out a worldwide survey of stakeholders on corporate reporting on non-financial issues (ECC Kohte Klewes, 2003). This organization found that the food and agriculture sector was far from being considered the best industry sector for reporting quality by its stakeholders, with only 10.1 per cent of respondents believing that it was a leader.

But increasing numbers of F&B companies are producing ever more detailed sustainability reports. However, even among the very large, global companies that we researched, managers revealed a lack of confidence in the quality of environmental and social reporting. Managers recognized the importance of conveying publicly what the company is doing in these areas, but were frustrated at not being able to focus more fully on these aspects. The excuse given? Again, internal emphasis on short-term financial outputs...

For the more progressive companies, the trend is towards creating sustainability reports that are separate to the annual financial report, with a mix of environmental and social performance data and information. While we were researching this study, two companies had only just produced their first sustainability reports, having produced an environmental report for several years before that. This change of direction corresponded in both cases to significant changes in outlook and strategy concerning sustainability in the company, in particular, top management engagement. Some managers we spoke to felt strongly that it does not advance the principle of mainstreaming sustainability in the business when separate reports are produced:

> *Analysts look at the annual report and not the sustainability report. Sustainability should be part of the business reviews in the annual report. Sustainability should not be considered as a specific item separate to the business.* (BCS10, Senior business manager, Business development)

An increasing tendency, we found, is to view the internet as a repository for detailed information:

> *There should be a summary of social and environmental performance information in the annual report. All other detailed information should be on the corporate website.* (BCS40 – Senior sustainability officer)

KPMG found that while there was a tendency with existing reporting for the F&B industry to focus on issues related to compliance with codes and guidelines, such as ISO certification, there is nevertheless increasing recognition of hot topics – such as climate change and supply chain issues (KPMG, 2002). However, at the time, less than one third of these reports were independently verified, thus putting into question both transparency and credibility. In general, the corporate sense of obligation to report on social and environmental criteria, and even to include external verification, is evolving in Europe. France introduced new legislation in 2001 making such reports obligatory for all French companies listed on the Paris Stock Exchange. It looked like the UK would be making a similar move in 2005 but the legislation failed to get through. Such developments make business and sustainability managers in the industry look more seriously at the Global Reporting Initiative (GRI),[19] a multi-stakeholder process and independent institution whose mission is to develop and disseminate globally applicable sustainability reporting guidelines.

Sustainability officers considered the existing form of these guidelines overly complex. As a result, they have tended to review the guidelines, be selective about what they use, and ignore the rest. It was clear that the GRI guidelines were gaining in credibility and being increasingly looked at by companies as their guideline for reporting content. Nevertheless, according to GRI, in 2004 only 17 F&B companies were reporting according to the GRI guidelines, including Chiquita, Danone and Diageo. Other major players in the industry such as Unilever and Cadbury Schweppes were not included in the GRI list. Yet, Unilever and Cadbury Schweppes were included by the global reporters 2004 survey of corporate sustainability reporting (Standard & Poor's, 2004) as amongst the top 50 best practice reporters in industry. This demonstrates that GRI had not as yet gained its place as 'the' standard as yet. One sceptical executive commented to us, while waving a comprehensive survey he had carried out on the use of the GRI within the industry:

> *To get all the information together required for the GRI, the average global company would have to spend US$5 million to achieve that level of reporting – the sheer effort needed to consolidate the information required is substantial.* (BCS34 – Business manager, Communications)

We found general scepticism within the industry with regard to the GRI, as may be expected from such a relatively new initiative. After all, financial reporting took decades to achieve the level it has reached today, and, as can be witnessed by the many recent corporate financial scandals already mentioned, perfection is far from attained. So it will be with social and environmental reporting; only perhaps more so, considering both the fuzziness and complexity of the concepts being dealt with and the lack of satisfactory indicators, particularly for the social aspects. At the time of writing, the GRI was developing sector-specific guidance that should help companies produce more relevant reports.[20]

Some managers overwhelmingly felt that the impact of such reports was primarily internal, and not external:

> *I am not sure how many external people actually read our report. Its main impact has been internal; it helps to drive the agenda internally.* (BCS24 – Senior sustainability officer)

Clearly, the formality of the process involved in developing a sustainability report, convinces employees of how seriously the company is taking sustainability, while making complex concepts more tangible and clearer in employees' minds. A first reading of a sustainability report may be the first time that the status of the corporate strategy and its action on sustainability issues becomes apparent to managers:

> *Our first environmental/social report was mainly written to create awareness amongst our 100 operational companies.* (BCS39 – Top management, CEO)

Consumer organizations complained about the inefficiency of corporate sustainability reporting for informing consumers about sustainable choices:

> *All those glossy brochures ... and the consumer is still totally confused about what companies are doing about sustainability The social and environmental reporting of companies benefit employees more than they do consumers.*

The survey carried out by ECC Kohte Klewes (2003) revealed that, in fact, few shareholders, investors, consumers and even employees actually read non-financial reports thoroughly despite their statute of primary stakeholders. However, we had ample proof during our interviews that the very existence of such reports and the effort that goes into them renders an organization more credible to its own employees.

However, at one leading company where we interviewed, we came across an interesting counter-perspective; the view that to be openly public about environmental and social behaviour, beyond compliance, was either risky or should not be necessary if the reputation of the company is rock-solid. The problem with such a defensive approach is that it quickly permeates the internal fabric of the company and affects managerial mindset, as is reflected in the comments of a manager from that company:

> *The ethic is that if we do not communicate, then we are less open to criticism. There are small areas where we could improve and win favour with the rating agencies – but there is an internal view that we should anyway be trusted as we are such a reputable company.* (BCS24 – Senior sustainability officer)

Interestingly however, this same company was economically extremely successful and this manager felt there was no pressure to revise the corporate communications strategy either:

> *Looking at our economic success – if we were doing something really wrong, this would be reflected in the figures somewhere along the line. But there is no significant pressure and nothing is felt important enough to do significantly more about our 'stumbling blocks'. As a result, we are mainly taking small steps.* (BCS24 – Senior sustainability officer)

7 Synthesis

The analysis that we have presented in this chapter suggests that there is substantial scope for increased exploitation of a BCS within the F&B industry. In each area examined, it was clear that implementing sustainability brought challenges because of tension created between the complexity that sustainability presents to the company, and the struggle of companies to match and manage that complexity internally with frameworks, systems, tools, structures, processes and the necessary human resources and values that allow smooth integration of these concepts into business strategy. For many F&B managers, getting their heads around the implications of sustainable development for their business is a daunting challenge. From supply chain challenges to marketing techniques, sustainability can lead to new ways of working and reflecting on how companies do business. However, although there are interesting experimental pilot projects going on in the supply chain in the most progressive companies, the industry is still as a whole more firmly anchored to tried and true business models.

Sustainability issues have the potential to have more of an impact on business operations and value creation than currently. Various examples of how the F&B industry might better manage these issues according to a strategic approach have been discussed. In this sense, clearly, there is a BCS awaiting better exploitation. However, it is also clear that its significance is currently interpreted very differently from company to company, from manager to manager. And companies are extremely careful about a roll out that is currently slow and halting.

This slow yet constant progress experienced by industry leaders in trying to outreach the BCS within their organizations, upwards in the supply chain and downstream through marketing initiatives, illustrates the difficulties of finding a breakthrough solution to the business case. Managers from both the manufacturing sector and retail were guarded about the potential for 'leapfrogging' effects:

The question for us is always, 'How fast and how far?' We are mainly taking small steps. (BCS24 – Senior sustainability officer)

We find it difficult to communicate the small steps that manufacturers are making. These steps are too small to make a substantial difference. That is why they have such difficulties in convincing consumers that their products are sustainable. (BCSBM13 – Retailer)

A stakeholder we interviewed confirmed that that the industry was moving slowly but that considerable progress had been made in the recent past (the interview was in 2004):

On a scale of one to ten in terms of integrating these aspects into strategies through alignment, the food industry is at two to three; yes, only the beginning. The industry still has a long way to go. The majority of companies are not doing much. However, although the experience is very much step by step, results have been encouraging. The industry has made considerable progress in the last five to eight years: Ten years ago, only four or five companies were doing something! (BCSBM33)

We deduce from these remarks that CSM in the industry will probably pay in the long run, but moving more quickly to integrate environmental and social factors does not necessarily make good business sense to most companies in the short to medium term. There are different business cases for different situations and they tend to be very company specific, depending on a number of factors; type of product, cultural context, type of market, company history, level of public exposure, brand recognition benefits and so on. Business cases are often not fully exploited because awareness, tools and guidelines needed to identify issues, and therefore risks are lacking. A fundamental problem is that the sector is lagging behind in terms of linking risks across different functions within companies. Because of extreme financial pressure on the sector, the focus is on incremental improvements rather than more holistic risk management.

Moreover, incentive systems are focused on short-term results and do not motivate staff to tackle sustainability issues in a more hands-on way. In addition, training and competence-building programmes are not currently oriented towards reinforcing the essential system of values that managers need in order to make CSM a part of their way of doing business. But the F&B business environment is far too volatile for a lackadaisical approach to its multiple risks to continue. It is hopeful that leading F&B companies have moved away from looking at sustainability from a purely cost perspective and are in a phase of exploring value creating potential. The majority of companies we included in our study see economic potential in CSM. However, the level of achievement throughout the industry is still relatively low, considering that there were so many large, global and progressive companies included in our sample and that much remained to be done even at these companies. We identified a number of internal barriers, including management mindsets and resistance; internal factors completely within the company's control. There is potential to further roll out and develop the business case.

Many of the examples we cited show that, although sustainability gives an opportunity to some, particularly branded companies to establish rare, firm-specific, non-imitable characteristics that can be the source of the sustained competitive advantage so promoted by academics and sustainability heroes alike, only a handful of companies are truly working on sustainability as a strategic objective. Nevertheless, we also found examples of companies emulating better practice and identifying how they can differentiate from other companies in these areas.

Let us not underestimate the impact of incremental steps either. To quote Plutarch, 'Steady, continuous efforts followed by periodic but purposeful thrusts are irresistible, for this is how time captures the greatest powers on earth' (Plutarch c.46–120 A.D.) For truly sustainable development, what is required is more 'purposeful thrusts' to join with incremental efforts already being made.

Notes

1 See also Winn 1995.
2 See www.guardian.co.uk/famine/story/1,12128,862655,00.html
3 See Ackerman, 1975 and World Economic Forum, 2002.
4 See www.unglobalcompact.org
5 Consult www.unilever.com/environmentsociety/newsandspeeches.
6 The process of identifying, analyzing and responding to social and political issues that can impact a firm (see Johnson, 1983).
7 See, for example, how Jack in the Box, a children's fast-food restaurant, reacted to accusations of being responsible for deaths of children as a result of E.Coli infections (Ulmer and Sellnow, 2000).
8 See Winter and Steger (1998) for a discussion on the limitations of traditional 'issue management' models.
9 See www.saiplatform.org
10 See www.glifood.org
11 See www.rainforest-alliance.org/news/2000/chiquita.html
12 One of the most potent greenhouse gases.
13 See www.greenpeace.org
14 See www.sustainable-palmoil.org
15 See www.msc.org/
16 See www.panda.org/about_wwf/what_we_do/marine
17 See 'Fishing for the Future – Unilever's sustainable fisheries initiative at www.unilever.com, and the MSC website at www.msc.org
18 A method of measuring overall corporate performance that looks at a number of factors in addition to traditional financial aspects.
19 See www.globalreporting.org/guidelines/rep_sector.asp
20 See www.globalreporting.org

References

Ackerman, R.W. (1975) The social challenge to business. Cambridge, MA: Harvard University Press.

ActionAid International (2005) 'Power hungry; Six reasons to regulate global food corporations' (Johannesburg, SA).

Adams, D. (1979) Hitchhikers guide to the galaxy. New York: Harmony books.

Adams, R. (1990) 'Green consumerism and the food industry: Early signs of big changes to come', *British Food Journal*, 92(9): 11–14.

Allen, J. and Root, J. (2004) 'The new brand tax', *Wall Street Journal Europe*, 13 September. New York, A7.

Aon (2005) 'Food, drink and tobacco sector report, 2005: An inconsistent approach to risk', London, UK.

Aon (2006) 'Risk report: The year ahead', London, UK.

Argenti, P.A. (2004) 'Collaborating with activists: How Starbucks works with NGOs', *California Management Review*, 47(1): 91–116.

Aroq Ltd. (2003a) 'Global fish market: Trends and issues', just-food.com

Aroq Ltd. (2003b) 'The organic food industry demystified', just-food.com

Arthur D. Little (1998) Realising the business value of sustainable development – An Arthur D. Little survey on sustainable development and business. Cambridge, UK.

Arthur D. Little (2002) Corporate responsibility in the food industry: Too hard to swallow? Cambridge, UK.

Ashcroft, E. and Goldberg, R.A. (1996) 'Nestlé and the twenty-first century', *Harvard Business School Case Studies*, Harvard Business School.

Atkins, R.C. (1992) *Dr. Atkins' New Diet Revolution*. New York: Avon Books.

Baas, E., Van Battum, S., Voorbergen, M. and Zwanenberg, A. (1999) 'The world food markets: Market trends and driving forces for international food companies', Utrecht, NL: Rabobank International.

Baas, H.J.A., van Potien, A.J. and Zwanenberg, A. (1998) 'The world of food retailing: Developments and strategies', Utrecht, NL: Rabobank International.

Bartolomeo, M., Daga, T. and Familiari, G. (2003) 'Green, social and ethical funds in Europe', Avanzi SRI Research/SiRi Group.

Becker, B., Huselid, M. and Ulrich, D. (2001) 'The link between people and strategy', *Financial Times*, London, UK: 6.

Blake, S. (2003) Globalisation of the food industry. Aroq Limited.

Bonini, S.M., McKillop, K. and Mendonca, L.T. (2006) The trust gap between consumer and corporations, *The McKinsey Quarterly*, Number 2.

Brown, L., Flavin, C. and French, H. (2000) State of the World 2000: The Worldwatch Institute. London, UK: 8.

Carpenter, G. and White, P. (2004) Sustainable development: Finding the real business case. *Corporate Environmental Strategy*, 11(2).

Carroll, A.B. (1979) A three dimensional model of corporate performance. *Academy of Management Review*, 4(4): 497–505.

Chang, L. (2004) Groupe Danone builds a major market in China. *Wall Street Journal*.

Christian Aid (2004) Behind the mask: The real face of corporate social responsibility. London, UK.

CIAA (2002) Industry as a partner for sustainable development: Food and drink: Confederation of Food and Drink Industries of the EU.

CIAA (2006) Data and trends of the European Food and Drink Industry – www.ciaa.be.

Clarkson, M.B.E. (1995) A stakeholder framework for analyzing and evaluating corporate social performance. *Academy of Management Review*, 20: 92–117.

Coase, R. 1937. The nature of the firm. *Economica*, 4: 386–405.

Collins, J.C. and Porras, J.I. (2000) *Built to Last – Successful Habits of Visionary Companies*. London, UK: Random House Business Books.

Consumentenbond (2002) Dossier MVO; Maatschappelijk verantwoord onderemen, ook een consuentenzaak; Summary: Conclusions on CSR research from a consumer perspective. Den Haag, NL.

Cowe, R. (2002) Developing value: The business case for sustainability in emerging markets. SustainAbility Ltd and International Finance Corporation.

CSR Europe (2003a) Competence building to mainstream CSR across businesses, *Working document*: CSR Europe, European Commission and Social Affairs Directorate General and Caisse des Dépôts et Consignations.

CSR Europe (2003b) Sustainability, responsibility: The business contribution to sustainable trade.

Davidson, H. (2003) Managing brands across stakeholders. *European Business Forum*, Summer (14): 85–7.

Davis, I. (2005) The biggest contract. *The Economist*, 28 May. London.

Davis, I. (2006) Plot your course for the new world. *Financial Times*, 12 January, London, UK: 12.

Diageo (2003) Corporate citizenship report. London, UK.

Drake Beam Morin (2001) CEO turnover and job security, *Special Report*. Boston, US.

DTI and Corporate Responsibility Group (2003) Changing manager mindsets.

ECC Kohte Klewes (2003) Global stakeholder report 2003: Shared values? Bonn, DE.

Edelman PR Worldwide (2002) NGOs: The fifth estate. *PR News*, 58(7): 1.

Elghamry, N. (2001) Procter & Gamble forced to withdraw GM snack. *European Chemical News*.

Engardio, P. (2006) Business prophet: How strategy guru C.K. Prahalad is changing the way CEOs think. *Business Week*, 23 January.

EPA (2000) Green dividends? – The relationship between environmental performance and financial performance. Washington, DC: United States Environmental Protection Agency.

Ethical Performance (2002) Child labour findings spur firms into action, 4(4): 7.

Ettenberg, E. (2003) *The Next Economy: Will You Know Where Your Customers Are?* New York: McGraw Hill-Companies.

European Commission (1996) Commission communication to the European Parliament and the Council on Food, Veterinary and Plant Health Control. Brussels, BE.

European Commission (1997) Green Paper; The general principles of food law in the European Union. Brussels, BE.

European Commission (2001) Promoting a European framework for corporate social responsibility, *Green Paper*. Brussels, BE: Department of Employment and Social Affairs.

European Commission (2002a) Analysis of the possibility of a European action plan for organic food and farming. Brussels, BE: Commission of the European Communities.

European Commission (2002b) White Paper: Corporate social responsibility. Brussels: Department of Employment and Social Affairs.

Fawer-Wasser, M., Butz, C. and Vaterlaus-Rieder, C. (2001) How sustainable is the food Industry? – A study of environmental and social compatibility of food and beverage companies. Bank Sarasin.

Fischer, G., Shah, M.M. and Van Velthuizen, H. (2002) Climate change and agricultural vulnerability. Johannesburg, South Africa: WSSD.

Forum for CSM, IMD, 21 and 22 November 2005: 'Great expectations? Corporate value chains – How far up, how far down?'.

Forum for the Future (2003a) Sustainability and business competitiveness: Boosting business competitive advantage through corporate social responsibility and sustainability. London, UK.

Forum for the Future (2003b) Sustainability and business competitiveness: Measuring the benefit for business competitive advantage from social responsibility and sustainability: Forum for the Future/Department for Trade and Industry, UK.

Fox, T. and Vorley, B. (2004) Top to bottom. *Elements*: 20–3.

Freeman, R.E. (1984) *Strategic Management: A Stakeholder Approach*. Boston, MA: Pitman Publishing Company.

Freeman, R. E. (1998) Stakeholder theory. In P. Werhane, and R.E. Freeman (eds), *The Blackwell Encyclopedic Dictionary of Business Ethics*. Malden, MA/Oxford: Blackwell Publishers.

Friedman, M. (1962) *Capitalism and Freedom*. Chicago, IL: University of Chicago Press.

FSA (2003) Review of research on the effects of food promotion to children: Final report. Glasgow, UK: FDA/University of Strathclyde.

Future Foundation and Work Foundation (2004) The ethical employee. London, UK.

Galbraith, J.R. (1977) *Organisational Design*. Reading, MA: Addison-Wesley.

Galbraith, J.R. (1995) *Designing Organizations: An Executive Briefing on Strategy, Structure and Process*. San Francisco: Jossey-Bass.

Giampietro, M. (1997) Socioeconomic constraints to farming with biodiversity. *Agriculture, Ecosystems and Environment*, 62: 145–67.

Goldman Sachs (2007a) Global Investment Research. Global Food and beverages report, 8 February, 2007.

Goldman Sachs (2007b) Global Investment Research. The GS Sustain Focus List, 22 June, 2007.

GreenBiz.com. (2006) China and India spotlighted in annual State of the World Report. 17 January, 2006.

Gunther, M. (2003) Tree huggers, soy lovers and profits. *Fortune*: 68–72.

Hardy, L. (1999) The lure of school marketing. *American School Board*, October.

Hawken, P. (1994) *The Ecology of Commerce*. New York: HarperCollins Publishers.

Henriques, I. and Sadorsky, P. (1996) The determinants of an environmentally responsive firm: An empirical approach. *Journal of Environmental Economics and Management*, 30(3): 381–3.

Heugens, P. (2002) Strategic issues management: Implications for corporate performance. *Business and Society*, 41(4): 456–8.

IACFO (2003) Broadcasting bad health: Why food marketing to children needs to be controlled. World Health Organization.

IITA. (2002) Child labor in the cocoa sector of West Africa: International Institute of Tropical Agriculture sponsored by USAID, USDO, ILO.

Innovest (2003) Monsanto and genetic engineering: Risks for investors. New York: Innovest Strategic Value Advisors.

Ionescu-Somers, A. (2006a) Consumer organizations. In U. Steger (ed.), *Inside the Mind of the Stakeholder: The Hype Behind Stakeholder Pressure*. Hampshire, UK: Palgrave Macmillan.

Ionescu-Somers, A. (2006b) Corporate customers and suppliers. In U. Steger (ed.), *Inside the Mind of the Stakeholder: The Hype Behind Stakeholder Pressure* (forthcoming). Hampshire, UK: Palgrave Macmillan.

IUF, UITA, and IUL (2002) The WTO and the world food system: A trade union approach. Geneva, CH: International Union of Food, Agricultural, Hotel, Restaurant, Catering, Tobacco and Allied Worker's Associations.

Jenkins, H.W. (2004) Don't let mad cow make you crazy. *Wall Street Journal* (Europe). 5 January. A7.

Johnson, J. (1983) Issues Management: What are the Issues? *Business Quarterly*, 48 (Autumn): 22.

Johnson, W.B., Natarajan, A. and Rappaport, A. (1985) Shareholder returns and corporate excellence. *Journal of Business Strategy*, 6(2): 52–62.

Jones, A. (2003a) British tastes harm sustainable fishing. *Financial Times*. 15 September. London, UK. 1.

Jones, A. (2003b) Drinks makers sued over age target. *Financial Times*. 27 November. London, UK. 15.

just-food.com (2003a) Logic of McDonald's organic move. 28 January.

just-food.com (2003b) Nestlé expresses concern over food prices – report. 4 March.

just-food.com (2003c) UK: GM crops fail environment safety trials – report. 3 October.

just-food.com (2003d) UK: Tax on fatty foods proposed to fight obesity. 9 June.

just-food.com (2003e) USA: Fastfood could be physically addictive, claim scientists. 30 January.

just-food.com (2003f) USA: FDA announces trans fat labelling rule. 10 July.

just-food.com (2003g) USA: McDonald posts first ever quarterly loss. 24 January.

just-food.com (2003h) USA: McDonalds slams new obesity lawsuit. 21 February.

just-food.com (2004a) Chiquita forced to make 'protection' payments in Columbia.

just-food.com (2004b) Global trends in ethical foods: Fair trade and sustainability go mainstream – Definitions and drivers in the ethical foods marketplace. 2.

just-food.com (2004c) UK: Co-op highlights nutrition info of major brands with on-shelf labelling. 21 September.

just-food.com (2004d) UK: Quality more important element of good value than price – research. 2 November.

Klein, J.G., Smith, N.C. and John, A. (2004) Why we boycott: Consumer motivations for boycott participation. *Journal of Marketing*, 68(July): 92–109.

Klein, N. (2001) *No Logo*. London, UK: HarperCollins.

Kong, N.T., Salzmann, O., Steger, U. and Ionescu-Somers, A. (2002) Moving business/industry toward sustainable consumption: The role of NGOs. *European Management Journal*, 20(2).

KPMG (2002) Best practice for the food and drink sector: Global Sustainability Services, KPMG International.

Lang, T. and Heasman, M. (2004) *Food Wars; The Global Battle for Mouths, Minds and Markets*. London, UK: Earthscan.

Lankowski, L. (2000) *Determinants of Environmental Profit: An Analysis of the Firm Level Relationship Between Environmental Performance and Economic Performance*. Helsinki: Helsinki University of Technology.

Leatherhead Food International (2000) *Dancing with the Devil: Crisis Management in the Food and Drinks Industry*. Leatherhead, UK.

Lewis, G.J. (2004) Uncertainty and equivocality in the commercial and natural environments: The implications for organizational design. *Corporate Social Responsibility and Environmental Management*, 11(3): 167–77.

Lewis, S. (2003a) Reputation and corporate responsibility: Market and Opinion Research International.

Loh, J. and Wackernagel, M. (eds) (2004) *Living Planet Report*. Gland, CH: WWF-World Wide Fund for Nature.

Mann, R., Adebanjo, O. and Kehoe, D. (1999) An assessment of management systems and business performance in the UK food and drinks industry, *British Food Journal*, 101(3): 238–44.

Marketing Week (2003) Thinking green won't drive you into the red. 17 April. London, UK. 32.

Mason, J. (2004) Special report – Sustainable business: A matter of necessity and not choice. *Financial Times*, 14 October.

Mason, J. and Firn, D. (2004) Monsanto sees seeds of food revolution in Europe. *Financial Times*, 19 March. London, UK. 6.

Mason, T. (2003) Diageo urges sensible drinking. *Marketing* (July 10): 15–16.

McKinsey (2008) Making talent a strategic priority. *McKinsey Quarterly*: January, 2008.

Michaels, E., Handfield-Jones, H. and Axelrod, B. (2001) *War for Talent*. Harvard Business School Press.

Morgan Stanley (2003a) Low-Carb Craze: Good for dieters, bad for companies – Industry overview. Morgan Stanley Equity Research.

Morgan Stanley (2003b) Obesity: A lingering concern, *Consumer staples:global insights*: Morgan Stanley Equity Research.

MORI (2002a) The ethical consumer. London, UK: Market & Opinion Research International and the Cooperative Bank.

MORI (2002b) The public's views of corporate responsibility. London, UK: Market & Opinion Research International.

MORI (2004) Captains of industry survey. London, UK: Market & Opinion Research International.

Moules, J. (2004) Planting the seeds of fair trade. *Financial Times*, 9 September. London. 8.

Murray, S. (2004a) Giants snap up organic mouthfuls. *Financial Times*, 14 October. London, UK. 5.

Murray, S. (2004b.) What's in a name? A crisis will tell. *Financial Times*, 9 March. London, UK. 4.

Nestlé (2003a) Nestlé and water: Sustainability, protection, stewardship. Vevey, CH.

Nestlé (2003b) Today farmers suffer from depressed coffee prices. What can be done? Vevey, CH.

Nestle, M.(2002) *Food Politics*. Berkeley and Los Angeles, CA: University of California Press.

Observer, The (2004) Handle with care: Can prawns give you cancer? Is Scottish salmon deadly? Will chicken from the Far East kill you? OFM uncovers the truth about food scares. London. February 15.

OECD (1998) *The Future of Food: Long-Term Prospects for the Agro-Food Sector*. Paris, France: OECD Publications.

Ohmae, K. (1983) *The Mind of the Strategist*. Harmondsworth: Penguin Books.

Oxfam (2004a) Oxfam Briefing Paper 61: Dumping on the world; how EU sugar policies hurt poor countries.

Oxfam (2004b) A raw deal for rice under DR-CAFTA: How the Free Trade Agreement threatens the livelihoods of Central American farmers, *Oxfam Briefing Paper 68*.

Peel, M. (2004) Bitter chocolate for children. *Financial Times*, 21 December. London, UK. 13.

Peters, T.J. and Waterman, R.H. (1982) *In Search of Excellence: Lessons from America's Best Run Companies*. New York: Harper & Row.

Peterson, D.K. (2004) The relationship between perceptions of corporate citizenship and organizational commitment. *Business and Society*, 43(3): 296–319.

Placet, M., Anderson, R. and Fowler, K. (2005) Strategies for sustainability. *Research Technology Management*, 48(5): 31–41.

Porter, M. (1980) *Competitive Strategy: Techniques for Analyzing Industries and Competitors*. New York: The Free Press.

Porter, M.E. (1985) *Competitive Advantage: Creating and Sustaining Superior Performance*. New York: Free Press.

Prahalad, C.K. (2004) Why selling to the poor makes for good business. *Fortune*, 150(10): 71–2.

Prahalad, C.K. (2005) Aid is not the answer. *Wall Street Journal*. New York. A8.

Prahalad, C.K. and Hammond, A. (2002) Serving the world's poor, profitably. *Harvard Business Review*, 80(9): 48–57.

Prahalad, C.K. and Hart, S.L. (2002) The fortune at the bottom of the pyramid. *Strategy and Business*, First quarter.

Prakesh Sethi, S. (1994) *Multinational Corporations and the Impact of Public Advocacy on Corporate Strategy: Nestlé and the Infant Formula Controversy*. Netherlands: Kluwer Academic Publishers Group.

PriceWaterhouseCoopers (2003a) Reputation Assurance TM: Managing your most valuable asset.

PriceWaterhouseCoopers (2003b) Uncertain times, abundant opportunities. *5th Annual Global CEO Survey*.

Quelch, J.A. and Harding, D. (1996) Brands versus private labels: Fighting to win. *Harvard Business Review*, January–February: 99–109.

Quist, J. (2000) Environmental assessment of shopping, cooking and eating scenarios in the Netherlands. *Background Report*: SusHouse Project.

Rabobank International (1998) The world of food service. *Market Study*. Utrecht, Netherlands.

Ramus, C.A. (2001) Organizational support for employees: Encouraging creative ideas for environmental sustainability. *California Management Review*, 43(3): 85–105.

Rappaport, A. (1986)[1998]. *Creating Shareholder Value: A Guide for Managers and Investors*. New York: Free Press.

Rappaport, A. (1998) Competitive advantage and shareholder value. *Directors and Boards*, 22(2): 36–9.

Reichheld, F. (1996) *The Loyalty Effect: The Hidden Truth Behind Growth, Profits and Lasting Value*. Boston, MA: Harvard Business School Press.

Reinery, I. (2004) Corporate responsibility industry report: Food and beverage. Munich: Oekom research.

Rosegrant, M.W., Cai, X. and Cline, S.A. (2002) *World Water and Food to 2025: Dealing with Scarcity*: International Food Policy Research Institute (IFPRI) and the International Water Management Institute (IWMI).

Salzmann, O., Steger, U. and Ionescu-Somers, A. (2005) Quantifying economic effects of corporate sustainability initiatives: Activities and drivers *IMD Working Papers*. Lausanne, CH: International Institute for Management Development.

Salzmann, O., Leitschuh-Fecht, H., Steger, U. and Ionescu-Somers, A. (2004) The challenge of sustainable consumption and the role of business as a solution, *IMD Working Papers*. Lausanne, CH: International Institute for Management Development.

Sandor, R. and Flatz, A. (2001) The DJSI – a story of financial innovation. *Environmental finance* (December 2001–January 2002).

Schaltegger, S. and Figge, F. (1997) Environmental shareholder value. Basel: University of Basel (WWZ) and Bank Sarasin.

Schein, E.H. (1992) *Organizational Culture and Leadership*. San Francisco, CA: Jossey-Bass.

Schlosser, E. (2002) *Fast Food Nation*. London, UK: Penguin Books.

Schwartz, M. (2003) *How the Cows Turned Mad*. Berkeley and Los Angeles, CA: University of California Press.

Sissell, K. (2004) Monsanto suspends biotech wheat R&D program. *Chemical Week*, 166(17): 9.

Sleep, C. (2005) just-food.com editor's weekly highlights. *just-food.com* (302).

Smith, A. (1776) *An Inquiry into the Nature and Causes of the Wealth of Nations*, edited by Edwin Cannar. London: Metheun and Co., Ltd. (first published in 1776), 1904.

Smith, N.C. (2003) Corporate social responsibility: Whether or how? *California Management Review*, 45(4): 52–76.

socialfunds.com (2000) Shareholders urge McDonalds to go GE-free. 26 May.

Standard & Poor's (2004) Risk and opportunity: Best practice in non-financial reporting: Standard & Poor's, SustainAbility, UNEP.

Steele, J. (2004) Coca-Cola to drop advertising in schools. *Telegraph*, 26 January. London, UK.

Steger, U. (1998a) A mental map of managers: An empirical investigation into manager's perceptions of stakeholder issues. *Business and the Contemporary World*, X(4): 579–609.

Steger, U. (1998b) *The Strategic Dimensions of Environmental Management*. London: Macmillan Press.

Steger, U. (ed.) (2004) *The Business of Sustainability: Building Industry Cases for Corporate Sustainability*. London: Palgrave Macmillan.

Steger, U. (ed.) (2006) *Inside the Mind of the Stakeholder: The Hype Behind Stakeholder Pressure* (forthcoming). Hampshire, UK: Palgrave Macmillan.

Steger, U., Amann, W., Salzmann, O. and Ionescu-Somers, A. (2005) *Sustainability as a Complexity Challenge*. Paper presented at the International Sustainability Conference; Strategies for a Sustainable Society, Basle, CH.

Steger, U., Humm, C. and Ogunsulire, M. (2001) Monsanto's genetically modified organisms: The public outcry: IMD.

Steger, U. and Ionescu-Somers, A. (2001) Unilever Indonesia: Linking business strategy to job creation, *IMD Case Study: 3-1042*.

Steger, U., Ionescu-Somers, A. and Nick, A. (2006) Transforming the global fishing industry: The Marine Stewardship Council at full sail *IMD Case Study: 2-0083*. Lausanne, CH: International Institute for Management Development (IMD).

Steger, U., Ionescu-Somers, A. and Amann, W. (2002) Hindustan Lever – Leaping a millennium, *IMD Case Study: 3-1073*. Lausanne, CH.

Steger, U., Lehmann, J.-P. and Ogunsulire, M. (2001) Under the spotlight: It's always Coca-Cola, *IMD Case Study: 3-1043*: International Institute for Management Development.

Steger, U. and Raedler, G. (1999a) Marine Stewardship Council (A): Is a joint venture possible between "Suits and Sandals"? *IMD Case Study: 2-0080*: International Institute for Management Development.

Steger, U. and Raedler, G. (1999b) Marine Stewardship Council (B): Departing in unchartered waters, *IMD Case Study: 2-0081*: International Institute for Management Development.

Steger, U., Salzmann, O. and Ionescu-Somers, A. (2003) Flirting with the enemy: The WWF/Lafarge conservation partnership (A), *IMD Case Study: 2-0101*. Lausanne, CH: International Institute for Management Development (IMD).

Steger, U. and Winter, M. (1998) Predicting where the pressure groups will strike. *Mastering Management*: 9–13.

SustainAbility, Global Compact, and UNEP (2003) The 21st century NGO: In the market for change.

Sustainable Food Laboratory (2005a) *Report of Sustainable Food Lab Review Meeting*. Earth University, Costa Rica.

Sustainable Food Laboratory (2005b) *Sustainable food lab design studio*. Salzburg, Austria.

Technoserve, McKinsey and Company (2003) Business solutions to the coffee crisis: http://www.technoserve.org/TNSCoffeeReport_Master.pdf.

The Economist (1993) The food industry. 4 December. London, UK.

The Economist (2002) Battling against big food. 19 December. London, UK.

The Economist (2003a) Big food v big Americans; Thin end of the wedge. 5 July. London, UK. 71.

The Economist (2003b) Cheap chow. 6 March. London, UK.

The Economist (2003c) Danger at the manger. 14 August.

The Economist (2003d) Did somebody say a loss? 10 April. London, UK.

The Economist (2003e) Don't just sit there. 21 November. London, UK.

The Economist (2003f) Drops on parched soil. 5 July 2003. London, UK. 73–4.

The Economist (2003g) Far less scary than it used to be. 26 July. London, UK. 23–5.

The Economist (2003h) Forgive debt, not theft. 20 May. London, UK.

The Economist (2003i) Harvest time: New research sends mixed signals on genetically-modified crops. 17 October. London, UK.

The Economist (2003j) Living with the enemy – Non-governmental organisations and business. 9 August. 49–50.

The Economist (2004a) Another gene genie out of the bottle. 19 May. London, UK.

The Economist (2004b) Big Mac's makeover, *Special report: McDonalds turned around.*

The Economist (2004c) Business: Profits and poverty; Face value. 372(8389): 62.

The Economist (2004d) Daring, defying, to grow. *The Economist.* 5 August. London, UK.

The Economist (2004e) Two-faced capitalism. 22 January. London, UK.

The Economist (2004f) Wal-Mart: How big can it grow? 15 April. London, UK.

The Economist (2005a) Europe's farm follies; The EU's agricultural policy. 8 December. London, UK.

The Economist (2005b) Junior fat: Obesity and advertising. 14 December. London, UK.

The Economist (2005c) Making a meal of it. 7 May. London, UK. 57–8.

The Economist (2005d) Things go worse with Coke – Coke v Pepsi. 17 December. London, UK.

Thorpe, B. (2000) Successful UK strategies for getting GE foods off supermarket shelves: http://thewitness.org/archive/may2000/may.keepwatch.html.

Tickell, S. (2004) The taste for commodities: Who benefits? *SustainAbility Radar, The Commodities Issue*: SustainAbility.

Timberlake, L. (2006) *Catalyzing Change: A Short History of the WBCSD.* Geneva, CH: World Business Council for Sustainable Development.

Tomkiewicz, J. and Hughes, R.E. (1993) The managerial implications of gender-based perceptions of social responsibility. *International Journal of Management*, 10(2): 237–42.

Tomlinson, R. (2004) Troubled waters at Perrier. *Fortune*, 150(11): 173–5.

Tsang, A.S.L. (2000) Military doctrine in crisis management: Three beverage contamination cases. *Business Horizons*, 43(5): 65–73.

UK Food Group (1999) Hungry for power. London, UK.

UK Food Group and Sustain (2002a) The CAP doesn't fit: Sustain and UK Food Group recommendations for reform of the Common Agricultural Policy. London, UK.

UK Food Group and Sustain (2002b) The common agricultural policy: How the CAP operates, the key commodities, competitors and markets for the European Union. London, UK.

UK Food Group and Sustain (2002c) The Common Agricultural Policy: Options for reform and their potential impact. London, UK.

Ulmer, R.R. and Sellnow, T.L. (2000) Consistent questions of ambiguity in organizational crisis communication: Jack in the Box as a case study. *Journal of Business Ethics*, 25(2): 143–55.

Unilever (2002a) Fishing for the future: Unilever's sustainable fisheries initiative. London, UK: Unilever.

Unilever (2002b) Growing for the future II: Unilever and sustainable agriculture.

Unilever (2005) Trip management; The next big thing.

Urry, M. (2001) Iceland warns again on profits. *Financial Times*. March 16. London, UK. 21.

Vorley, B. (2003) Food, Inc: Corporate concentration from farm to consumer: UK Food Group.

Webster, K. (2004) Profitable partnerships. *Accountancy Magazine*. March.

Wells, M. (2003) Pepsi's New Challenge, *Forbes Magazine*, 171: 68.

Williams, F. (2004) Diabetes now seen as a bigger killer than AIDS. *Financial Times*. Thursday, May 6. London. 8.

Winn, M.I. (1995) Corporate leadership and policies for the natural environment. In J.E. Post (ed.), *Research in Corporate Social Performance and Policy. Sustaining the Natural Environmental: Empirical Studies on the Interface Between Nature and Organizations*. Greenwich, CT: JAI Press.

Winter, M. and Steger, U. (1998) *Managing Outside Pressure: Strategies for Preventing Corporate Disasters*. Chichester, West Sussex: John Wiley & Sons Ltd.

World Bank (2004) Urgent action needed to avoid global fishing crisis, *Press Release*: The World Bank Group.

World Commission on Environment and Development (1987) Our common future: From one earth to one world. London, UK: Oxford University Press.

World Economic Forum (2002) Global corporate citizenship: The leadership challenge for CEOs and Boards.

World Health Organization (2000) Obesity: Preventing and managing the global epidemic, WHO Technical Report Series 894. Geneva: WHO.

World Water Council (2000) World water challenges for the twenty-first century, *Press Releases*. The Hague.

WTO (2004) Trade and environment at the WTO. Geneva, CH: World Trade Organization.

WWF (1996) Marine fishes in the wild, a species status report: World Wide Fund for Nature.

Young, W. and Welford, R. (2003) Benchmarking retailers on ethical trading. *JCC*, 10 (Summer).

Index